Remnant of a Past

A Journey of Discovery and Hope

Sharon M. Brunner, MSW

Freedom Eagles Consulting and
Research Associates, LLC
Sault Ste. Marie, MI

Copyright 2011 by Sharon M. Brunner

All rights are reserved. No part of this book may be reproduced, stored in a retrieval system, or transmitted in any form by any means, whether electronic, mechanical, photocopying, recording, or otherwise, without prior written permission of the copyright holder, except by a newspaper or magazine reviewer who wishes to quote brief passages in connection with a review.

Editorial, sales, distribution, rights and permissions inquiries should be addressed to Freedom Eagles Consulting and Research Associates, LLC, 4599 East Five Mile Road, Sault Ste. Marie, MI 49783, USA.

Front Cover by Sarah Tule

First Printing, 2011

ISBN 978-0-615-49680-1

Published by
Freedom Eagles Consulting and Research Associates, LLC
4599 East Five Mile Road
Sault Ste. Marie, MI 49783 USA

Email: sbrunner4599@gmail.com

Prophesies

We knew this is the wealthiest part of this continent, because here the Great Spirit lives. We knew that the White Man will search for the things that look good to him, that he will use many good ideas in order to obtain his heart's desire, and we knew that if he had strayed from the Great Spirit he would use any means to get what he wants. These things we were warned to watch, and we today know that those prophecies were true because we can see how many new and selfish ideas and plans are being put before us. We know that if we accept these things we will lose our land and give up our very lives.

-Dan Katchongva, Hopi

Keepers of the Earth

A long time ago the Creator came to Turtle Island and said to the Red People, "You will be the keepers of the Mother Earth. Among you I will give the wisdom about Nature, about the interconnectedness of all things, about balance and about living in harmony. You Red People will see the secrets of Nature. You will live in hardship and the blessing of this is you will stay close to the Creator. The day will come when you will need to share the secrets with other people of the earth because they will stray from their spiritual ways. The time to start sharing is today.

-Don Coyhis, Mohican Writer and Consultant

Spiritual Security

They do us no good. If they are not useful to the white people and do them no good, why do they send them among the Indians? If they are useful to the white people and do them good, why do they not keep them at home? They [the white men] are surely bad enough to need the labor of everyone who can make them better. These men [the missionaries] know we do not understand their religion. We cannot read their book --they tell us different stories about what it contains, and we believe they make the book talk to suit themselves. If we had no money, no land and no country to be cheated out of, these black coats would not trouble themselves about our good hereafter. The Great Spirit will not punish us for what we do not know.

-Red Jacket, Seneca Orator

Respect

A lot of our kids--I say you think you are an Indian just because you wear red bandanna or war dance. Not being Indian. Have to respect yourself, others, Elders, and everybody else. Then you are an Indian.

-Jennette Timentwa, Colville Lake Tribal Elder

Community

All affirmed the central role of Indian prophecy, the bond between Indians and "Mother Earth," the existence of sacred "powers" by which ritual specialists benefited their people. They agreed to restore spiritual practices, encourage native language use, and combat alcoholism and family disintegration.

> -Little Star,
> Unknown American Indian

Seven Generations

Look behind you. See your sons and your daughters. They are your future. Look farther and see your sons' and daughters' children and their children's children even unto the seventh generation. That's the way we were taught. Think about it--you yourself are a seventh generation.

> -Leon Sheandoah, Onondagan Elder

The Human Family

O Great Spirit, who made all races, look kindly upon the whole human family, and take away the arrogance and hatred which separates us from our brothers.

> -Cherokee Prayer
> Unknown American Indian

Source: Schaef, A. (1995). *Native Wisdom for White Minds - Daily Reflections Inspired by Native Peoples of the World.* New York: Ballantine Books.

This book is dedicated in memory of
all the ancestors who suffered before me and for those
still plagued from the aftermath from the acts of genocide,
discrimination and assimilation. I wish everyone the best
on their journey to finding peace.
Megwetch Gitchi Manito (Thanks Creator)
for your guidance during this project.

ACKNOWLEDGEMENTS

I would like to express my gratitude to the members of my masters' thesis committee, Dr. Jane Swanson, Chairperson, Dr. Martin Reinhardt, and Dr. Jerry Johnson for their support and guidance on the original project. I would like to thank Mr. Robert Van Alstine for his provision of valuable materials and pay tribute in memory of Van Alstine as a historian. I would like to thank interview participants for sharing accounts of their family history and boarding school experience. The Cabin Fever Writers' Group, later referred to as the Creative Endeavors Group and many others for their support in this process, their emotional support and by reviewing the text of this book to give input. I also want to thank a dear friend, Betty Wilson, whose valuable work I hope reaches publication. Members of the Healing Foundation for Aboriginal People provided a lot of information about the process taken to provide healing for those who were forced to attend the Residential schools in Canada. I also want to thank my family who tolerated my involvement in this process. I want to extend my gratitude to Joyce Brown-Moore for taking the time to provide me with edit suggestions. Most importantly, I want to thank my husband, Don Brunner, who provided a vast amount of support during this entire process. All input, positive and negative was received and examined fully.

Table of Contents

Introduction.. 1
Chapter I Beginnings............................. 23
Chapter II Traditional Period......................... 46
Chapter III Eagle and Coyote Travel with Columbus............................ 71
Chapter IV Eagle and Coyote's Adventures with French Settlers 95
Chapter V Power and Control through Patriarchal Domination and the Church 114
Chapter VI The Realization of Manifest Destiny 146
Chapter VII Eagle and Coyote Infiltrate the Holy Childhood Boarding School........... 174
Chapter VIII Life on the Rez 208
Chapter IX Eagle and Coyote's Day in Tribal Court 229
Chapter X Remnants of a Shattered Past.......... 257
Chapter XI A Journeys End 290
Chapter XII One Step at a Time 311
Notes 348

Appendix History of Federal Indian Education Policy 359
Glossary.. 364
Bibliography 368

Introduction

What Happened to the Indian People??

Why This Book Is Necessary

Native Americans continue to be the most neglected minority in the United States. Many legislative actions, such as the creation of boarding and residential schools and reservations have caused great angst for the Native American people. As a result of centuries of being subjected to discrimination, genocide and assimilation, today's Indian population is plagued with a multitude of societal ills, including alcoholism, domestic violence, child abuse, child neglect, suicide, unemployment, and an array of mental health issues. Indian people continue to experience higher rates of diabetes, cardiovascular disease, pneumonia, and influenza. The death rate due to alcoholism is seven times the national average. The unemployment rate for Native Americans is 2.5 times the national average, and 32 percent of Indian people live in poverty as determined by federal guidelines. The suicide rates of Indian people are almost twice the national average and homicide rates are more than twice the national average. [1] The Sault Ste. Marie Tribe of Chippewa Indians' seven county service area in Michigan have a suicide rate of 17.4 deaths per 100,000, compared to the suicide rate of 11.2 per 100,000 for Michigan, and the national rate of 10.8 per 100,000. [2]

According to a report developed for Congress in 2004 by the U.S. Council on Civil Rights:

"Native Americans are 770 percent more likely to die from alcoholism, 650 percent more likely to die from tuberculosis, 420 percent more likely to die from diabetes, 280 percent more likely to die from accidents, and 52 percent more likely to die from pneumonia or influenza than the rest of the United States, including white and minority populations....

"Diabetes is one of the most serious health challenges facing Native Americans, resulting in significant morbidity and mortality rates. In fact, American Indians and Alaska Natives have some of the highest rates of diabetes in the world, with more than half of the adult population in some communities having the disease...

"Although the tuberculosis rate among Native Americans is declining, it continues to disproportionately affect this population in the number of cases and severity of disease. Tuberculosis is an airborne disease, frequently occurring among people living close together, with poor ventilation, a demographic disproportionately populated by Native Americans. The American Lung Association reported that in 1998, the incidence rate of tuberculosis among Native Americans was 12.6 cases per 100,000 persons, which was more than five times the rate of 2.3 for non-Hispanic whites. By 2002, the tuberculosis incidence rate had dropped to 7 cases per 100,000, approximately twice that of the overall U.S. population, though mortality rates remain six times higher...

"Native Americans are at a higher risk for mental health disorders than other racial and ethnic groups in the United States, and are consistently overrepresented among high-need populations for mental health services. The Surgeon General reported that this overrepresentation might be attributed to the high rates of homelessness, incarceration, alcohol and drug abuse, stress and trauma in Native American populations.

"The most significant mental health concerns today are the high prevalence of substance abuse, depression, anxiety, violence, and suicide. Substance abuse, most notably alcoholism, has been the most visible health disorder crisis. Depression is also emerging as a dominant concern. These two illnesses are commonly attributed to isolation on distant reservations, pervasive poverty, hopelessness, and intergenerational trauma, including the historic attempts by the federal government to forcibly assimilate tribes…

"…Depression is the most serious emerging mental health disorder in the Native American population. One of the troubling indicators of the toll it takes on Native Americans is reflected in suicide rates… The suicide rate for Native Americans continues to escalate and is 190 percent of the rate of the general population… In fact, suicide is the second leading cause of death for Native Americans 15 to 24 years old and the third leading cause of death for Native American children 5 to 14 years old…

"Despite a significant demand for mental health services, there are approximately 101 mental health professionals available per 100,000 Native Americans, compared with 173 mental health personnel per 100,000 whites. With a greater need for mental health specialists, but fewer for treatment, Native Americans frequently go without the necessary care for substance abuse, depression, anxiety, suicide ideations, and other mental health conditions."[3]

Native American women suffer from the highest rate of domestic violence; more than any other ethnic group in this country. The rationale for the higher rates of violence dates back to the period of time when this country was being colonized. Cultural imperialism was introduced in this country by the Spanish and at a later date by the Euro-Americans, meaning all people who migrated from Europe to settle in this country. This imperialism destroyed many Native American rituals and introduced a foreign system based on patriarchal domination. For example, in the past, when crimes were committed, oftentimes those committing the crimes would be ostracized from the villages, seriously threatening one's survival. The population of many villages was sparse; hence, it was not prudent to commit a crime against anyone in the village. Indian people worked together to take care of the needs of the entire village, and protected one another. Things changed drastically when the Europeans arrived in this country.

Many mental health issues today can be traced to their origins from previous generations who attended the boarding and residential schools and were forced to reside on reservations. Warren Petoskey in his book *Dancing*

My Dream explains what he and his father went through. His father attended the Carlisle Boarding School. Warren's family had to walk on eggshells because they did not want to upset his father. My mother was forced to attend the Holy Childhood Boarding School in Harbor Springs, Michigan. She told me about her boarding school experience. She recalled girls being hauled from their beds at night by the nuns. Also, children were whipped with a rubber hose because they wet the bed. This institution appeared so huge and cold to her. My mother told me that as a child and teenager she raged a lot. I watched her rage during my childhood and as an adult.

As a mother, she was emotionally absent, and I remember trying to seek even a small amount of validation. I wanted so much for her to smile at me. To make matters worse, my father was an alcoholic. My father's alcoholism and the ghosts from his childhood made him fly off into fits of rage with little or no provocation. My childhood was laced with physical and sexual abuse, neglect, and exposure to domestic violence. I know by firsthand knowledge what it is like to not be nurtured and protected by people who are supposed to have responsibility for my care and well-being as a dependent child. Most of my life I walked on eggshells for fear of rocking the boat. Taking caution in regards to extremely tenuous relationships laced with abuse was like carefully tiptoeing through a mine field, trying to avoid being blown up.

I was also raised with the burden of being given too much responsibility starting at a very young age. My training included taking responsibility for others' feelings, and I was forced to take on the caretaker role for the family. My worth was determined by how much I did for others, leading me to some serious unresolved shame issues. My feelings, needs and wants were not considered important by my parents, others and later on myself. As a result, I neglected to take care of myself most of the time, which had a very negative impact on every aspect of my life. My sense of helplessness and hopelessness set me up to be victimized over and over again.

As a result of the different forms of abuse I suffered, I developed Post Traumatic Stress Disorder (PTSD). I believe many of the attendees and those who had a family member who attended the boarding and residential schools are plagued with PTSD and/or other mental health issues. Because of my own personal trust issues, I would alienate myself as a protective measure. With PTSD, especially when it is caused by abuse, trust of others is not a part of the picture. As a result of the pain I was feeling, I would sometimes lash out at others, which in turn would cause further alienation. In turn, I felt extremely lonely on many occasions. A great number of Indian people reported they have felt extreme loneliness at certain points in their lives. I struggled when dealing with authority as do many other Indian people.

If I experienced a "trigger," I would go into a tailspin and then into a deep depression, sinking into depths of despair. I would have difficulty accomplishing even the smallest tasks, such as getting out of bed in the morning. A trigger is a cue associated with a past experience related to the cause of a person's PTSD, such as real or threatened acts of abuse. I worked through the exercises in a book on PTSD and completed many of the activities suggested to overcome this dreadful disorder, as well as seeking other various treatment modalities. Because of PTSD, I had difficulty with jobs, relationships and my own personal growth. I know what it feels like to be held prisoner by the ravages of PTSD and shame issues inflicted by self-serving, abusive individuals. Recovery has been a long arduous road. Happily, I can report that I have become a more balanced and content person.

    I fear many people with PTSD are either being treated for depression, are not receiving any treatment at all, or they are self-medicating by the use of alcohol or drugs to numb their pain. Many children in the boarding and residential schools were exposed to and/or experienced physical, spiritual, emotional and sexual abuse. Historical distrust has prevented a large number of Indian people from obtaining the help they need. If the triggers are not dealt with for individuals suffering from PTSD, PTSD will not go away. The acts of discrimination, genocide, and assimilation were chronic acts of abuse that many Native American people experienced.

    Until recently, some of the people who have been abusive to me were still in my life. It was difficult, but I had to remove myself from their lives. Healthy boundaries had to be set. I sought to deepen my spirituality in many ways and became a part of community activities to address feelings of loneliness and helplessness. I worked at taking care of my four selves; physical, intellectual, emotional and spiritual.

Living the examined life has also led me down a path of discovery and healing. It is so important to examine closely what is working and not working in your life and come up with a plan to address your unmet needs. Throughout most of my life I have been interested in finding out about my roots and how my roots affected who I am today. I pursued an undergraduate degree in sociology and counseling, and a master's of social work degree. The process associated with the completion of my master's thesis involved researching the experiences of Indian people who attended either a missionary or a federally run boarding school. These individuals came from three different tribes and resided in various locations in Michigan. The missionary boarding school was located in Harbor Springs, Michigan, and was referred to as the Holy Childhood boarding school. The federal school was located in Mt. Pleasant, Michigan. I found out something of interest: those interviewed who attended the missionary boarding school all had the same phobia, fear of the dark. The persons interviewed who attended the federal boarding school did not report having this fear.

More people were interviewed for this project. I did not use the real names of those interviewed when I made reference to them in this book to protect their anonymity. Some of Indian people interviewed resided in Canada and attended either the Spanish or Shenwauk residential school in Canada. The Spanish Residential School was a Catholic missionary school, while the Shenwauk school was nondenominational, resembling the federal boarding school in Michigan. Three people had family members who had attended boarding schools were interviewed to study the effects of intergenerational stress. I compared my findings with my experiences of being raised by someone who was forced to attend a boarding school, my mother.

In regard to my recovery, I have also become a healer, and a Reiki master. Reiki involves a noninvasive approach to energy balancing as a way of addressing the stresses and physical problems people are experiencing and this service is coupled with life coaching. I am currently an adjunct professor at a tribal community college. I have served as a member of a Child Welfare Committee since 1989 for the Sault Ste. Marie Tribe of Chippewa Indians (Sault Tribe), and I have worked side by side with the prosecuting attorney for the Sault Tribe for two years while I was completing my internship for my master degree. I provided assistance in preparing for child welfare cases, which was a part of my internship when I was working towards my master's degree. Also, during that time, I completed extensive revisions on the Child Welfare Code for the tribe.

I visited many tribal communities located in the western states conducting reviews with teams of reviewers for the national Head Start Office. I ended up visiting the Wounded Knee site on four separate occasions, which strongly suggested to me that I was definitely being presented many signs about the strife many Indian people have been exposed to and/or experienced. I firmly believe I need to do something about these problems and help a very troubled people of which I have a connection. During the 1980s and 1990s, I worked for the Sault Tribe's Johnson O'Malley Program, providing cultural, recreational, and educational programs for tribal children and their families. Following that experience, I worked for the tribal Head Start program until I was accepted as a Head Start reviewer and chose to pursue a master degree. What I learned from my review experience, my masters' thesis project, my Child Welfare Committee experience, and other valuable opportunities also served as the inspiration for this project.

    A magnitude of resources, my personal life experiences, and the experiences of those I interviewed for this project have been used to unveil what actually happened, what consequences evolved from what happened, and what can be done for those who have been harmed by historical trauma. I used the works of Anishanaabeg authors and other esteemed authors including, Edward Benton Benai and Rainbow Eagle, for some of the narration. The history of Indian people has been carefully delineated throughout this book. Some of the topics may appear to be repeated over and over again; however, this repetition is due to the seriousness and importance of the topics. Different voices are used throughout the text to demonstrate the harshness, and diversity of the Native American and Euro-American populations. Whenever possible, I apply humor, usually in the Eagle and Coyote renditions.

About the Book

I begin this book with the history of my Ojibwe ancestors going back as far as the 1300s in the *Traditional Period* chapter. Information about other tribal entities is used as a way of associating what has happened throughout history. The words Indian, Indian people, Anishanaabeg (plural) or Anisahanaabe (singular), Native American people, and tribal people are used interchangeably. Others are called Europeans, white people, and Euro-Americans. This was not done out of disrespect. Traditionally many Indian people looked at the colors of red, white, yellow and black as representing the four races and all were considered brothers and sisters of the Anishanaabeg.

What was known as the Indies today was known as Hindustan in 1492. The word "Indian" came from Columbus' description of the people he found. He was an Italian who did not speak or write Spanish very well, so in his written accounts he called the Indians, "Una gente in Dios," a people in God. Therefore, the given name of Indian is a perfectly noble and respectable word. Columbus thought he landed in the West Indies. Thus, those residing in the area in which he landed were referred to as Indians.

At one time, the Anishanaabeg were a noble and courageous people. Euro-American colonizers came to this country and exploited the Indian people which in turn took away a lot of their self confidence. They were used for slave labor, their land and other necessary resources that would ensure their survival was taken from them. Stereotypes such as the uneducated "Drunken Indian" have fueled the negative public image of Native Americans to this day. Years of being despised and defamed, most of it unjustly, has resulted in a large group of downtrodden people. Many Indian people have lost hope. African Americans, other people of color as well as the female population of all races have been discriminated against in this country. In the effort of streamlining and utilizing the best examples for addressing the critical effects of past trauma, the focus will be mainly placed on the Anishanaabeg for this book.

Women are mentioned in this book in various places, because women were highly revered and respected by the Indian people and many Indian people believe that one of the reasons for the world being off balance is the lack of value placed on women. Indian women filled prominent positions and aided to preserve the Native American heritage. Respect of both males and females is necessary to obtain balance in all cultures.

The Indian people had their children taken away, they were told they could not participate in their traditional and spiritual practices, and they were relocated to useless plots of land referred to as reservations. Their freedom has been violated in many ways, which has led to boredom, dissatisfaction with life and a sense of hopelessness and helplessness. As this was occurring, they were being referred to as "dirty savages" and other derogatory names. Coupled with these acts of discrimination, these individuals were shown ways in which to parent by those who promoted the acquisition of wealth, material goods, and the viewing of wives and children as possessions, concepts introduced by the patriarch and capitalist societal belief system. When you own something, you can do what you want with it. Thus, people have been objectified, including women. Look at the way women are portrayed by the media. Indian people were also ostracized, and then objectified.

As described in the *Traditional Period* chapter, the Anishanaabeg believed nothing was to be owned or possessed; the animate and inanimate contained spirits. The land on which they resided, was graciously provided to them by the Creator and must be respected. Children were cherished. Animals were placed on the Earth to provide protection and food and were highly valued. Many of the legends passed down from generation to generation included animals providing valuable lessons. In the past, Indian people possessed the wisdom of how to live in harmony with the environment. They knew Earth as the Mother who would provide them with food, clothing, and shelter. Before the onset of the European takeover, these individuals did experience solidarity and a sense of contentment as a result of their strong ties to their family of origin.

When the Europeans came to this country, they were further advanced in technological development, which was foreign to the Indian people. Europeans possessed the need to control and own anything crossing their paths. The concept of the "buying" and "selling" of land was another foreign concept for the Indian people. Treaties were used to delineate the relationship between the United States government and Indian tribes. The treaties included provisions, which established reservations, procurement of supplies, and payment for the land that was taken from the Indian people. One could possibly allude to the treaties being created in good faith by all parties. However, as the land became more populated by the Europeans, payments to the Indian people required by the treaties became too costly for the government. Other expenses such as the building of the railroads were considered more important.

In 1871, it was determined that Indians would be controlled by Congressional legislation instead of treaties. The treaties put into place before 1871 would still be considered valid and upheld. From 1778 to 1871, 371 treaties with Indian tribes were put into place and ratified by the federal government. However, most of the treaties were broken.

The chapter *Power and Control through Patriarchal Domination and the Church* covers the harmful effects of those who have misinterpreted the Bible and what these faulty perceptions have done to women and Indian people. The false perceptions of those who interpreted the Bible for their own self-serving reasons has caused people to either abandon an adaptable form of spirituality suited to their needs or seek a source of organized religion for their salvation. There is nothing wrong with organized religion if that is the right path for you. I encourage all people to seek different ways of exploring their spirituality to find what best serves their personal needs and not fall prey to those who only think one way is the right way.

    I described the history of the Roman Catholic Church and the Church's campaign to denounce the Gnostic practices associated with paganism. In my opinion, the faulty interpretation of the book of Genesis has caused more harm than any other legislative act in history and has introduced the concept of domestic violence. I witnessed a man say to his wife at a bible study meeting that she had to cook all the meals because of what the book of Genesis portrayed. Since, women were behind all the evil in the world, they had to be submissive to men. As you are aware, it was depicted that Eve gave into Satan's persuasion, thus, opening the door to Satan and his corruption. Satan has always been referred to as a male. That's an interesting point to consider. Another man made the comment to me personally that women are at fault for all the evil in the world, so women must continue to pay for what Eve has done. If you can own women, you can own children. So the book of Genesis has also propagated the practice of child abuse and neglect.

    The story of our modern way of looking at the world began approximately 500 years ago when the Church took it upon itself to maintain central authority over the European inhabitants through imperial rule. The Churchmen set themselves up as the sole gatekeepers to the divine, and did alleviate complete deterioration of the human condition after the collapse of the Roman Empire by redirecting hostilities to other entities. The crusades are a good example of this. The Church also maintained its control by introducing and enforcing specific Christian beliefs. However, absolute power has been known to lead to absolute corruption. The Church, in its attempt to maintain its control of the masses, and build their wealth, decided to circulate dogmatic beliefs, such as the fear of God, to increase attendance at their services.

      Science was beginning to bring into question the beliefs propagated by the Church, and the Church was losing some of its credibility. Galileo and Copernicus challenged the Church's dogma concerning the solar system, mathematics, and things happening in the universe, such as the orbiting of the planets. The Church wanted people to believe that Earth and humans were the center of all life. The Gnostics promoted the mystical wonders of the universe, and the importance of women concerning their association with the divine, beliefs supported by the Ojibwe people in the past before the arrival of the Europeans. The Church was beginning to lose its foothold. To offset the loss of credibility, the Church and other forms of imperial rule annihilated their opponents, people who defied their beliefs. The Gnostics challenged Christian and other beliefs of those in authority, so they were eliminated. Galileo and Copernicus were also put to death for challenging the Church's viewpoints.

It is difficult to even imagine how little European people knew about the physical processes of nature. Little knowledge existed to explain the organs in the body or the biology of plant growth. Thunderstorms were angry gods, and people needed to seek forgiveness, or more accurately humans had to pass the spiritual test. Another way in which the Church maintained its control was by the compilation of a variety of texts that supported their self-serving goals. The Bible was endorsed as God's word, and only the priests could be in possession of these important messages. They worked endlessly to prevent the population from having direct access to any holy texts. If individuals wanted to make it to heaven, they had no choice but to follow the dictates of powerful Church leaders.[4]

      The *Realization of Manifest Destiny* chapter covers the various acts of discrimination, assimilation and genocide that are still occurring in the United States today and the beliefs propagated by the rationale that set forth Manifest Destiny was the driving force. Information about the signing of the *Declaration of Independence* and additional efforts to do what was set forth by President Thomas Jefferson, such as the *Louisiana Purchase* was also covered in this chapter. He managed to sidestep the British Government. England was still in control of the 13 colonies. Jefferson decided to push into legislation the establishment of the United States during a time of political unrest. West of the 13 colonies, states were being developed and joining the union, which was referred to as the United States. In regard to the "Indian problem," Jefferson thought he would participate in what he considered to be the most humane of the options. He decided to work towards assimilating the Native American people by the introduction of agriculture.

Andrew Jackson was not so kind. He pushed the *Indian Removal Act* through Congress and worked toward pushing the Indian people to the western part of the country or decimating them completely. Great numbers of Indian people lost their lives as a result of Jackson's legislation. He was the driving force behind the "Trail of Tears." Other legislative decisions that had a major impact on the Native American people are also covered in this chapter.

The Euro-Americans coerced the Indian people to relinquish more of their land by the extermination of the buffalo. They were starved and forced to move to reservations and rely on the government for food. Reservations were constructed where the land was considered the least desirable. The Dawes Allotment Act along with the Allen and Sedition Acts, were methods of allotting land to Indian people in an attempt to disintegrate Indian treaty land bases. These acts reduced the Indian land claims from 140 million acres to less than 50 million acres in 46 years. The education and land policies were put into place to undermine the culture of the Indian people, by uprooting them from their homes and enforcing a disciplined education, along with a coerced hatred of their Indian heritage.[5]

As early as 1842, there were 37 Indian schools established by the new Bureau of Indian Affairs (BIA).

The BIA was created by the War Department. Boarding and Residential School legislation came into effect during the 1880s, and the design for these institutions was fashioned after military encampments: highly structured routines; the wearing of uniforms and/or used Euro-American clothing; and marching in formation. Students were expected to stare ahead during classroom instruction and not communicate with one another at all during most of their stay at these institutions. These routines were enforced in all the schools. As a result of these highly regimented environments, the children, or more appropriate and accurate in most cases, teenagers who left these institutions, did not establish an ability to think for themselves. A recipe for disaster was created as the result of the abuse that every child who attended these boarding and residential schools either witnessed and/or was a victim of involving various forms of abuse; physical, sexual, emotional, and spiritual.

I used the *Remnants of a Shattered Past* chapter to relay the results of the historical trauma that was inflicted on Indian people. This information can be used to help all who have suffered at the hands of the oppressors. Oppression is a method of control, separating one group from another to enhance a feeling of superiority. Be it: racial, gender, socio-economic and/or religion/spirituality based. All have paid as a result of past and current acts of oppression. As a result of historical trauma, a vast number of Indian people may be suffering from Post Traumatic Stress Disorder, shame, malignant trauma, Residential and Boarding School Syndrome, loss of culture, and difficulties with communicating with others. Many Native American people are struggling with maintaining relationships, securing employment, and wrestling with serious problems, such as domestic violence, suicide, child abuse, child neglect, health related disorders, and substance abuse.

Alcoholism is addressed as a symptom and not of and in itself concerning the possible causes of dysfunction for Indian people. Alcohol has been recognized for destroying lives and has torn apart families. What has set alcohol apart from other addictive substances is its universal acceptance and association with common bonds between people. The media portrays what great fun can be had by all when ingesting alcoholic beverages. Local establishments, such as bars and saloons, have become profitable business enterprises. Happy hours and cocktail parties are held to entice people in their ventures to look for love and/or companionship, relax with friends, and to hold important business dealings. Wine is symbolic with various religions as a form of communion and other religious practices. Alcohol consumption dates back to approximately 12,000 BC. During the period of ancient Greece, Plato applauded alcohol's social and medicinal characteristics.[6]

Alcohol is here to stay and we need to get to the root cause of why people are abusing this substance. One in ten American adults has a "drinking problem." [7] I described in the *Remnants of a Shattered Past* chapter how PTSD is associated with the use of alcohol. Many individuals who suffer from PTSD use alcohol to deaden the pain they are experiencing. It's not that Indian people won't stop drinking alcohol, they can't stop. Remember I suffered from PTSD, I would go out with friends and never plan on getting drunk, but had difficulty stopping. Many times I left bars wishing I didn't have so much to drink. I no longer have problems with alcohol since I have gotten rid of PTSD and have dealt with most of my shame issues. I consider myself a work in progress. Also, remember my personal history included my mother's attendance of a boarding school and my childhood was laced with abuse and neglect. The description of my life experiences fits with what most Indian people have also experienced.

Proactive forms of healing are described in the *One Step at a Time* chapter. There needs to be a retraining from destructive thoughts and actions to achieve more positive behaviors, moving towards the practice of true community building activities, such as looking out for one's neighbors. The purpose of this chapter is to clearly demonstrate that there is hope for individuals and communities to become healthier. Many ways exist for those who seek a path of healing.

I describe the history of Indian people with the help of Eagle and Coyote, my protagonists. They traveled through time to reveal the truth as experienced by Indian people of the past and present. Eagle and Coyote are fictional characters developed to present the information in a different manner, adding clarity to the events occurring throughout the saga of the Indian people. They possess many gifts, such as being able to communicate telepathically and they can also shape shift and spirit travel. All these gifts were bestowed upon them by the Creator. Eagle and Coyote travel with Columbus, visit an Early French settlement, explore life at a boarding school and on a reservation, and fill the roles as prosecutor and case worker for tribal court. They surmise what they learned from their travels in the chapter *A Journey's End*.

The Eagle and Coyote stories were my way of bringing to life several settings to get a feel for what life was like for Indian people throughout history. These renditions were derived from a variety of sources including interviews with Indian people, a vast amount of research, personal employment opportunities, and my personal life experiences. The history of other tribes were used to assist with presenting a clearer picture of how the policies set forth by the government and other initiatives to take care of the "Indian problem" impacted the Indian people today and what can be done to fix the problems that still plague the Anishanaabeg.

Chapter I
Beginnings

The Anishanaabeg, meaning the original people, were settled in small villages and lived in peace and harmony, with the exception of an occasional battle against a competing tribe over resources. Battles were fought amidst formidable unity that existed within each tribal community. These resources consisted of valuable hunting and fishing grounds, along with land rich in edible plants and berries. Providing for one's family and the village as a whole was of the utmost importance. A strong sense of community was endemic. Their form of tribal leadership and the seeking of spiritual balance provided a cohesive relationship between all villagers within these tribal communities. The Anishanaabeg had respect for all, including women, children, animals and Mother Earth. Gratitude was extended to the Great Mystery for meeting all their needs. Nothing was taken for granted. Colorful renditions of their ancestral history and valuable lessons were taught while they sat around the camp fire.

Eagle and Coyote pretend to be members of another Ojibwe tribe when they visit an Ojibwe village to find out about their culture and spiritual beliefs. The tribal people welcome Eagle and Coyote and invite them to participate in their tribal activities. Eagle and Coyote learn a lot from the elders and other tribal members. Join them as they explore life with a traditional Anishnaabeg village.

Traditional Ojibwe Village in the 1300s

"You are getting heavy. Let's sit a bit over on that mountain top while I catch my breath."

Eagle gracefully landed on a large rock near the top of the mountain. While perched on the rock, they begin observing an Ojibwe village. The Creator requested they learn about the customs, beliefs and values by observing and participating in the daily activities with an Ojibwe tribe. The villagers were settling down for their midday meal. An elder gives thanks for the meal they were about to eat and for everybody's hard work during the morning hours.

"You know, Coyote I am looking forward to observing the people at this village. I'm glad the Creator sent us on this mission," said Eagle.

"Remember the tribe we visited in the southern part of western hemisphere? They built those elaborate canals and had these raised farmlands," recalled Coyote.

"I do. And remember the pyramids of the Mayans and Aztecs?" asked Eagle.

"Those were amazing. Some of the tribal communities have been progressing for centuries," stated Coyote.

Eagle and Coyote returned their focus to the Ojibwe villagers.

"One of the men prayed for the deer's spirit and thanked him for providing his family with food after he shot the deer this morning with his bow and arrow," said Eagle.

Eagle went on to explain information about the Ojibwe language. "He referred to the deer as *wawahkeshi*. The Creator told us, when he endowed us with the ability to understand and speak the Ojibwe language, it is a descriptive language like many other tribal languages."

"*Wawahkeshi* represents gentleness and innocence. These animals serve as a reminder to the Indian people to establish a strong healthy connection with children before exposing them to additional people and other strange energies and instills a remembrance of the traditions, which are natural and suitable for family units,"[8] Coyote added.

"The animal kingdom does provide the Indian people with a lot of meaningful values and guidance," said Eagle.

"When I watch *wawahkeshi* run in the woods, they appear so graceful and peaceful," replied Coyote.

"Yes, they do."

"Let's talk about that *waboose* (rabbit) who gave up his life for us yesterday. He was just running around playing with his brothers and sisters and here you swooped down and picked him up," replied Coyote.

"I know he was tasty and all, but he did have a spirit," implied Eagle as she mournfully thought about the rabbit.

"Even though the Creator made *waboose* one of the most common preys, they do have significant meaning for Indian people. The *waboose* represent to the Indian people fertility and new life,"[9] said Eagle.

"Hey! You know we can pray for that *waboose* right now can't we?" pleaded Coyote as he bent his head down preparing to pray feeling a little guilty.

"Yes. Let's pray for the spirit of the *waboose* and thank him for providing us with nourishment," replied Eagle.

They used the words the hunter used and solemnly prayed for the waboose they dined on the day before. After they prayed, they curled up and took a short nap together.

As Coyote was wiping the sleep from his eyes, he noticed Eagle was smiling while she was sleeping.

That must be some dream she's having.

Subconsciously feeling eyes resting on her, Eagle slowly opened her eyes to find Coyote staring down at her.

"Listen, you silly fool, I don't do that to you when you're sleeping," scowled Eagle as she sat up and starred back at Coyote.

"I'm sorry. Must have been some dream. Would you like to tell me about it?"

"No. It's none of your business," replied Eagle.

"Have it your way."

"Okay. Have it your way. I miss my mate. I've been longing for him for a couple of weeks now," exclaimed Eagle and she tried to hide the tears she was starting to shed.

"Well then, why didn't you just say so," replied Coyote indignantly.

"I just did," retorted Eagle.

"Let's not waste anymore time. We have to continue observing these people," stated Eagle as she tried to gain composure.

"Look at those children. One of them is playing with a bow and arrow. You see that boy over there?" asked Coyote.

"Yeah, I see him," replied Eagle.

"Did you see how the girl handled the bow and arrow? She was giving a demonstration to that younger boy," stated Coyote

"He caught on fast didn't he," replied Eagle

"Yes, he did."

Women were pounding deer hides and hanging them on a long pole. Younger children were chasing each other. The older children were working alongside the adults copying what the adults were doing.

"What are they going to do with all those deer hides?" asked Coyote.

"I don't know. We are going to have to change into human forms, then go and find out more about this tribe and what they are up to," said Coyote.

"I think you're right," replied Eagle.

"You think I'm right. What day is it? You never say I'm right," exclaimed Coyote.

"Yeah, I think you're right," said Eagle, trying to hide her smile.

"Do you think we have all our strength back after the last shape shift episode?" asked Coyote.

"I think we'll be okay," stated Eagle.

"What's going to be our story when we reach the village?" asked Eagle.

"I think we should be visitors from another village who speak the same language as they do," replied Coyote.

"That could work," responded Eagle.

"I don't want you to spend most of your time trying to woo the women," stated Eagle as she tapped her talons on the ground.

Ignoring Eagle's comment, Coyote asked, "Are we going to be related, like sister and brother or something else? How can we explain that we're not together if you know what I mean?"

"It sounds like you don't want it to look like you have an attachment to me so you are available to the women," stated Eagle.

"You don't want to rob me of my fun do you," asked Coyote as he stared at Eagle in a stern way.

"Okay, have it your way. We can be cousins from the same clan," responded Eagle as she was trying not to let her frustration towards Coyote get the better of her.

"Thanks, Cousin."

Shape shifting took a few minutes as they prepared their spirits and minds to adjust to their new identities. Coyote transformed into a handsome young man. He had long black hair tied back in a braid with an eagle feather held by sinew at the end of the braid. Sinew was a waxy thread made out of the intestines of animals. He was almost six feet in height and sported a slim build with a muscular chest. Coyote's dark brown eyes were dancing with an air of mischief and curiosity.

His loin cloth was made from bear skin. He wore bear skin moccasins laced tightly to his feet by leather straps made of bear hide.

Eagle's transformation took the form of a statuesque, beautiful young woman. Her dark brown eyes represented deep pools of sincerity and knowledge. She was of medium build and medium height. Her long black hair was tied in a braid with strips of leather dyed with the juice of blueberries, which turned the leather deep purple. These were used to tie the bottom of her braid in which an eagle feather was securely fastened. She wore a dress made of deer skin. Blue and red flowers were painted on the bottom of her dress. Her moccasins were trimmed with porcupine quills colored a deep purple and red. She walked with a confident stride.

Their eyes stared straight ahead as they contemplated their encounter while they walked down a trail, created by years of trampling feet, to the village of Ojibwe people.

****

An Ojibwe man approached Coyote and Eagle as they got close to the village. He stopped sculpting the bone he was working on as soon as he saw them. The man had bronze skin and long black hair that was kept in one long braid that hung down the center of his back. He wore a loin cloth made of deer skin. His feet were bare. His dark brown eyes looked at Coyote and Eagle intently as he welcomed them to come and sit with him. He told the woman who was standing off in the distance to round up the other men and women so that they could meet their new visitors.

Coyote used the Ojibwe words for eagle woman and big wind when they introduced themselves. The Ojibwe word for big wind is *Chi Nodin* and Eagle Woman is *Migizi Kwe*. It was reported by the Creator that both names are highly revered by the Ojibwe people. Their new names will be used from this point forward when Eagle and Coyote are interacting with the people of the village.

Standing Crow, the man who greeted them, was the first to introduce himself. He was a young man, perhaps in his early 20s. The elders sitting around the table were the first to be introduced by Standing Crow. He happened to be the son of the chief of the village. The chief's name was Running Bear.

Standing Crow introduced his mate, Crane Spirit. She smiled warmly while he told Migizi Kwe and Chi Nodin his children's names, which were Song Bird and Dancing Bear as he pointed to them. They were sitting close by on the ground with the other children. Standing Crow asked Running Bear to take over the discussion as he sat down.

Running Bear stood up and introduced himself and gave his clan name, which was the Crane Clan. He asked the visitors why they are visiting their village.

"We heard about other Ojibwe villages. Migizi Kwe and I, since we like to explore, we decided to take off on foot and see if we can find more villages like ours. We have been traveling for three days. We are very tired, hungry, and are wondering if we could rest a while at your village," asked Chi Nodin.

"We would be happy to provide you with lodging in one of our wigwams," replied Running Bear.

"What sparked your curiosity about other villages?" asked Running Bear.

"We were visited by people like you. They told us they came from a village, which took four or five days of travel, so we thought we would go exploring and see if we could meet people like ourselves," replied Migizi Kwe.

"Are you two wed?" asked Standing Bear.

"We can't marry because we are both from the Eagle Clan," said Magizi Kwe.

"We can't marry within our clan either," replied Standing Bear.

Migizi Kwe and Chi Nodin had several objectives to accomplish for the Creator. It is important to have an understanding of the tribal people regarding their values, activities and customs. He needs to be prepared should they ask for his help in prayer and to help make a determination of what to do if problems arise.

Running Bear made arrangements regarding where Migizi Kwe and Chi Nodin would be staying and what they had planned for their day. The elders were going to continue stitching the birch bark for the canoes. The men were going fishing and hunting. The women were gathering berries and preparing deer hides.

The men were informed that deer were plentiful over by the meadow where the white tailed hawks were seen perched. This was foretold by a dream that Swift Water had the other evening.

    Standing Crow stood and started retreating to his wigwam to get his hunting gear, Chi Nodin followed suit.

    Migizi Kwe helped a young mother strap a cradle board to her back with a small baby in it. They joined the other women, all carrying black ash baskets to a clearing to the west of them. Migizi Kwe was surprised to see how many blueberries had grown in the field. She stood by the woman she helped with her baby and began picking the delicious fruit. The work was tedious, but rewarding. With twenty or so women picking they had the baskets filled in only a few hours. Black bears were off in the distance eating berries right off the bushes. The bears and women did not pay attention to one another. They just kept about their business.

    The women carried the berry filled baskets back the village and wrapped the baskets in deer hides to protect the berries from animals and insects. Some of the men returned from fishing and the women assisted with the cleaning the fish they caught. A couple of the men had dug a hole in the ground and placed the cleaned fish in a large basket. The basket was covered and placed in the hole. The hole was covered with dirt and a fire was made on top of the hole. The fire was stoked continually by the fire tender.

    Some of the other men shot two deer with a bow and arrow. Chi Nodin counted the 12 velvet covered points on one of the deer. The deer were placed on a bear hide. The men conducted a prayer for the deer's spirit and thanked Gitchi Manito for providing them with the deer for their village. The men took turns pulling the bear hide back to the village.

The atmosphere of the village was filled with the satisfaction of a day well spent accomplishing the goals for the village. A couple of men and women ripped the hide from the freshly killed deer and hung the carcasses from a nearby tree by straps made of deer hide. The hides were strung on a long horizontal pole to dry before cleaning.

The elders worked on sewing large strips of birch bark together for a couple of hours. Afterwards they went into the woods in search of three of the medicinal plants, sage, cedar and sweet grass. These herbs are used for a variety of spiritual and/or healing practices and aid in communication with the Creator.

Running Bear spoke, "There are two young people, a girl named Red Robin and a boy named Fast Elk, who took their journeys and passed through one stage in their lives and are entering another. It's the responsibility of the elders to demonstrate how to use the medicines they have gathered. A medicine bag was made for both the girl and the boy by the elders. As foretold by our ancestors, four Medicine Men with the colors of the dawn painted on their foreheads came out of the eastern sky, each carrying a live otter in his hand. The otters served as medicine bags. The Medicine Men restored life to a young man who had been dead eight days. We have been instructed to continue with the traditions of our ancestors by carrying medicine bags in the event that we may need to help some of our people. Now that these young people have passed through the portal into adulthood, they have the responsibility to care for others also."[10]

"What was used to make the medicine bags you are using today at the ceremony?" asked Eagle, as she feared his answer may be a live animal.

"We used deer hide," replied Running Bear.

White Wolf, an elder, explained the rite of passage activities and about the ceremony the villagers were holding during the evening.

"A small wigwam was made for Red Robin by her mother. Red Robin has fasted for four days and four nights in that wigwam and has reached maturity. We have been preparing for a feast in honor of these two special people for a couple of days. *Wawahkesi* offered his life to us this morning and will be prepared for the feast. Since this is the first summer of her womanhood, Red Robin could not have berries, fruit or vegetables until after she matures. She has to pick her own strawberries for tonight's ceremony. The *Medewiwin* (Medicine man) will drum, sing, and then hold a spoon with berries up to her mouth four times and pull the spoon away from her each time. On the fifth time, the spoon is brought to her mouth and she can eat the berries."[11]

"Why does it have to be four times?" asked Migizi Kwe.

"The number four symbolizes the four directions, the four sacred plants, and the four stages in the life of the Anishanaabeg. Our four sacred plants are sage, tobacco, cedar and sweet grass. We use these plants for healing, purification and calling in our ancestors," replied White Wolf.

"Thanks for the explanation," said Eagle.

"Fast Elk, the young boy who has come of age, has been in his tree fort, which was made by his father. He has been fasting for the past six days. He has had a vision that he will be a great warrior and is permitted to come back to the village and partake in the feast too. The feast will be held soon after the berry ceremony," noted White Wolf.

"May I ask a question?" asked Migizi Kwe.

"Yes, you may," responded White Wolf.

"What do you do when a couple gets married?" asked Migizi Kwe as she thought longingly of her mate.

"We just had a marriage ceremony last week," replied White Wolf

"You did? Who was married?" asked Migizi Kwe.

"It was Blue Thunder and Laughing Fox," said White Wolf.

"Can you tell me about that ceremony?" asked Migizi Kwe.

"There isn't a ceremony. The young man plays the courting flute and if the young girl is interested, she will invite him to visit with her at her parents' wigwam. The couple is watched closely and not left alone. The young man will bring over a deer he has killed to prove that he can take care of his family. If the parents approve of him, they invite him to stay and feast on the venison with them. The young couple will go away for a few days by themselves, which serves as their wedding ceremony. The couple may live in her parents' wigwam and after a while build a wigwam of their own. Or perhaps build a wigwam of their own soon after they are wed. It is very rare, but the couple may reside with the man's parents."[12]

"That includes all of the festivities for marriage?" asked Eagle to clarify that she was told everything tied with weddings.

"That's all," replied White Wolf.

"In our village there has been trouble surrounding the male choosing more than one wife. That doesn't always set well with the first wife and they may move out and return back to her parents' wigwam."

"Would you like to learn about anything else?" asked White Wolf as she adjusted her deer skin dress.

"What do you do about discipline especially, towards someone who has killed another in the village?" asked Coyote.

"We let the family of the one who is deceased decide on the punishment. Sometimes the one who caused the death is put to death by a male clan member of the deceased. Sometimes the murderer is adopted by the family. These problems do not readily occur because we have to rely on one another for our survival," replied White Wolf.

"Let's talk about cheerier things. Are there special celebrations tied with a child's birth?" asked Eagle?

"*I hope you are paying attention Coyote. We have to report to Gitchi Manito all this information. I saw you* staring at those young women just now." (Migizi Kwe is reaching Chi Nodin telepathically).

"Don't worry cousin. I am catching everything," responded Chi Nodin.

"Remember the parents and elders watch the young men and women closely. We don't have time for you to court, wed and dump some unsuspecting woman before we are done here."

"You're right. I will try to show some restraint."

White Wolf was staring at them trying to figure out if they were ready for her to tell them about child birth and didn't know if she should disturb the two or not.

Migizi Kwe noticed White Wolf's reaction and said, "I'm sorry, I was thinking about the way our village practices the wedding ceremony. Our village does it the same way."

Nice save, cousin.

Migizi Kwe smiled at White Wolf and said, "Please tell us about the birthing ceremony."

"If the baby is born at night, drums are pounded loudly. The men, other than the newborn's relatives, work together to see if they can take the baby from the father and mother. The child's relatives throw water on the attacking party. The men fight and wrestle. The men, who secure the baby, bring the baby to the chief and the chief carries the baby four times around the fire while the people are singing a song with words meaning 'we have caught the little bird.' These activities are carried out to make the child brave by hearing so much noise as soon as it is born."[13]

"That sounds like fun," responded Coyote as he smiled and winked at one of the women who caught his eye.

"We celebrated the birth of a little boy born to Wild Rose and Goose Feathers six nights ago. Do you want to hear about our naming ceremony?" asked White Wolf.

Chi Nodin and Migizi Kwe nodded in response.

"The naming of a child can happen in many ways ranging from visions or dreams, to the selection being made by the child's parents of common names or nicknames of the deceased."

"See that young girl over there?" asked White Wolf as she pointed to the left of them.

"She received her name from a dream that Standing Crow had the night before she was born. Her name is Rainbow. Standing Crow dreamed of a thunder storm and then after the storm there was a beautiful rainbow. It was so radiant he thought the new child must be called this name in honor of all rainbows. So she was," said White Wolf as she smiled at the young girl when Rainbow heard her name and turned her attention to source of the conversation.

"Dreams for our people are a way we learn how to do new things. Much of our wisdom and knowledge comes from dreaming, then doing what our dreams suggest. Carrying out the tasks described in our dreams tests our strength. Our ability to dream and to remember our dreams is taught to us when we are children. Fasting, isolation, and meditation give us the ability to commune with our guardian spirits," reported White Wolf.

"I am sorry. I am rambling on and on. You probably know all this," stated White Wolf.

"I love hearing about what you do at your village," said Migizi Kwe as she smiled at White Wolf.

"Come here, Hawk Vision, and tell them more about the importance of dreams," pleaded White Wolf. Hawk Vision was standing a short distance from where they were sitting.

Hawk Vision sat down, arranged her deer skin robe, and turned to Migizi Kwe and Chi Nodin "Many of our people have dreamed great dreams of things that have happened in the past or will happen in the future. I saw myself in a large house built of logs surrounded by people with very pale skin. None of my people have ever dreamed about something like that before. Stands Alone had this dream about a brown bear, and he could be heard calling out for the brown bear when he was in danger. It is said that when you dream of an animal you can become that animal. He was wounded and the men thought they could hear the cry of the brown bear. When the men got to where they thought he was lying, they could see a brown bear off in the distance running away from the area," said Hawk Vision, as she watched the visitors intently.

"It's time to go to the feast. I was coming to get you when you asked me to sit down," said Hawk Vision.

"We are making a fire tomorrow night to give thanks and ask for guidance for those who just entered a new passage in their lives at a sweat lodge ceremony," said Hawk Vision.

"Would it be alright if we participated in that event?" asked Migizi Kwe.

"I will ask the ones who will be running the lodge," responded Hawk Vision.

The feast was spread out on the table where they sat when they first arrived at the village. Chi Nodin was amazed to see sweet potatoes, corn and tomatoes along with berries and lots of venison. He could hardly wait to dig in.

Running Bear asked his father to give the prayer before they began eating.

"Oh, Gitchi Manito
Megwetch for this food.
Megwetch for the safety of the men
Who hunted today to bring food to this table.
Megwetch for the vision that Fast Elk received on his journey.
And the coming of age for Red Robin.
We pray along with Gitchi Manito
To ask for guidance for this young man and woman
And to keep our village healthy and safe
As we move into the future.
Megwetch to the four directions.
Oh, Megwetch"

Everybody around the table responded by saying "ah ho."

The feast was as delicious as it looked. As planned, Migizi Kwe and Chi Nodin were learning a lot about this culture as they participated in all the activities.

Red Robin and Fast Elk were presented with their medicine bags by an elder of the village. The villagers sang and danced around the fire into the evening until everybody was exhausted. They sat around a large camp fire while the elders told legends associated with *Nanabazoo*. One of the legends an elder told relayed information about the first porcupines.

"A long time ago porcupine was like the Anishanaabeg. He had really soft skin. Porcupines ate the same things. They ate greens and tree buds and things like that. They would climb trees to get away from the wild animals. One day, this porcupine was out gathering in the woods. He was out in the field by the edge, and he was eating when across the field comes a great big wolf. So he gets in the top of a tree as far as he could get so the wolf could not reach him. The wolf goes away."

"He is in that same field again and a bear comes across, growling and growling at him. The porcupine runs and climbs the tree where the bear can't reach him. The bear is trying to reach up and grab him. The porcupine is safe."

"So the bear goes away and the porcupine climbs back down, and he wants to get something to eat, so he is out in the field and he is eating. He's under a hawthorn bush eating the berries that are on the ground and he keeps eating. And the thorns are picking him in the back and hurt him. And he gets this idea. So he gathers these branches and ties them in a ball and crawls underneath the bush and then he goes out to find food. A wolf tries to bite him and the porcupine is curled up underneath. He continues eating. Then Nanabazoo sees him with the bushes on him, and porcupine told Nanabazoo that he had to do something."

"Everybody is trying to eat me so I have to protect myself by putting these branches on my back."

"Nanabazoo says, I will help you."

"Nanabazoo made a clay pack and put it on his back and he stripped the branches and put the thorns in the clay. So the wolf sees the porcupine and tries to bite the clay pack and he got thorns stuck in his mouth and in his face and the wolf runs away howling."

"Then the bear comes along and he sees the porcupine and thinks that he would be a good meal so he takes a swipe at him and he runs away crying with thorns sticking out of his paw. And that is how the porcupine got its quills," said the elder.

****

"Who is this Nanabazoo? He sounds like he has a lot of the same gifts."

"Did you hear that he was a trickster too?" responded Migizi Kwe.

"Yeah cousin, I heard".

"Do you think there is some connection to me and Nanabazoo?" asked Chi Nodin.

"I think there might be. We are going to have to ask the Creator."

Chi Nodin was feeling all smug about himself and before he knew it time slipped away, and it was time to retire for the evening. Migizi Kwe and Chi Nodin shared wigwams with other young men and women. Migizi Kwe stayed in a woman's wigwam and Chi Nodin, much to his chagrin, slept in a man's wigwam.

Sleep came quickly for Migizi Kwe and Chi Nodin. Their slumber was laced with fanciful dreams of a faraway land. Oftentimes Migizi Kwe and Chi Nodin would have the same dream at the same time. They were in a meadow. There were these large creatures and they were riding on them, moving swiftly through the forest. They came upon a hill, then a pond. They got off these creatures and swam under a waterfall.

****

The next day, the villagers scurried off to accomplish their many chores. Evening came, and before they settled down for the evening meal, a discussion was held regarding the sweat lodge ceremony. Chi Nodin was given permission to participate in this ceremony.

The sweat lodge was constructed with bent poles and covered with deer hides. Six men entered the lodge at a time. The elder men entered the lodge last so that they could sit near the eastern doorway and run the lodge ceremony. Chi Nodin was asked to sit out until the second round. The fire tender handed in rocks by utilizing a long pole with deer antlers attached by sinew on the end of the wooden pole. The leader of the lodge received the rocks by using a small set of deer antlers without wooden extensions. As the rocks were placed in the center of the lodge, the attendees greeted the rocks or grandfathers as they were referred to, by saying "*Boozhoo Mishomis.*"

The rocks were placed in the center of the wigwam, water was sprinkled on the rocks and the rocks were caressed with sweet grass. The leader in the lodge said a prayer and the group sang after he sprinkled the rocks with water three times. The steam from the rocks symbolizes the communication emanating from the grandfathers. All the men in the lodge were given a chance to say their prayers and possibly sing if they felt the need to do so. Chi Nodin found the voice of the Ojibwe and sang the songs too. These songs rang with familiarity which baffled Chi Nodin.

****

"Boy, it was really hot in there. At one point I thought my skin was going to melt off," he told Migizi Kwe when they snuck off alone for a couple of minutes that evening.

"I was told by the women that the Creator only makes it as hot as you can stand it," replied Migizi Kwe.

"I was really moved by the singing and praying," stated Chi Nodin.

"We prayed for the four leggeds, our sacred items like our eagle feathers, and our loved ones. We thanked the Creator for all he has given us. If I had any questions when it was my turn to pray, I could ask the Creator what I needed to know. Or another way, I was told, was to ask the leader of the sweat lodge about something I was wondering about and he would ask the Creator and grandfathers for me in the lodge. I could meet with the leader of the lodge before the lodge ceremony began to let him know what I needed to find out," stated Chi Nodin.

    "This has been a very interesting experience," stated Chi Nodin.

    "I can't wait to share with the Creator what we have learned," stated Migizi Kwe as they headed back separately to the village to avoid suspicion.

    "Those people were so nice. They were willing to share everything with us."

    "I know" replied Eagle.

Chapter II

Traditional Period

Dancing around the fire
telling stories,
food abundant.
Forests filled with animals,
fields plentiful with berries.

Armed against intruders,
opposing tribes of yore.
Clans provided leadership.
Egalitarian rites abound.
Grateful for all bestowed.

Blessed by the Great Mystery,
industrious, content and prosperous,
dreams, visions and prophecies.
The esteemed Mother Earth
held in highest regard
by the Anishanaabeg

Prophesies and Migration

   The Anishanaabeg have a history dating back 50,000 plus years on the continent known as North America, also referred to as Turtle Island. Before the 1300s, the Ojibwe resided in the St. Lawrence River Valley area now known as Newfoundland. The future of the Anishanaabeg was foretold by the prophets of the Seven Fires. The vision included a move westward, or the

Anishanaabeg would perish. Some of the native people scoffed at these predictions, and others believed these words to be true.

The seven prophets predicted a time during the Fourth Fire, when men with pale faces would visit their villages. If they came in peace offering gifts, life would be wonderful. The white people and the Anishanaabeg would share resources, knowledge, and build stronger communities. If the white people came with fire power and/or death faces, the Anishanaabeg will confront a doomed future. The death face and the brotherhood face may appear to be very similar. The Anishanaabeg were warned the brotherhood face could feign one of suffering; however, in reality these visitors' hearts may be filled with greed for the riches of the land in which the Anishanaabeg were residing.

The Fifth Fire would be a time of great struggle for the Indian people and result in a vast depletion of their population. The Sixth Fire represented a time when the children were taken away from their homes and taught to adapt the practices of a different culture. The Fifth and Six Fires depended on what the white people did during the time of the Fourth Fire.

During the Seventh Fire, new people will emerge. These people will retrace their steps. These steps will take them back to the elders. Some of the elders will be silent out of fear. Many elders have fallen asleep and will awaken with nothing to offer and only a few may be available to guide other Anishanaabeg on their journeys. It was prophesized that if the white people chose the right road, the Eighth and final fire will be lit, which represents peace, love, and unity amongst all. If the white people make the wrong choice, then the destruction, which the Europeans brought with them when they came to this country, will cause much suffering and death to all of Earth's people.[14] The Eight Fire may also represent a time of revelation when things, good and bad, will be revealed to all. Today, many Indian people believe the time of the eighth fire is quickly approaching.

Because of these prophecies, some of the people migrated northwest to the Quebec area. Others continued their migration to the west to the land where food grows on the water (wild rice), known today as Minnesota, or the Bahweting area, known as Sault Ste. Marie, Michigan. They fished, trapped and later were in the lumber business.

The Lenni Lenape were considered the original people and later were referred to as the Anishanaabeg. The Lenni Lenape were known as the Grandfathers, from whom many tribal nations such as the Ojibwe were derived. The migration has connected the Ojibwe to many other tribes such as the Blackfoot, Cheyenne, Cree, Shawnee, Miami, Passamaquaddy, Penobscot, and Wampanoag. During a more recent migration westward, the Ojibwe traveled with descendents of the Odawa and Potwatomi tribes and settled in Michigan.[15] These three tribes were referred to as the Three Fires. Each tribe worked together to provide for the needs of all. They utilized similar dialects of the Algonquian language as a mode of communicating with one another. The joint cooperation of the Three Fires Confederacy ensured protection and control over the Three Fires' territorial claims from other tribes. Today, these tribes are still referred to as the Three Fires. However, they function as separate entities lacking the unity that existed in the past.

Tribal Leadership

The Indian people had a form of leadership in place in which respect for all tribal members occurred naturally. The Ojibwe tribes as well as other tribal communities were made up of clan systems that served as a form of leadership. Seven original clans existed for the Ojibwe people. These have been, but are not limited to, the Crane, Loon, Fish, Bear, Marten, Deer, and Bird.[16] Clan members believe they have a special relationship with the clan animal. This relationship delineated the specific role each member of certain clans possessed in consideration to tribal leadership. The clan system is still utilized today to varying degrees with various tribes.

All members of the same clan, blood relatives or not, were considered brothers and sisters. Members of the same clan could not marry. The clan and kinship networks created a blanket of security for the villagers, and created a strong commitment to giving and sharing that was endemic of the tribal culture. The Anishanaabeg lived in areas abundant with wild game, fish, and edible plant life such as berries, acorns, and fruit. The tribal people did not take this abundance for granted.

The abundance of food afforded the Anishanaabeg time to participate in various ceremonies. The villagers danced, sang, played games, and built the tools they needed for food gathering, farming and other necessities. They had an optimistic view about life in general and continually planned for their future. Cooperation was involved in providing sustenance for the village as a whole, and all able villagers worked diligently to provide for the well-being of the community.

Language

The origins of the Ojibwe language were associated with the Algonquian or Algonkin language groups. The language was derived originally from the Lenape people who defined the linguistic connection to those who were considered close relatives such as the Mohican, Nanticokes, Shawnee, Cheyee, Penobscots, Passamaquaddy, Wapanoag, Odawa, Potawatomi, Mesquakie and others.[17] Language is a descriptive mode of communication for various cultures. One word can have multiple meanings. For example, the word bakade meaning black or blackened in the Ojibwe language can have a deeper meaning. The Anishanaabeg blackened their faces before they entered the woods on a vision quest to enhance their spiritual connections. Knowledge of the language is paramount to understanding the meaning of stories, prayers, and songs. Language and culture are intertwined.

Public speaking was practiced and perfected by many of the Anishanaabeg. The Ojibwe language explains human emotions and actions as well as natural phenomena. The speaker recalled events by using language to instill detailed images. The Anishanaabeg were good listeners also. It was considered a form of respect to listen intently to those who were speaking. Children were strongly encouraged to listen. They would be responsible for passing down the traditional information to their children and grandchildren. Children were taught to speak well and portray the exact meanings of what they wanted to relay to others. The stories and legends provided entertainment along with the teaching of valuable lessons and a way of providing historical information.

      Stories passed down from the ancestors were laced with moral teachings such as not being greedy, the necessity of giving to others, and being kind and respectful. The teachings were often indirect, so the listener had to pay attention fully in order to develop an understanding of the message being conveyed. The Anishnanaabeg relied on oral tradition to teach many important lessons. The telling of stories was a way of relaying historical and cultural information in a tried and true method that has continued to be practiced today in many tribal settings.

Child Rearing Practices

Childbirth was celebrated with feasting. The child and mother were inseparable for the first year of the child's life. During the traditional period, the educational process occurred in three phases. In phase one, a child would be strapped onto a cradle board, referred to as a *dikinagan,* for most of the child's first two years to learn the life skills of observation and listening. They watched the adults in the village work and learned about the habits of people and animals. Their observation skills were enhanced as they matured from infant to a young child. Surrounded by nature, they observed and listened to the communication between animals and people. The art of listening was fostered further through seeking wisdom on their search to learn the deeper meaning of things. Today, listening and observation skills are still held in high regard with many Indian people.

The second phase began at approximately age seven. From one year of age until adulthood, girls were cared for and nurtured by their mothers, grandmothers, and aunts. All female adults in the village, other than their mothers, were considered aunts, and all these caregivers provided training to prepare them for adulthood. They received training on how to raise crops, to gather plants and berries for food, and to provide other necessities for the home. Another lesson involved how to make nets for fishing. The making of fishing nets consisted of gathering basswood or nettle cord, learning how to dry these materials, separating the fibers by wetting them and drawing the fibers through their mouths, how to roll the fibers, and how to tie the netting fiber in different patterns to enable the fisherman to catch different kinds of fish.

Young women were trained on how to tan animal hides, which included the removal of flesh, washing off the blood stains, soaking the hide, scraping off the fur, soaking the hide in deer brains, scraping the hide again, and then stretching the hide on a wooden frame. Tribal women also needed to learn how to use the bow and arrow so they could provide protection for the children and themselves when the men were away on hunting expeditions. Many tribal women were proficient in hunting and fishing.

At the age of seven, fathers, uncles, and older male cousins provided boys with lessons on hunting and fishing. Concerning the construction of canoes, boys were taught how to remove bark from birch trees and how to shape the wood for flooring and gunwales. They were given instruction about how to gather and combine spruce resin with grease and black powder of cedar to coat the canoe as an adhesive and sealant. Another important lesson involved learning how to make bows and arrows used in hunting. When the young male had his first successful kill, the whole village celebrated. The kill was served as the main part of the feast.

The third phase of the educational process consisted of the search for wisdom. The search extended into late adulthood. This involved a quest to know the entire story of things, events and happenings from the simplest to the most complex, through the many layers of meaning; learning the whole of things.[18]

The elders, adult males and females provided teachings to prepare the youth for their path in life. It was important to learn how to live in a gentle way with humbleness and respect accomplished through prayer, fasting, and listening to everything. The beliefs associated with the path of life included the following:

- Honor Gitchi Manito (The Creator).
- Honor elders.
- Honor our elder brothers (all animals are considered to be elder brothers because they were here before humans, and they are relied on for teachings, as well as for sustenance).
- Honor women.
- Keep promises and uphold pledges.
- Show kindness to everyone.
- Be peaceful in body and spirit.
- Be courageous.
- Be moderate in dreams, thoughts, words and deeds.[19]

Children were disciplined in many ways. They were ignored if they were tale bearing, and scolded if caught lying. When children quarreled with their peers, they would not be permitted to play with those children. Stealing usually resulted in the child returning the stolen object to the person it was stolen from. Older children often received spankings for stealing. Sometimes fear was used, but not to the extent that it was harmful to the children. Instilling fear about certain things was often a safety measure. For example, to prevent children from playing on a hill that was considered dangerous, the parents would put a scarecrow at the top of the hill to scare them, and the children never went back to the hill again.[20]

Boys and girls could play together when they were younger, but as they matured, it was not allowed. The children would copy the adults doing various chores, such as housekeeping, caring for dolls, hunting, fishing, and dancing to prepare them for adulthood. All age groups participated in a variety of games of chance and games involving dexterity, such as lacrosse. The use of games served as a part of the learning process.

The purpose of traditional Ojibwe educational practices was to prepare the young people to provide for the needs of the community. Children were also taught how to develop a meaningful relationship with the Great Mystery. These teachings were part of the balance of their life journeys and beyond into eternity. If one only learned about life skills without the benefit of obtaining knowledge about the spirit, it was believed this individual would live a life without purpose or any significant meaning. The entire village provided care, supervision, and instruction to the children. Essentially, all adults were responsible for the security and protection of all the children in the village. Also of equal importance in the learning process was the exploration of everyone's roots.

Creation Story

    The Anishanaabeg, like other cultures, had a creation story that was continually recited to provide lessons for all tribal people. In the beginning, *Gitchi Manito* created the universe as we know it today. He created Grandfather Sun and Grandmother Moon, Mother Earth and Father Sky. On the earth, he created all things, living and nonliving. He created life on the earth, in the sky, and in the water. He created the plants, rivers, four-legged and winged creatures, and the swimmers. After this was done, he created one of the greatest mysteries of all, the four seasons, to bring harmony and balance to all.

    After all creation of animate and inanimate entities was completed, then the Creator made man. After he created the first Anishanaabe, the Creator instructed him in a dream to name all things in the language given to him, Anishinaabemowin. So the first man went about his journey and named all things he saw, the animals, insects, birds and fish. He told *Gitchi Manito* in a dream he finished what was requested of him. Then the Creator gave the first man his name, which was Nanaboozho. Whenever the Anishanaabeg meet and greet one another, they say a part of his name, *Boozhoo*, meaning hello.

    The creation story tells how the Anishanaabeg originally migrated to the Great Lakes region from the East Coast. The Anishanaabeg resided peacefully until the villagers became restless and unsettled. Selfishness and competitiveness took over the lives of these inhabitants. The Anishanaabeg were at war with one another and they were not on the red road. Hatred and other forms of dysfunction ran rampant through the entire Anishanaabeg nation. The creator looked down at these settlements and decided to cleanse the earth with water to renew the earth, its inhabitants and begin anew. Many creation stories contain a flood as a part of the cleansing process.

    After this cleansing, Nanaboozho found refuge on a log with many animals. All of these animals tried to swim to the bottom to retrieve a piece of dirt to rebuild a land base. Many of them tried and failed. Then, the smallest, weakest of the four leggeds was able to accomplish what the other animals could not. That animal was the muskrat. However, the muskrat gave its life to bring up the dirt, which saved all the other animals and Nanaboozoo. The muskrat's lifeless body floated to the top of the water with the dirt clenched within his little hand. Nanaboozoo placed this dirt on the turtle's back and created the land, which today is referred to as Turtle Island.[21] The telling of creation stories has carried significance throughout the history of the Anishanaabeg.

Spiritual Practices

The most important event in an Indian child's life was, and continues to be with many tribal entities, the receipt of personal identity through a naming ceremony. The given name permitted the child to have a place by the tribal fire and be a part of the tribal thoughts and discussions. The name was a gift from the spirits, inherited through a naming ceremony by the person bestowing the name, usually soon after the child's birth. The given name was to be respected for its origin within the tribe and cherished by the one receiving it. The children's names would come to the leaders and other adults in the village through dreams and visions.

Sometimes children would receive the name of a namesake who passed on. Two people in the same village could not have the same name simultaneously.[22]

      Dreams were considered significant, so children were taught at an early age how to take notice of them. By examining their dreams closely, predictions of good and bad events and other necessary information could be derived. While they were still innocent, they were encouraged to walk alone in the woods to commune with their spirit guides. Their faces were blackened with coal before they ventured on this journey. Fasting also occurred during the time the young men and women were coming of age to assist with seeking direction for their adult years.

      Ceremonies were held to celebrate various stages in the lives of the villagers.

Ghost suppers were held to honor those who passed on. The ghost supper has been a traditional fall ceremony of Anishanaabeg people throughout history. The time when leaves are falling on the ground was considered a time for remembering and honoring those who walked on. The ghost supper has been held in many different ways. One common denominator includes the serving of the favorite foods of the ones who are being remembered. Usually a place is set at the table for the one(s) who passed on. The plate was fixed with a variety of the loved one's favorite foods and left for the entire evening.

Ancestry has been paramount for Anishanaabeg people. Ghost suppers served as an avenue for family stories and fond memories of the deceased. Families would visit another home and eat the food they prepared. Then that family would be invited to their home and so on. This fostered community awareness, and encouraged community trust and sharing.

The sweat lodge ceremony was another way Indian people united for a common purpose, which was to commune with the Creator and other spirit guides. Other tribal entities may conduct sweat lodge activities in a different manner. The sweat lodge ceremony served as a vehicle to give thanks, and pray to *Gitchi Manito* and the attendees' spirit guides. These ceremonies continue to be held today.

The lodge is constructed in a dome shape and made from bent poles and covered with animal hides. Today, tarps are often used. The door is located on the east side of the lodge. The east represents new beginnings and is where the sun rises. Attendees are instructed to enter the lodge in the eastern door and circle around clockwise until they are sitting next to the person who entered before them. Minimal clothing is appropriate to permit the spirit guides to roam freely within a person's psyche and body. Jewelry is not permitted because it may distract the spirits.

      The leader of the lodge gives direction on how each person is to enter the lodge and what order they will be sitting in the lodge. The leader instructs the fire tender to bring in the grandfathers, which are the hot rocks that have been heated by the sacred fire. The gathering of these special stones is a ritual in itself. Only the leaders of the sweat lodge can gather the rocks.

      The tender of the fire distributes one rock or a few rocks at a time and the attendee(s) may greet the grandfather by saying "*Boozhoo Mishomis.*" Sometimes the leader is the only one who says the greeting to the grandfathers as they are passed into the lodge. The leader sprinkles water on the rocks and then caresses the rocks with sweet grass. After the rocks are brought into the lodge, the door is closed. Songs are sung with the beating of a drum to call in the spirits.

Each person is given a chance to speak after the songs are sung. Each speaker introduces themselves after saying *Boozhoo Gitchi Manito,* which is saying a formal hello to the Creator. The introduction includes the persons name and totem (*dodem*) in the native language. Prayers for themselves or others in need would be said last. It is important to give thanks first to show appreciation for all the Creator has provided. Some of the things attendees would be thankful for are the four leggeds, the air, water, and food the Creator has provided for all of his people.

The ceremony can last up to four rounds. A round consists of each person having an opportunity to speak. The door is opened after each round. The attendees often drink cedar water. A private discussion may be held before and after this ceremony with the sweat lodge leader to explore answers to some of the questions an attendee may have. After the ceremony, a small feast is usually held and everyone partakes in comfortable banter with one another. Prior to eating, a small plate of food is prepared and offered to the Creator at the fire. The description of the sweat lodge ceremony is based on the author's personal experience. Other tribal entities may conduct sweat lodge activities in a different manner. These ceremonies continue to be held today.

Pow Wows are also considered spiritual events and continue to be held throughout most of North America. They are a way in which the Anishanaabeg socialize and celebrate their heritage. The term " pow wow" comes from the Algonquian derivative of "Pauau". It originally meant curing ceremony. Pow wows signify a time in which Anishanaabeg could sing, dance, feast and give gifts.

The main emphasis of this spiritual practice continues to be with the powers of nature, which are Father Sun, Mother Earth, mountains, rivers, clouds and animals. The traditional female and male dancers celebrate Mother Earth's gifts. Different forms of dancing are used to elicit rain for crops, preparation for hunting, food gathering, healing, and warfare as well as a way of extending respect and giving thanks. Many of these dances are handed down from generation to generation.

Another form of dancing is referred to as the jingle bell dancing. These dancers ward off illness and disease. The young woman or girl has a dream and is given instruction to become a jingle dress dancer during that dream. Today the bells for the dancer's regalia are made from the tops of chewing tobacco containers. There are teachings to be learned prior to wearing the dress. Teachings involve the physical, spiritual, emotional and mental balance needed to walk a good road or the red road.

The Four Sacred Plants

The four sacred plants are used in many of the spiritual ceremonies. Four sacred medicines provide balance, protection and cures for the Anishanaabeg and other cultures throughout history. The four sacred plants are tobacco, sage, sweet grass and cedar. The plants carry much significance, such as their representation of the four directions and the four stages in one's life. The four sacred plants have been used throughout history in spiritual and healing practices. Other herbs and spices are also used under the direction of a medicine man and other spiritual healers.

Tobacco (*Samah*) represents the Eastern direction, which is symbolized by the color yellow. It is used to establish a relationship between the energies of the universe, primarily the Creator. Tobacco has been used in offerings to the Creator as a medium of communication. Tobacco was offered to the Great Mystery when an animal or plant gave of itself. It can be placed on the earth after asking the higher powers to provide guidance. Tobacco holds vast importance with creating a bond between earthly and spiritual realms. Elders have given instruction to hold the tobacco in the left hand so it is closer to the heart. Tobacco is provided to medicine men and other spiritual leaders before they provide spiritual services. These services include the seeking of spiritual guidance, sweat lodge ceremonies, and spiritual and physical healing.

Cedar (*Keezhik*) represents the southern direction, which is symbolized by the color red. Cedar serves as a purifier. It is burned while praying to the Great Mystery during meditation. Many traditional women keep it in their left pocket. A person will have the stamina and courage to survive if times are difficult when the aroma of cedar is breathed in. Cedar is burned to bless and clean a house before moving into the home. The smoke has cleansing powers. Smudging occurs while the herb is being burned. Cedar is also boiled in water and served as a tea for healing purposes. Elders have given instruction to place cedar in shoes; then only goodness will come their way.

Sage is also considered to have cleansing and other spiritual properties. Sage (Sukodawabuk) represents the western direction, and is depicted by the color black. Native Americans have used sage in smudging for the release of unclear thoughts and the cleansing of their homes of bad spirits and negative energy. Smudging involves the burning of sage and the smoke is used for healing and cleansing purposes. Individuals using these herbs must have clear and admirable intentions. The root of the sage plant was used for healing by the Ojibwe in the following three ways: as an anti-convulsive, on wounds to stop bleeding, and as a stimulant. The Potawatomi used it as a poultice for sores persisting for long periods of time. It serves as a purifier and provides a signal to the Great Mystery of one's need for help.

Sweet grass (*Weengush*) has also provided many healing and spiritual properties for those who use it, and represents the northern direction and the color white. It is also used for purification. Sweet grass symbolizes the hair of *Nokomis Akin* (Grandmother Earth). When sweet grass is braided, the three sections of the braid characterize mind, body and spirit. The smoke from burning sweet grass is known to be repugnant to all evil beings and deters their powers. It is tied with many sacred and cultural objects and events. When used as a smudge, the individual is to fan the sweet grass smoke first in front of the heart, second to the mind and third around their body and lastly return the smoke to the head. For example, the men's traditional grass dance regalia are symbolic of this sacred plant. A braid of sweet grass is tied to the dancer's belt. The colorful yarn or fringe that is a part of the regalia symbolizes sweet grass swaying in the wind as the dancer dances around the dance arena. Sweet grass has been used to make coiled baskets called unity baskets. The very small baskets were used to keep children's naval cords in them.

  The four sacred plants are often utilized in sweat lodge ceremonies, pow wows, ghost suppers, naming ceremonies and other spiritual practices. The four sacred plants complete the circle of life. Their smoke can provide cleansing for the mind, body, spirit and soul. They can remove negative energy and refresh those who use them. It has been very important for the Anishanaabeg and other cultural groups to bestow gratitude for all the Great Mystery has provided to them. Keeping the idea of gratitude in their minds and the proper use of all the sacred plants helps those who use these sacred plants to convey their personal meaning of thankfulness.

In the days before the United States and Canada were settled by Europeans, there were no political boundaries. Many of the tribes were nomadic hunters and gatherers. Weather and the availability of food sources played a role in deciding where the Anishanaabeg would live. The Indian people were industrious, prosperous and predominantly content. Prosperity consisted of being able to celebrate the abundance of food, support from community members, resilient leadership, and strong spiritual ties with the Great Mystery. Leadership in traditional Indian communities maintained solidarity amongst all community members. The Anishanaabeg practiced an undying gratitude for all bestowed upon them. In 1620, many European people settled in the Great Lakes area and the way of life of the Anishanaabeg changed drastically.

Chapter III
Eagle and Coyote Travel with Columbus

After Columbus' arrival to the Western Hemisphere others followed suit, and millions were dehumanized, families torn apart, societies collapsed and civilizations destroyed as the result of colonization. Mankind still suffers from the effects of the racist ideology that justified slavery, assimilation, discrimination, and genocide. For more than 500 years, the dominant culture has practiced discrimination and segregation based on skin color and gender, which in turn has prevented unity and has aided them to maintain their power and control. With every dark cloud, there is often a silver lining. Much can be learned from the mistakes of the past. As a result of past acts of destruction, it has been discovered that the Native American population has demonstrated extreme resilience.

Europe during the 1400s was a tumultuous place laced with corruption, greed and pandemonium. The population of Europe was sparse compared with that of today and was under the rule of kings and feudal governments. The aftereffects of the ruins of the Roman Empire blanketed Western Europe. Muslim rule prevailed in Spain from 756 until the 1400s. As a result, the Spaniards developed a formidable and brutal military culture to counteract the control of their opponents, the Muslims. Around the same time, the Catholic Church exercised monumental power across the majority of the European continent. During the enduring relationship between the Church and the Roman Empire, the elite took pride in defining themselves as superior, segregating themselves from non-Christian societies in and out of Europe. Christian and Muslim religious practices endemic in Europe during this time period were militant.

  The Muslims were more tolerant of the Christians than the Christians were of them. The Muslims recognized their religious beliefs were based on Judaic traditions, and had similarities to Christianity. Both acknowledged Christ as a prophet and a conveyance of universal truth as revealed by God. According to the Muslims, it was their duty, as it was for Christians, to inform all humanity of this divine message. The struggle between the Muslims and Spaniards endured for nearly seven centuries and established the Europeans' insight of how they should deal with non-Europeans. The Muslims constructed a formidable military force with the collaboration of many Muslim groups that led the way to controlling a major port city, Constantinople, in 1453. The takeover of Constantinople led the way to Muslim rule over much of Eastern Europe.

  During this time of unrest, Christopher Columbus was born to an Italian weaver in 1451. Throughout much of his lifetime, Columbus became a man of deep-seated convictions. Columbus possessed strong Christian beliefs. He also believed he could travel west from Spain and reach Japan and China and held onto these convictions up until his death. For years he was persistent with trying to convince rulers of various countries in Europe to fund his expedition. He was not able to persuade the king of Portugal, or the rulers of England and France to fund his first voyage and spent years trying to convince Ferdinand and Isabella, rulers of Spain. The Spaniards and other European countries were preoccupied with taking over specific ports and land holdings from the Muslims.

Eventually, the Spaniards started experiencing military success and captured the port of Seville. A link to the continent of Africa was established, forming a base for trade and served as a conduit for expeditions against the Arabs in the Mediterranean area. In 1469, the marriage between Ferdinand and Isabella consolidated the armed forces of Castile and Aragon leading to the final annihilation of the Moors. The last Moorish king submitted to the rule of the Spaniards. Then the Spaniards overtook Grenada. Columbus was witness to this takeover in 1492.

On March 31, 1492, Ferdinand and Isabella strived to strengthen Christian influence in their kingdom by banishing Jews from Spain. The queen's ruling applied to 300,000 Jewish people who did not practice Christianity. Many of the Jewish people avoided extradition by professing the Catholic faith. After the ruling was enforced, Jewish people suspected of infidelity concerning the Church were referred to as "marranos" meaning pigs. New laws were put into place and as a result Jewish blood was considered at fault for their Christian infidelity. Because they were tainted due to their bloodline, their sinfulness could not be eliminated by baptism. Thus, they needed to be banished.[23]

During this time of religious unrest, Columbus finally persuaded Ferdinand and Isabella to fund his first voyage. The rulers wanted to convert the natives to Christianity and the thought of a source of untapped wealth was another reason why they agreed to support Columbus in his ventures. He insisted on being appointed viceroy, meaning governor, of the newly discovered lands and demanded ten percent of the gold, spices, and trade that he found.

Columbus was never fully aware of the significance of his discovery. It was the precious metals and other finds that led to the rise of European capitalism in the newly discovered land. As a result, there was a gradual transfer of political and economic power from Europe to the Americas. Columbus made three additional voyages to unchartered lands before he was forced to retire because he lost his foothold with the ruling class. Columbus spent his last lonely years in Spain before his death in 1506.

Towards the end of the 1400s, a belief existed of a land resembling paradise far to the east of Europe. Mystical wonders like the biblical Eden and the fountain of youth were believed to exist. It was believed these faraway lands were free from the strife the Europeans faced at home. Initially, Columbus referred to the people he discovered in the Western Hemisphere as children of God. Columbus imagined his good fortune led him to the Golden Age. He wrote to his royal patrons after meeting the first inhabitants of the newly discovered land:

"So tractable, so peaceable are these people, that I swear to your Majesties there is no better nation on earth. They love their neighbors as themselves, and their discourse is ever sweet so and gentle, accompanied with a smile, and though it is true that they are naked, their manners are decorous and praiseworthy."[24]

The "Columbus as the discoverer" myth that has been handed down to the present day propagated the belief of which voices were to be listened to and which were to be ignored. Columbus never set foot on North American soil. The native peoples of the Caribbean, the discovered, were later portrayed as lacking feelings or thoughts. To explain as simply as possible, what happened over five hundred years ago was a group of heavily armed Europeans invaded a country to claim and control the lands of a large group of people, the indigenous.

Columbus found that riches were not readily obtainable, and did not want to return to Spain empty handed during his first voyage. He took it upon himself to capture many of the native people and take them back to Spain, hopeful of making a profit. A massive raid was conducted and 1,500 Arawaks [Tainos] were abducted. Men, women and children were imprisoned in pens, which were guarded by men and dogs. Columbus' ships could not carry more than 500 slaves so only the ones considered the most valuable were loaded aboard. The Admiral told those under his command they could do what they wished with the remaining captives. The native people who were not wanted for any purpose were released and they ran in all directions like lunatics, women dropping their infants in the rush, running for miles without stopping, fleeing across rivers and mountains. The terror inflicted on them is unimaginable.

      Of the 500 slaves taken to Spain, only 300 arrived alive. They were put up for sale in Seville by Don Juan de Fonseca, the archdeacon of the town. The slave trade proved to be unprofitable because so many of the slaves died. Columbus turned his focus to obtaining large amounts of gold. However, he continued to make the tribal inhabitants, slaves for his own use or to be sold, which in itself demonstrated that these native people possessed little or no value to the Spaniards.[25]

      The beliefs of the native people presented a paradoxical point of view to the Europeans. One side demonstrated a people who did not live within the confines of a civil society, lacking the concepts of marriage, property and law. Common ownership and a lack of selfishness are also trademarks associated with innocence and natural virtue. The laws that beset civility defined the boundaries between what was considered a savage existence and that of civilized society. The heightened awareness of these differences created confusion concerning people of color when the Spaniards discovered the New World. Many circumstances, such as the Black Death, military conflicts and the shift towards a market economy, also led Europeans to adopt a highly competitive mindset.

      Bartolome' de Las Casas was disheartened when he heard of the brutal treatment and exploitation inflicted on the native people. He based his beliefs on what he thought needed to occur in the new land, which involved the spreading of their interpretation of God's word. According to Las Casas, that was why God permitted the discovery of this foreign land. He devoted his life to serving as an advocate for Indian people.[26] However, there were stronger powers at play overriding his efforts.

In 1493, before the Pope turned over South America to the Spaniards, he gave them a proclamation. The Spanish conquistadores were ordered to read this declaration to the native people mandating that they should:

"… Recognize the Church as your Mistress and as Governess of the World and Universe, and the High Priest, called the Pope, in her name, and His Majesty in Her place, as Ruler and Lord King…

And if you do not do this… with the help of God I shall come mightily against you, and I shall make war on you everywhere and in every way that I can, and I shall subject you to the yoke and obedience of the Church and His Majesty, and I shall seize your women and children, and I shall make them slaves, to sell and dispose of as His Majesty commands, and I shall do all the evil and damage to you that I am able. And I insist that the deaths and destruction that result from this will be your fault." [27]

This document removed all responsibility from the Spaniards and gave them authorization to do whatever they felt necessary to conquer and exploit the native people. Thus heinous atrocities were inflicted in the name of Christianity with the Pope's blessing.

The takeover of native land and resources continued after Columbus made his discoveries. From 1519 to 1521 Hernando Cortes and 400 Spaniards set foot on the Yucatan peninsula. These Spaniards defeated an empire of 200,000 Aztecs. At the time of this invasion, 50,000 Aztec men were prepared for battle. The takeover was possibly made feasible by a rumor that Montezuma believed Cortes was the god Quetzalcoatl and that was how Cortes became feared and gained so much power over the Aztecs. This was the first time the Aztecs were exposed to horses and firearms. Another explanation for the depletion of the Aztec population involved disease, possibly after he obtained notoriety as their new found god.

A picture was painted demonstrating the beliefs and practices of the times when Columbus invaded the New World and claimed this land for Spain. He was following the instructions of the rulers of Spain and the Church. It has been extremely difficult to fathom that they felt it necessary to wield such brutality on people who welcomed them into their country. Gaining a better understanding of the mindset of the European culture with their strong competitive and military attitudes of this time period may help make things more comprehensible.

As much as Columbus' actions appear deplorable, his actions did represent the mindset of the religious, political and economic forces of that time period. Celebrating Columbus' discovery has provided validation for the abuse of the Western Hemisphere's native people, the destruction of their societies, and the brutal enslavement of many people of color. Today, many tribal communities use Columbus Day as a day of mourning concerning what happened to their ancestors and to celebrate their unity against the oppression of the European culture. The only thing to celebrate is the 500 plus years of resistance.

Eagle and Coyote are sent on a mission to find out about Columbus' first voyage. They learn about the native people who lived there and how Columbus and his men treated those unfortunate people. This story was based on information obtained from several resources. It is difficult to sugar coat the truth. The stage was set by giving information about the mindset that was endemic during the days when Columbus set sail. This story relays the harshness of Columbus' actions and the start of hundreds of years of exploitation faced by native people. The reader will learn about the condition of the ships and the sailors' plights, about the inhabitants and the land that was discovered, and the end results of Columbus' first voyage.

****

The Year is 1492

"I am not sure I want to go on this venture with you," said Eagle as she anxiously looked at the vast ocean.

"Oh, come on. You can do it," retorted Coyote.

"You remember how much I struggled with that big fish. It almost brought me to my death."

"Yeah, but you survived to tell the story," replied Coyote.

"Yes, I did. Just thinking about that fish gives me the willies," said Eagle.

"You should have known a swordfish was going to be too big for you to handle."

"I know, but I thought we could eat off that swordfish for at least a couple of days. You know once I get something in my talons I can't usually let it go."

"The Creator has requested we visit the ships that are being commanded by Christopher Columbus, so we will need to cross the ocean and join the crew on his ship," stated Coyote firmly.

"I guess that means putting my fears behind me."

"You know there's a way of getting around this," stated Coyote.

"Tell me what you have in mind, Coyote."

"I think we should have our spirits do the traveling. What do you think?"

"You know, you may be on to something. We can join the spirits of some of the sailors and discover what the Creator wants us to find out," responded Eagle as she tapped her talon on the ground pondering the possibility of spirit travel.

"We definitely have to protect our vessels while we are on this endeavor because they will be left unattended for quite some time," stated Coyote.

"We should find a safe place for our bodies to rest while we are on this adventure," said Eagle.

"You're right. Look at that abandoned nest up there," said Coyote as he looked upward to a nest that was on top of a tall pine tree.

"You know, even from here that nest looks big enough for the two of us," replied Eagle.

Eagle picked up Coyote and flew to the nest at the top of the tree.

"This is a turkey vulture nest. Look at the feathers that were left behind," stated Coyote.

"This isn't hatching season. That's been over for a couple of weeks, so we should be safe here for a while," stated Eagle as she was flattening some of the leaves that were lying on the bottom of the nest.

Eagle and Coyote began preparing for their journey. They provided protection for their bodies by putting a spell around the entire nest to ensure that no being could harm them. Coyote curled up with Eagle. Eagle had to remain partially sitting since her wings were so large and Coyote snuggled under her wing. Before preparing their spirits, they visited Columbus' ship with their minds' eye so they would know what direction to travel. The human souls they selected to embody with their spirits were chosen. Coyote picked a deckhand, and Eagle chose a low ranked officer.

They began the process of spirit imaging. Coyote's spirit ball was a spectrum of swirling colors of blue, purple, orange, red and yellow. Eagle's spirit ball was mostly white, laced with green and blue colors spattered throughout the surface of the ball. Their spirits were readily permeable by their minds. Their minds gave their spirits instruction on where to go, and after a short period of time, they arrived on the deck of Columbus' ship.

Eagle and Coyote's spirits had already sought permission to join the spirits of the sailor and officer. Joining the spirits was completed very quickly, and they were communicating with one another. The sailor's name was Samuel and the officer's name was Henrico. Both of their spirits were unsettled and extremely unhappy. Eagle and Coyote, when in their spirit form, had to talk to one another telepathically. This form of communication was done as little as possible, as to not arouse suspicion.

******

"Where's Samuel? I need him up on deck immediately," demanded Senior Officer Luis.

"What do you need sir?" replied a shaky Samuel after another sailor retrieved him.

"You need to swab the deck before sunset."

The sailors were treated like servants. They did not have their own living quarters. The crew worked in four hour shifts, and when they were off duty, they slept anywhere they could find space. Their duties consisted of pumping bilge, cleaning the decks, working the sails, and checking the ropes and cargo. Columbus often spent days without sleep. Only the captain had his own private sleeping quarters. The sailors' lives were hard, and they often died from disease, hunger, and thirst. Religion was the central focus of their lives, and their days began with prayers and hymns and ended with religious services in the evenings. The sailors received one hot meal a day, cooked over an open fire in a sandbox on deck. Their diet included biscuits, pickled or salted meat, dried peas, cheese, wine, and freshly caught fish.[28]

****

A storm was brewing off in the horizon. The sailors were battening down the hatches. The howling wind and rain ripped against the ship. The sailors were being tossed and turned from one side of the ship to the other. Samuel was hanging onto a beam. His face was streaked with terror as he closed his eyes and prayed the ship would weather the storm.

"I'm telling you, I don't think I have ever been more scared Coyote. Are our sailors going to survive this storm?"

"We can only pray along with the sailors. I think the Creator already knows the ships will reach land."

"I think you're right."

"I hope so. Samuel is saying this "Hail Mary" prayer over and over again. He's terrified. I don't know how much more he can handle."

"Well, I hope his prayers work and I hope you are right about the Creator already knowing we're going to find land."

The storm passed the following day. Only a couple of sailors lost their lives when they were thrown overboard because of the high winds. The three ships only needed a few minor repairs.

****

"Bartolomeo, what are you doing? Get over here and eat with your brother" demanded Columbus.

"We really lucked out with that storm. I have to tell you, brother, on a few occasions I thought I could see my life flash before my eyes," said Columbus.

"Do you think we are going to find land soon? Some of the men are becoming a little mutinous," said Bartolomeo as he scoffed.

"You know, we've been on the sea for at least a month, and it is wearing on me, too. I love the smell of the sea, but seeing land would be much appreciated," stated Columbus.

Columbus' ships covered approximately 150 miles a day. His crew used a compass for direction and a chip log and reel to measure speed. The chip log was a large reel with over 700 feet of line wound up on a large wooden spool. A triangular piece of wood was located on the front right side, which was thrown over the side of the ship. It created a large amount of drag that stayed where it fell in the water, and the ship could sail away from it. The rate at which the line ran off the reel represented the speed of the vessel. The rope was knotted and spaced along the line at intervals of 47 feet, 3 inches, representing the distance the ship sailed in 28 seconds, if traveling at one nautical mile per hour. If two knots ran off the reel in 28 seconds, the ship was traveling two nautical miles per hour. The term "knots" was derived from the tying of knots on a rope and is still used today. The reel was usually held by two sailors. One sailor, usually the sailing master, tossed the chip and counted the knots. Another sailor was placed in charge of the sandglass to track the time. Columbus relied on his experience, intuition, observations, and guesswork to determine his ship's position.[29]

"If my calculations are correct, we should be seeing land in a couple of days. The Indies were supposed to take just a little over a month to reach," reported Columbus.

Columbus was a collector of a large amount of books and the Bible was a great source of inspiration for him. Columbus was influenced by the written works of Pope Pius II's *Historia Rerum ubique Gestarum,* which was published in 1477 and Cardinal Pierre d'Ailly's *Imago Mundi* published in the 1480s. Columbus derived his image of the world from these books and was determined to prove he could reach the Far East by traveling westward.[30]

"I can't wait to see land. The days are beginning to seem endless," said Bartolomeo.

"There may be unfriendly people and animals living on the land," added Columbus.

"Let's make sure we have our guns and ammunition ready just in case some of the animals are vicious," stated Columbus.

"I will meet with the officers and tell them that we may be seeing land soon and to be prepared," replied Bartolomeo.

"Thanks."

****

"Do you know what we have to do Emilio?" asked Francisco.

"Yes, we have to have our matchlock muskets armed and ready. I will assist with cleaning the stocks," said Emilio.

"I think we brought plenty of gun powder," said Emilio.

Henrico was huddled over a musket as he slid a stick with a rag tied to it into the barrel. As he redrew the stick, he turned the rag around to the clean side and attached it to the stick. The rag came out cleaner the second time. Henrico tossed the rag to one of the sailors to clean. The sailor ran the rag over the washboard several times and hung it to dry on a nail that was pounded into one of the sideboards.

"Henrico does not have any respect for the sailors. He treats them like garbage," said Eagle to Coyote telepathically.

"I know Samuel hasn't eaten today. His head is pounding, and he still has to clean the starboard deck before he can retire to the dining hall."

"The conditions on this ship are deplorable, the rats, the food, and the sleeping conditions. I couldn't stand one day working as hard as these sailors do. Could you imagine if we were in human form? I am so glad you suggested spirit travel," said Eagle.

"Columbus reported to the officers that they might see land in a couple of days."

"I wonder what we are going to see."

"I don't know Coyote. I hope your spirit is providing comfort for Samuel's spirit."

"I am doing the best I can. He's pretty downtrodden and feels like there is very little hope that he will survive this journey."

"That's so sad. Henrico isn't happy either. He can't wait to set anchor."

"I hope we discover what the Creator wants us to learn."

"The Creator wants us to find out Columbus' reaction to finding the native people and his rationale for what he does after he makes this discovery."

"This is a tall order, isn't it, Coyote?"

"One of the tallest."

"I think it would be best to visit the spirits of Columbus and Bartolomeo."

"Why didn't we do that in the first place?"

"I don't know."

"Let's get cracking because I think they are going to discover land soon," said Eagle.

Eagle and Coyote's spirits communicated with the spirits of Columbus and Bartolomeo, and they were given permission to join the spirits of these two men.

****

"Tierra! Tierra," exclaimed Rodrigo de Triana at two hours past midnight on October 12, 1492 as he was serving as a lookout on the Pinta. A pension of ten thousand maravedis a year was going to be rewarded to the sailor who spotted land first. This was two thousand maravedis less than what a sailor made in a year. However, Columbus took the money for himself and stated he had seen several lights the night before. [31]

The captains of the Pinta and Nina set anchor close to the shore. The Santa Maria was the bulkiest of the three ships and could not be anchored close to land. The sailors from this ship had to take small rowboats to the shore.

Columbus was not impressed with the Santa Maria. The ship was not suited for sailing near reefs and shallow waters. The Nina and Pinta were known as caravels, which meant these crafts could be navigated more easily. A caravel did not have much cargo space, but these vessels were able to sail over difficult or shallow waters.

****

Meanwhile on land the native people were viewing the ships as they were approaching the shore.

"Do you see what I see father? Those things coming from the water, the home of the powerful spirits," exclaimed Amiq to his father.

"I wonder what these great spirits want from us," inquired Ramez.

"I don't know father. Remember I saw something like this in my dreams. In my dream, the visitors coming to our land had pale faces and powerful thunder sticks," replied Amiq.

"Go alert the rest of the village," ordered Ramez.

Amiq ran back to the village to warn the other villagers.

****

Green foliage and lush flowers of many colors peppered the land as Columbus walked along the shoreline. The sand on the shore was white and pristine. The sailors were in awe of the beautiful scenery. Brightly colored birds chirped and cawed as they flew above. The large branches of the palm trees swayed in the gentle breeze. Columbus stared at the magnificent view as he made his way further into the forest down a narrow path with the crew and officers from the ships. A clearing was spotted a hundred yards ahead of the weary travelers.

Columbus ordered the sailors to have their weapons ready to fire.

A small group of villagers approached the sailors. They had bronze colored skin. Their bodies were of a slim build and muscular. Their long black hair was braided and tied with twine.

The tallest man in the group waved for the rest of the group to stay. He approached the large group of sailors. His smile revealed perfectly straight teeth, which shined in the sunlight like pearls. He extended his hand and waved for them to follow him to the village.

"What do you think about this?" inquired Columbus as he waited for a response from Valante, an officer of the Santa Maria.

Valante appeared to be unsure, and he responded by shrugging his shoulders.

Henrico walked up to Columbus and said, "I think we are going to be alright. These people don't appear to have any weapons."

"Are you sure? They could have people hiding in those huts ready, to pounce on us as soon as we get near the village," said Emiliano, an officer of the Nina, as he looked at the huts anxiously.

"We discovered this land and I am not going to let a few strange people stop us. They are like animals, naked, and the color of their skin is like no other I have ever seen," stated Columbus.

The sailors were invited to sit down around a fire, and the native people introduced themselves in a strange language.

Columbus stared thoughtfully at the native people. *Their tongue is unintelligible. They don't understand a thing we're saying. How are we going to find out where the treasures are located? Did we take a step back in time when we landed on this ancient barbaric land or did we actually come across the people of the Golden Age? These people seem almost perfect. They welcomed us and appear to be so friendly, not only to us, but to each other as well. They have this gentle attitude with visitors, and they treat each other with the utmost respect.*

****

"We have searched high and low and can't find any treasures, and we can't communicate with these people to find out where their treasures are kept," said Columbus as he fervently placed his hands on his hips to demonstrate his frustration.

"The other soldiers are starting to talk about us. They think we are soft and need to put our foot down with these savages," stated Bartolomeo.

"I know, brother. I've been thinking about the very same thing. We need to come up with a plan," replied Columbus.

******

"*I think we may have an opportunity to feed these individuals' spirits with some good psychic energy.*"

"I know Eagle, but we may drastically change the future if we do so."

"What's wrong with that?"

"The Creator only wanted us to observe and report."

"We need to see how things play out then," replied Coyote telepathically, as he sullenly retreated back into the spirit that he was visiting.

****

"I have an idea. Why don't we take as many of these creatures as we can capture and take them back to Spain? They can be used as slaves and sold for a profit. I promised Isabella and Ferdinand I would bring them back valuables," said Columbus.

"I think we can take at least 500 back to Spain," said Bartolomeo.

"Let's inform the other sailors of our plans," said Columbus.

The sailors from the three ships were informed of their plans and instructed to construct cages to house the natives until they were ready to depart. The cages took a couple of weeks to build.

"We have all the cages built, Columbus. Now what?" asked Henrico.

"It's time to round up the savages. Get the best specimens and put them in the cages," replied Bartolomeo.

"Do you only want men?" asked Henrico.

"No. I want to take back both men and women," replied Columbus.

"What about the children? What do we do with them?" asked Emilio.

"Children wouldn't make good slaves. Let's leave them behind," replied Bartolomeo.

****

"I don't like this Coyote."

"I don't either. It sounds like these native people are going to be dragged from their homes against their will," stated Coyote as he tried to reassure Eagle.

"What is going to happen to this village," stated Coyote aghast at thinking about the villagers' future.

"I wish there was something we could do to stop this," replied Eagle.

"Me, too. I never felt so helpless," stated Coyote.

"These spirits we joined are so cold. It's like they don't bother themselves with what others are going through. They seem to only care about themselves. Are these the dark souls the Creator warned us about?" asked Eagle.

"I feel a little scared and leery of these dark spirits," stated Coyote.

"I think we need to return to our vessels soon and report to the Creator about what we learned from this venture," said Eagle.

"I think we need to be here for just a little while longer. Let's rejoin the spirits of the sailors we first visited and continue to see how this plays out," retorted Coyote.

"Let's do that," stated Eagle.

They returned to the spirits of the first two sailors and continued their observations.

****

"I will get everybody moving concerning the gathering of these savages," stated Emilio.

"We must get back to Spain and collect our fee for services rendered," said Columbus as he turned to locate the captains of the ships and tell them of their plan.

The horrified villagers were gathered and put in the cages. They were crying and screaming with terror. The other villagers, who were not captured, tried to run to the mountains and forests to hide. Some were lucky while others were drug back and beaten for trying to flee. The captains told the sailors they could do what they wanted with the rest of the villagers. The acts committed against them were unspeakable. Some of them manage to flee.

The captains were more than happy to plan their voyage back to Spain and collect their pay. Food was scarce on the ships so plans were made to take a lot of the food from the villagers to take on board the three ships.

****

Eagle and Coyote commanded their spirits to join their physical bodies as they traveled back to the turkey vulture nest where their bodies rested.

"I can't believe what they did to those people. Where did these people come from? Who are they? They all appeared to have no hearts including that Columbus," said Eagle as she sobbed uncontrollably.

"I know Eagle. It was horrible. It is going to take a long time to get the stench of this experience off of me," replied Coyote.

"I am going to ask my spirit guides to aid me in my healing from this experience," stated Eagle.

"Good idea," replied Coyote.

"The Creator is going to be sad when he hears about what happened and why Columbus did what he did," stated Eagle.

Eagle and Coyote curled up with one another in the nest and cried themselves to sleep.

Chapter IV
Eagle and Coyote's Adventures
with French Settlers

French merchants realized that the indispensable fur bearing animals, especially the beaver, were plentiful in North America. The fur-bearing animals were becoming rare in Europe. These furs provided the human wearer protection against the elements and served as a mark of social distinction. The native people who resided on the uncharted territories of what was later referred to as New France welcomed these visitors with open arms. New France encompassed present-day Nova Scotia, Quebec, and other surrounding territories in the Eastern portion of what is now known as Canada. Knowing little about the capitalistic motives of the Europeans, the native people were duped into forfeiting claims to a vast amount of this country's resources to satisfy the whims of a few wealthy people in Europe and fortune seeking entrepreneurs. The French may have appeared to be on friendlier terms with the native people; however, they had the same goals in mind, which involved the building of profitable endeavors without consideration for the needs of the native people.

Jacques Cartier, a Frenchman, traveled down the St. Lawrence Seaway to Quebec and Montreal in 1535 to establish trade with the Iroquois for an exchange of European goods for furs. The French developed unified relationships with numerous Algonquian tribes along the St. Lawrence shores and parts of what was known as New

France, encompassing much of current day Quebec and Nova Scotia. They settled in, or lived in close proximity to Indian villages.

The French encouraged the Indian people to carry out their Indian ceremonies, and also participated in many of these ceremonies. A canon was fired from a French settlement as a salute to honor and welcome an Indian chief who exhibited and/or carried a French flag to show his support for them. Welcoming ceremonies included gifts, such as guns, ammunition, kegs of rum, metal tools, blankets, clothing and beads. The French adopted many customs from the Indian people when they traveled with and settled near the tribal communities. For example, the mosquitoes and black flies could be a real nuisance, and the French learned how to smear their bodies with bear grease to prevent the bugs from biting them. [32]

During the 1580s, French trading companies were set up in the region of what was later referred to as New France. French frontiersmen were referred to as *coureurs de bois* or forest runners. Another name given to these brave men is voyageurs who happened to be canoeists or travelers. The reduction of the beaver population forced the *coureurs de bois* to go further into the interior of what is now known as Canada.[33] The fur trading business caused much calamity for the Indian people. Not only was the population of the beaver depleted, the population of the native people was decreased considerably through contact with the traders by the ravages of disease to which they had no immunity. Smallpox was the number one killer, with measles, scarlet fever, diphtheria, typhus, whooping cough, and influenza following suit. Also, the fur trade created an upheaval of tribal communities as they fought one another and joined forces with European allies to gain control of land bases and its resources.[34]

The missionaries usually lived with the Indian tribes while they sought to convert them to Christianity; the next order of business was to civilize the native people.[35] The missionaries known as the Jesuits became advocates for the Indian people. The main purpose of the Jesuits' work was to preach the Gospel in this newly discovered land. Their views were based on the belief that endorsed subordination of humans, plants and animals to a hierarchy based on devotion to the Trinity of Father, Son and the Holy Spirit. Democracy did not exist with this order and there was no communal form based on equality. The system supported the beliefs that superiors and inferiors existed. There were those who were destined to spread the word and maintain control and those who were followers. This system was put into place, according to the Jesuits, by a certain agreement and order.[36]

However, the Jesuits did not endorse the use of brandy as a trade item. Intoxicated Indians were unlikely candidates to be converted to Christianity. The Jesuits lobbied in Europe against the use of brandy. Their lobbying efforts were generally unsuccessful. If French alcohol was prohibited, it would be substituted with rum manufactured in British colonies.

Samuel de Champlain founded the small village of Quebec with 28 men in 1608. In 1630, 103 colonists resided in this community and by 1640, the population had grown to 355. Champlain was known as the "Father of New France." In 1627, Cardinal Richelieu who was an advisor to Louis XIII, formed the company of One Hundred Associates. Richelieu served as an advisor for Louis XIII. One of the goals of this company was to gather investors to provide an income for New France by promising land parcels. French aspirations in this newly founded territory were the expansion of mercantile business and agriculture. Richelieu's grand plan encompassed all lands between present-day Florida and the Arctic Circle. This Company of One Hundred Associates or New France was given the cartel in trade except in the cod and whaling industry, which was awarded to other European countries. The main mission of this company was to expand the fur trade with the Indians.[37]

  The French sought to build communities as significant as the British colonies. The French settlers numbered in the hundreds. The British colonies were more heavily populated and prosperous. Samuel de Champlain was appointed governor of New France, and he made it part of his plan to convert New France into a more prosperous region.

  Part of Champlain's mission to settle New France was to learn how to adapt to life in North America. Champlain ordered young French men to live with the tribal people learning their language and customs. Shiploads of marriageable women were transported to the new territory. Eager French governmental officials coerced settlers to relocate with cash payments. Bounties were paid as an incentive for couples to produce large families. Fines were levied on fathers of daughters who were unmarried after the age of 15. All of these sanctions were attempts to increase the population of New France.[38]

Eagle and Coyote visit a French settlement to explore life as French settlers. They joined other colonists daring to take part in Richelieu's and Champlain's proposed plan to build an affluent colony and provide security for New France and its properties against the British and their Indian allies.

1627 French Settlement (Now referred to as Old Quebec City)

"How did we get here? Is this a cave? There could be bears in this cave ready to attack us," said Eagle, as she was trying not to have her anxiety get the best of her.

"Now Eagle, you know the Creator would not put us in harm's way," replied Coyote as he tried to soothe her.

"I guess you're right. Remember your run in with that bear?" asked Eagle.

"I think we startled him and he was just reacting."

"Yes, but he did send us into flight to escape him," replied Eagle.

"Yes, he did."

"I think I am my own worst enemy. Something scary happens and I hold onto it forever. I need to learn how to let things go," said Eagle as she grimaced.

"Well, it can't be much fun having so many fears."

"Back to the task at hand. We have to shape shift so we can fit in with these people," exclaimed Eagle.

Tall pine trees were situated on the east side of the settlement. Eagle, carrying Coyote, flew up to the top of a pine tree to get a better look at the inhabitants. Wooden houses circled around a well. French soldiers, and a few men and women civilians, were strolling around the grounds. The men wore long dark colored coats atop cropped pants, while the women wore dresses made of dark fabric with some splashes of red to add color.

"I think I am going to like wearing that clothing. The people here seem to be in such good spirits," said Eagle as she studied the inhabitants.

"I think we are going to have fun here. They do seem to be in such good spirits," replied Coyote.

"The Creator told us our names were going to be Marie and Jacque. What is our last name?" asked Coyote.

"It's Marcheilles. We are going to be cousins of Samuel de Champlain."

"The Creator gave us the ability to speak and understand French. I am sure that is going to come in handy," said Coyote.

"He has done that with all the languages we have come across," said Eagle as she stared admiringly at the inhabitants.

"It is amazing how he can set things up like this so nobody is on to us," stated Coyote.

"Yes, I am always impressed with the gifts the Creator possesses," exclaimed Eagle.

Eagle shape shifted into a petite young woman with dark brown hair. Her hair was arranged on top of her head in a bun with ringlets strewn around her face. Her skin was white and her eyes were blue. Eagle donned a white petticoat, pantaloons, stockings, a black dress with red sleeves.

Coyote shaped shift into a young man of medium height with black hair that was tied back. He put on a set of trousers that were cropped at the knees, a white shirt, black coat and black boots.

"You do look dapper, Jacque, if I do say so myself," retorted Eagle.

"You are definitely easy on the eyes, Marie. I have to start getting used to your new name," stated Coyote.

"Let's find our house. The Creator told us our names would be on the outside of the house, and he said it would be the one closest to the well," said Marie.

"There it is. I see our names on the front of the house, and we are located next to one of the largest houses in the square," stated Jacque.

"That must be Samuel's home. Let's go inside our house and see what's waiting for us," said Marie.

There was a sitting area that shared a room with a kitchen and sleeping quarters. Large logs served as the legs for an oversized table. The table top was made from planed pieces of wood. Two high back chairs were placed at the table. A wood stove, which served as a cooking and heating source, was situated in the middle of the room. In the sitting area were two more high back wooden chairs. One four poster bed with a fluffy mattress filled with leaves sat in one of the far corners. The bed was covered with animal furs. Stacked on a couple of wooden shelves was more clothing for both Eagle and Coyote.

"I can handle this way of living," stated Marie as she rifled through the small assortment of dresses, pantaloons and petticoats.

"We have work to do, so let's get cracking," demanded Marie.

They walked into the courtyard, and Samuel walked over quickly to them and greeted them.

"You should see what we did with the main hall today. We put the finishing touches on it. Come with me. I can't wait for you to see it," said Samuel.

The streets were bustling with activity. Talk was emanating from some of the inhabitants about a party that was going to be held in honor of the newly constructed hall. By the looks of things, it appeared some of the men were already partaking in the drink. One man staggered, holding a flask to his lips. He dropped the flask to the ground when he discovered it was empty and sat on the deck of a small mercantile and began singing loudly. Another man sat next to him and shared what he had in his flask. They both commenced to singing while they slung their arms across each others' shoulders and began swaying back and forth.

"Check out those two fools. They can't wait until tonight to enjoy the festivities," stated Samuel.

"What is going on tonight, cousin?" asked Jacque.

"We are blessing the new town hall," replied Samuel.

"What were we planning on doing with the hall?" asked Marie.

"My dear, we are going to hold public meetings, ceremonies and the like in that hall. I can't wait until we have our first town meeting to discuss membership in the One Hundred Associates. Tonight it is going to serve as a banquet hall," replied Samuel.

"What is the One Hundred Associates?" asked Jacque.

"Cardinal Richelieu made arrangements with Louis XIII to give those who qualify a parcel of land to farm," responded Samuel.

"Are we on the list to receive land?" asked Marie.

"You are, since you are my cousins, but keep it under your hat for now," replied Samuel.

"Did we just make a killing on another fur delivery? Is that how we can afford such luxuries like the town hall and the festivities?" asked Marie.

"Those silly Englishmen think selling codfish to the Catholics to eat on Fridays is the way to go, but it takes six shiploads of fish to earn what we make on one shipload of furs. Things have been really booming in the fur trade. The women in France and other parts of Europe love to wear those hats."

"Speaking of Catholics, do you really think it is a good idea for Cardinal Richelieu to ban all non-Catholics from relocating to this area? I learned many Protestants are moving to the British colonies rather than denounce their faith," stated Jacque.

"The Cardinal is serving as an advisor to Louis XIII, so my hands are tied with that one," responded Samuel.

"Back to the topic of furs; are the Indians willing to provide you with all you want?" asked Jacque.

"We have some willing Indians who will brave those cold waters to trap the beavers for their pelts in exchange for containers made of metal, weapons and the drink."

Obtaining beaver skins might come with a few battle scars from the beaver's sizable teeth, when the hunter has to pull the animal from the cold frigid water by hand. Hunting for beaver pelts usually happened during the winter time when the pelts were the thickest. Sometimes these creatures hid in underground passages leading from their dams. Beavers were often conspicuous as they gnawed at saplings and small trees to construct their dams. Indian hunters who were very familiar with the streams and rivers could locate them more readily. [39]

"How long have you been working with the Indians?" asked Jacque.

"Since we arrived in Quebec and began setting up camp," replied Samuel

"Some of the Indians say they love spending time with us. We're more fun than those English. We have also traded tools so they can begin building log homes at their villages."

"Why aren't the British in the fur trading business?" inquired Jacque.

"They are, but New France is under our command, and they do not have the right to invade this region and tap into our resources. I do not think our freedom is going to last forever in the fur trading business. I heard through the grapevine the British were building an alliance with the Iroquois," reported Samuel.

Samuel, Jacque and Marie begin walking through Champlain's gardens behind his home. There was a variety of flowers as well as an abundance of beans, corn and squash. Venison was hanging to dry from a long pole that extended from his home. Fish were being cleaned by the hired hands.

"Your garden has done quite well this year Samuel," commented Marie.

"Yes, it has Marie. We used waste from fish to fertilize our gardens. The Indians showed us how to do that," replied Samuel.

"Enough garden talk. Let's go see the town hall," said Samuel.

The hall was a large building, the size of three or four of the homes. Two wood stoves to provide heat were situated on opposite walls. Twenty high back wooden chairs lined the walls on the south side of the building. Two large tables were set up near a cooking area. The tables were made with large planed boards atop bulky logs. The main door was sizeable, fashioned after a barn door. It was high and approximately six feet wide and locked by sliding boards into large braces. The ceiling was also high and there was a loft located on the west side of the building that served as a sleeping area for visitors. The windows appeared small for such a large structure and were covered with wooden shutters. Rough sawn logs were utilized for the floor. The walls and ceiling were made from large logs.

"Look at that door. We constructed the door like this so that it could not be easily knocked down if we were being attacked by the British and their allies. While you were gone on your hunting trip, we did a lot to fortify this building," said Samuel.

"The same consideration must have been given when the windows were put in," replied Jacque.

"The plan was to have a few windows so that we could shoot out of them, but they couldn't be too large to make us more of a target. The shutters close from the inside and were put into place for the same reason. Remember the plan of surrounding our settlement with tall wooden walls to provide protection," said Samuel.

"You mean the plan is to make this settlement into a fort? Yes, I do remember you telling me that," replied Jacque.

"I feel we may need more protection. The English believe all the land belongs to them, and I fear they may take action against us," stated Samuel.

"When are we going to get started on that project?" asked Jacque.

"The project has already been started. Some of the men have been cutting down some of those tall pine trees over there," said Samuel, as he pointed to the west of the settlement.

"What can I do to help, Samuel?"

"You can help by digging some of the holes for the long logs to be placed in. I hate to ask you to do this, but we need all the help we can get," replied Samuel.

"I will start first thing in the morning," replied Jacque.

"Probably not too early; we have some serious partying to do tonight."

"Am I invited to this party?" inquired Marie, who appeared to be hurt because she had not been included in the conversation.

"Yes, my dear. There are going to be lots of women at the party tonight," responded Samuel as he looked at Marie inquisitively.

"Jacque, I have to go home and pick out a dress for tonight."

"Ok. I guess I better get going too. I've got to chop some wood for the cook stove," said Jacque as he turned to leave with Marie.

"See you tonight around 6:00 p.m.," said Samuel.

"I hope we can figure out who's who at this party tonight," said Marie pondering the thought of meeting so many people who were going to be complete strangers.

"I think once everyone starts drinking, it's not going to matter."

"I hope you're right my friend," said Marie.

****

"Do you hear that noise," asked Marie as she looked towards the woods from the town square.

"I have never heard wolves or coyotes make sounds like that. It sounds like a wounded dog howling for its owner," replied Jacque.

"I want to check things out. I am a little concerned with all that howling. I wonder if a pack of dogs or wolves are wounded," said Marie as she started walking towards the wooded area with Jacque following suit.

Marie and Jacque came across a clearing, and a group of Indian men were standing in a circle, baying and hooting loudly as they passed a flask around.

"I bet they are passing around jugs of rum. I heard some of the townsfolk mention about how the Indians couldn't hold the drink," said Marie as she looked upon the unruly bunch of native men.

Just as Marie finished speaking one of the men threw a tomahawk at a tree trunk. It missed and hit one of the men in the upper portion of his leg. Blood gushed from his leg. He was bleeding to death. Marie and Jacque ran over to him, but it was too late. The man was already dead.

The drunken man was taken to the father and mother of the man he killed. A custom of the Indian people when someone is killed is that the family decides what to do with the person who killed their family member, accident, or no accident. Sometimes the person who committed the crime is adopted into the family to replace the dead family member. This time the parents of the man who died decided to have the guilty man put to death. Their decision was carried out quickly. The man's head was bashed in by a large club before many onlookers.

"I heard the mother saying that once the drink takes over there is no saving anyone from its evil grip," said Marie.

"Earlier today, before we went inside the town hall, I saw an Indian man trading his firearm for a jug of that rum. How is he going to protect his village or his family?" asked Jacque as a concerned look crossed his face.

"The French know the problems caused by providing rum to the Indian people. Why do they keep doing so?" asked Marie.

"Do you think they do so because it is easier to take advantage of someone who is drunk?" asked Jacque.

"I don't know. I see a lot of problems being created for Indian families if they keep providing them with rum," said Marie.

****

The town hall was buzzing with chatter and laughter as Marie and Jacque entered. Everyone turned to look at them. Since they were considered old timers to the settlement, they did not get much notice. Samuel came over to greet them. Men who appeared to be unattached were talking with some of the young single women. The women were batting their eyelashes and smiling sweetly to gain favor with potential suitors.

"Oh, this is ridiculous. Look what these women have stooped to in order to find a mate. The men in this settlement outnumber the women two to one. Being selective has gone out the window," said Marie as she rolled her eyes.

A large group of Indian men and women walked through the door and everybody turned their focus on these individuals. The men went over to the where the drinks were being served while the women stood against the wall.

A French man began playing the fiddle and an Indian man accompanied him by playing a small drum. People at the party started tapping their feet. After the second or third song was played, men started approaching the single women and asking them to dance. Some of the single French men asked the Indian women to dance with them. Following suit, a few married men asked their wives to join them on the dance floor.

"Mademoiselle, how about gracing me with your presence on the dance floor?" asked Jacque, as he extended his hand out to Marie.

"I would love to," replied Marie for the benefit of the onlookers.

"This is the first time I saw two different races mingle like this," stated Jacque.

"I think there are more than trade arrangements going on at this settlement," replied Marie.

"I know. The people at this settlement are gracious and fun to be with. They seem to have a real friendship with the Indians expanding beyond the trading activities. It sounds like the French are not on friendly terms with the English, and they may go to battle with them again sometime in the near future," said Jacque.

"I don't envy you tomorrow when you have to help dig the holes for the fort walls. I sense the urgency about the fort getting built," said Marie.

"I'm concerned about that, too," responded Jacque.

"Perhaps we can find out if the Indians who live around here have any enemies, maybe with another tribe for example. I wonder if they get along with the English, and if there is a battle, who they would side with?" inquired Marie.

"You remember what Samuel said. He said the Indians favored the French."

"I wonder if all Indians get along. We have met with several Indian groups, and they appeared to be very friendly," said Marie.

"I know, but everybody at one time or another has had enemies, even if it is with their own race. Wars are often fought over resources. Land is considered a precious resource when it comes to feuds of any kind," stated Jacque.

Looking thoughtfully Marie said, "Remember, Samuel told us the Iroquois were siding with the British."

"Let's approach Samuel and see what he has to say," said Jacque.

Samuel spoke of the Algonquin tribes who had fought against the Iroquois and other tribes in the past. He reported he witnessed some of these altercations and was amazed at the brutality of the warfare. It was usually brief and conducted as an ambush. He gave the following example: The Iroquois were sneaking up on an Algonquin village. The men of this village had been warned about this ambush so when the Iroquois were almost up to their wigwams, they attacked them from behind. The Iroquois couldn't react fast enough. Some were able to flee to the woods. Others were slaughtered in their tracks. Samuel reported that the Algonquin tribes had been able to stave off the attacks so far, but the war is not over.

    Jacque helped with the digging of the holes for the fort's logs for a couple of weeks. Meanwhile, Marie met with many of the women. She learned many of the married couples received payment, with the agreement that they would have as many children as possible, so the town would become more populated. Many of the women were asking Marie when they planned on having their first child. Marie replied that they were trying to conceive, but to no avail.

    I remember one of the elders telling me when we visited the Ojibwe village that young couples are not encouraged to conceive children if a war may ensue. It is not wise to bring children into the world during times of war. There was talk of a possible war, and these French couples are encouraged and even paid to conceive children thought Marie.

    Marie noticed the women were staring at her so she said the first thing that came to her mind. "The money would sure come in handy." As she said this, she noticed the stunned looks on the women's faces.

Marie recovered by adding, "A nice little bundle of joy would surely add to our lives."

Marie told the women she had to go home and prepare dinner. Jacque was waiting for her at their home. He was sitting by the woodstove, tossing in a couple pieces of kindling. Jacque was somewhat mesmerized as he watched as flames gathered on and around the wood. Marie surprised him as she opened the door to their home, and it made a very loud squeaking sound.

****

"We have learned a lot about this community and have gotten a flavor of what the French are like. The Creator wanted us to find out about the interactions between the Indian people and the Europeans. I am not sure what he wants to learn from this exploration, but I am sure he has his reasons," said Marie.

"Let's go back to the house and change back into our eagle and coyote bodies and fly out of here," said Eagle.

When Eagle spread her large wings and sprang into the air with Coyote in her strong talons, the memories of their existence were erased from the villagers' minds.

Chapter V
Power and Control through
Patriarchal Domination and the Church

The Loss of Deeper Meaning
Nature served as the Great Mystery's temple.
Women and children revered by all.
Wars not fought over spirituality.
Original forms of Christianity and traditional
Indian spirituality share similar ideals.

Roman Catholic Literalist mindset,
clouded views of what and who to worship.
Misinterpretations of the book, the Bible.
The masses swarm to Church
to hear their word of God.

The power of prayers is lost
due to fear and ignorance.
Many have suffered under acts of superiority.
Spirituality shrouded by denial,
from a loss of deeper meaning.

    All paths to "the divine" need to be respected and honored. Indian traditional spiritual practices, Buddhism, Christianity, and other forms of religion and spirituality consist of a vast amount of valuable lessons to be learned. Indian legends, the Koran, and the Bible hold mysteries to be discovered. Wise women and men from all races could lead the way to salvation and unlock the secrets to a life of contentment. The power of prayer has been known to provide healing and a feeling of comfort and a connection with the universe. Superiority instilled by rigid religious belief systems caused a vast number of people to suffer because all paths to the divine were not respected. The state of many Native Americans concerning poverty, domestic violence and other serious challenges is the result of a lack of spirituality in their lives. The Church and others in authority have wielded discrimination against women, setting most of the world off balance for thousands of years by the lack of matriarchal support and guidance. While certain aspects of religion have their place, most religions do not do enough to make a connection with the higher power to support a strong spiritual relationship with divinity.

Today, the unquestioning acceptance of modernization has deterred many from seeing divinity as a significant part of the modern world. All human societies have manifested a belief system that explains the story of their creation, phenomenon such as floods and other catastrophes. Many of the stories consist of moral teachings and the actions of divinity serving as important performers in unforgettable events throughout their history. According to documented records, the Hebrews managed to be the most prominent source in regards to their description of the ancient past. Considering the knowledge base of scientific information such as geology during the ancient times and the spread of Christianity, the Hebrew versions provided an irrefutable argument about how this world came about. Upon careful scrutiny, it was proven that Noah's flood could not have happened as reported in the Bible. Geological factors based on the discovery of animal skeletons do not support the Noah's ark happenings. Controversy about the age of this earth and other scientific data has revealed that this planet may have a very different past. Doubts about a belief system based on a book, the Bible, has shaken the religious and spiritual foundation for a multitude of people.

Patriarchal domination has wielded power and control over the masses as far back as early Greek civilization. One of the most flagrant examples of this is evident in the Church, meaning primarily the Roman Catholic Church. The Church either served as the sole ruler over the masses, or worked with the ruling class to provide governance during the time of the Roman Empire and after the collapse of the Roman Empire. Interpretations of biblical messages have been the catalyst for oppression, and are linked to the historical trauma for Indian people and other subjugated people of many races, especially women. Bloody skirmishes between opposing factions and acts of oppression have scarred many in the name of God and religion. A multitude of Indian people were forced to accept Christianity and abandon their traditional spiritual practices. However, it is essential as a part of being fully human to have the freedom to decide one's own moral standards. Freedom does not represent the absence of restrictions, it means finding the most liberating limitations.

David Marshall in his book *The Truth about Jesus and the Lost Gospels* makes reference to Christianity as the most liberating form of religion. He refers to stop lights and the stopping at such lights, which can be proven to be liberating as opposed to traffic jams. Rules are needed otherwise there will be chaos according to Marshall. However, traditional spiritual practices provided the freedom for Indian people to seek their own relationship with the divine, a form of spirituality that lent itself to guidance and support for Indian youth embarking on their spiritual journeys. These Indian youth were instructed on what to do, such as participating in vision quests, and analyzing their dreams, not what to think.

      Traditional spiritual leaders emerged thousands of years ago from small communal tribes as individuals who could explain mystical phenomena and offer ways to resolve problems. These explanations helped alleviate fear, sustain focus on cooperative efforts to accomplish tasks essential for survival, and maintain cohesion among everyone residing in those small villages. If one was to oppose the cultural values of their tribe, they would risk alienating themselves. Isolation most likely would result in death. Leaders were selected and earned the right to lead the village because of their acts of wisdom, kindness, bravery, and their concern for the well-being of the entire village.

      On the other hand, the hierarchy that evolved within church leadership created a 'top-down' mentality placing lay members at the bottom. Members were taught to believe they had to go through the priests to have a connection with the divine. Today, many Christian people often believe they possess the absolute truth, and everyone would be better served if they adopted their form of truth. This belief in their form of absolute truth endangers everyone's freedom. As a result of this narrow-mindedness, Churches have remained stagnant, and the following statements hold true for many of these religious institutions.

- Church is patriarchal: there's no room for full participation of women.
- Church is authoritarian: it attempts and oftentimes succeeds to enslave its members by deciding what they must believe and practice in every situation.
- Church is intolerant of other viewpoints. Individuals with different viewpoints are considered unsaved.
- Church appears to be a marketing scheme.[40]

Indian people did not fight over religion, and their form of spirituality was of a personal nature with the Great Mystery. Spirituality is the essence of one's soul, an individual's innermost nature, and represents the synergy in all things, animate and inanimate. Spirituality does not only represent tolerance and acceptance, it is the feeling of universal oneness and unity in diversity. It refers to a general sensitivity to moral, ethical, compassionate, and existential issues without reference to any religious doctrine. Spirituality is larger than religion, it includes an awareness of the connectedness of all that is, and accepts that all of life has meaning and purpose and is accordingly blessed. It could be defined as the animating force in life, symbolized by breath, wind, vigor, and courage and can be considered an active and passive process. Spirituality is inborn and exclusive to all people, and represents a tendency to move towards knowledge, love, meaning, hope, transcendence, connectedness, and compassion. [41]

   Before the onset of the European influence in this country, children were raised with traditional teachings to bolster their awareness of their personal spirituality journeys. These lessons consisted of what would become a way of life for them. These lessons included:

- "respect for all life forms and further sacred space
- love and honor for the Sacred Self
- responsibility of each individual for their spirituality, their own voice, and direction in life
- seeking and following a personal vision or purpose
- honoring various transitions in life: puberty rites, rites of passage, becoming an Elder, etc.
- living in the present moment, learning to manage fear
- each person has a right to make choices about their various journeys
- every journey has value, and all visions are to be honored

- all experiences of life have lessons for us to learn
- we learn from both daytime and nighttime experiences
- there are no mistakes in life
- spirit guides and Elders are available to provide advice and guidance, but the choice belongs to the individual
- everyone can honor the child and the Elder growing within
- the Creator gives us messages and signs to guide us
- as we learn more about ourselves (our gifts and limitations), we're more able to practice self-discipline and maintain personal integrity
- there is no such thing as bad; the only *change worlds* into a new experience of life
- like the bear, we must sometimes enter the cave of inner awareness in order to know ourselves better, find joy in the silence, and seek our own honey of truth
- healing means knowing and balancing oneself
- the beauty of life is in all directions
- life can be enjoyed fully, and personal power is strengthened when there is no guilt or self blame

- we are always connected and related to the universe" [42]

Conversely, religion is generally associated with a body of people adhering to a particular set of beliefs, practices, rituals and theory, and provides guidance for moral behaviors.

The commonalities of most religions are:
- All major religions basically teach the same things about moral and good behaviors and explain the rationale behind evil circumstances.
- Each religion only sees a portion of the truth, not the whole truth.
- Religious belief is culturally and historically biased.

According to Traditionalists and others who support the practice of meaningful spirituality, individuals don't have to be in elaborate churches to pray. The term "Traditionalists" was developed to refer to those who believe in what was considered pagan values including those practiced by traditional Indian people. The term, "God," "divinity," "the divine," and the "Creator" will be used from this point forward to define the higher being in order to be all-inclusive. Each form of religion and spirituality celebrates some higher being, and these terms appear to be the most widely used in this country.

Progress comes with many losses. Today, spirituality isn't considered real by many people. More and more people are concerned with the process of production and its association with monetary goals. Competition for "bigger and better" as well as the separation associated with competition has led to alienation. Technological advances are being developed at an astonishing pace, but rather than giving people more control of their lives, technology seems to be taking it away. As a result, what exists is an unhealthy level of dysfunction in most relationships, and direct person-to-person communication has been replaced by various types of technology.

Fear and ignorance has also served as a catalyst for deterring people from establishing and/or forming trust and healing. Ignorance and fear prevents the seeking of positive growth and change. Two major fears continue to be perpetuated: not being enough, and not having enough. A paradigm shift has occurred for millions of people who have deserted traditional religions and replaced these conceptual formats with materialism. The fear of "not having enough" fostered the greed of many religious leaders and rulers thousands of years ago, creating many difficulties existing today. These difficulties include the lack of community cohesiveness and an overall dissatisfaction with one's life. Religion came into existence to control the masses. Patriarchal domination was another way in which power was utilized to govern those considered weaker and oftentimes threatening.

Some people believe biblical patriarchy does not mean that man is dominant. It means man is to serve as head of his household as a provider and protector, and to love his household as our higher being loves all of creation; he should be willing to give his life for his family. Biblical patriarchy does not mean suppression of woman; quite the opposite. Both men and women were meant to be on a spiritual path together living out their lives as patriarchs and matriarchs in equality. The rigidity and pathological control by patriarchal domination has corroded religious practices, and rendered it meaningless and lifeless in many ways. All roles including leadership positions need to take on the matriarchal and patriarchal mindsets, which will help restore balance in the world.

Matthew Fox, in his book *The Coming of the Cosmic Christ,* proposes that civilization as it is known today has been forced to succumb to patriarchal domination and has put people out of touch with the core meaning behind Christianity. A very important component has been missing, which is the addition of the matriarchal mindset. The matriarchal mindset involves creativity and emotion, the nurturing elements necessary for any meaningful relationship. The patriarchal mindset represents the linear mode of thinking based on intellect. Intellect requires the balance creativity and an emotional standpoint can bring to the table. Without the feminine aspect, what remains can be cold and unyielding.

Fox makes the statement that Indian people had it right from the very beginning. They had a closer connection to their higher being, and spirituality was more meaningful for them. Their higher power, the Creator, communicated often with them through dreams, vision quests, sweat lodge ceremonies, and other traditional spiritual practices. Fox posed the question about the current existence of problems, such as drugs, alcohol and entertainment addictions, perhaps resulting from feelings of emptiness due to the lack of connection to the divine.[43]

When something is feared and enhances insecurities, the abolishment of the fear causing elements becomes probable. The spiritual practices of the Indian people were outlawed until the 1970s. The mystery of these ceremonies led to feelings of fear for the Euro-Americans. During this prohibition period, harmful sanctions were put into place to punish any Indian person who disobeyed and participated in traditional spiritual practices. Many Indian people secretly continued their spiritual practices. Others felt they had no choice, but to adopt Christian religious beliefs.

Concerning traditional spiritual practices, the spirit must come first and be nurtured in a way that creates a permeable wall for the divine to breach. Traditionalism involves a partnership with oneself. When things are in need of improvement, the solution is inside the individual's mind, soul and heart. Traditionalists believe everyone has everything they need inside of them to secure a relationship with the divine and to heal oneself in the following areas: spiritual, physical, emotional, and intellectual. Today, many Indian people are feeling a loss because they do not have a connection to the divine.

The Roman Empire's expansion covered most of present day Europe and the Mediterranean area. The Roman Empire was in control of this land base and its resources before the appointment of Julius Caesar in 44BC until 1453, when the Ottoman Turks (Muslims) took over Constantinople. The size of the empire and its lengthy existence led to Roman influence on language, religion, architecture, philosophy, law and government of countries around the world to this day.

    The Roman Emperors controlled the religious institutions and participated in the imperial cult system, which consisted of deceased emperors serving as demigods to be worshipped by all. Their successors would appoint demigods to enhance their own status. People have worshipped the Pope as if he were a deity. When false gods are worshipped, it was and continues to be easy to convert and covet "things" and these things such as gold begin serving as false gods. God, Jesus, and other higher powers become less and less real. [44]

    The Roman Catholic Church did everything in its power to sequester and control all pagan sacred documents. In 1945 an Arab peasant, named Mohammed Ali, found a whole library of Gnostic gospels hidden in a cave near Nag Hammadi in Upper Egypt on the bend of the Nile River. He uncovered a three foot tall red jar that contained 12 papyrus books bound in leather and additional book stuffed inside another. The books were written in an Egyptian language called Coptic, letters based on the Greek alphabet. These documents included the teachings of Christ and his disciples and speculations were made that they were written by Jesus' first disciples. The authors of these documents were followers of an ancient group called Gnostics. [45] Gnostics were considered mystics and progressive thinkers for that time period, which went against the Roman Literalist Church hierarchy. Throughout history, other groups who went against the Church were punished for their beliefs.

    The Gnostics existed before and during the onset of Christianity. The word "Gnostic" was derived from the word "Gnosis" meaning knowledge of God. Marshall in the book *The Truth about Jesus and the Lost Gospels* claimed that Gnosticism can be described as "salvation by knowledge." Marshall referred to knowledge of the self being the means to freedom according to Gnosticism.[46] The Gnostics were considered outrageous and even dangerous by the Roman Catholic Church. They did not support the idea that those who were seeking a relationship with their higher power had to do so with the aid of a priest. Their beliefs were based on a mystic knowledge and did not fit with the monetary and political wishes of the Church, associated with greed and control.

    However, the publicity the Roman Catholic Church gave the Gnostics served only to feed the interests of many of the inhabitants of the Roman Empire. The Roman Catholic Church took their interpretation of the Jesus story as a literal account of historical events, and thus they were referred to as Literalists. The Gnostics were imprisoned and/or put to death because they went against the beliefs of the Church. Another historical reason the Gnostics were obliterated was because some of the Gnostic divinities were female. [47] In essence, the Church managed to reduce the amount of people practicing a form of spirituality and a way of thinking to maintain its power and control.

One of the beliefs of the Gnostics involved their conviction that Eve was a courageous woman. As a result of Eve's receiving the apple, she moved humans closer to the attainment of many divine gifts. The eating of the apple represented the obtainment of knowledge. The false perception promoted by the Church was Eve was weak and brought her own bad luck by coercing Adam to partake in the eating of the apple delivered by Satan. Myths can have great power. Because of the impact of this creation story, women have had to endure a great deal of blame, shame and have been associated with darkness and evil. The story in Genesis, the first book of the Bible, with God's six-day creation, and inception of Adam and Eve portrayed God as tyrannical and trivial. Nakedness associated with sexual sin, female vulnerability and God's wrath were paramount in the message derived from this story. [48] The concept of a vengeful God caused a separation between people and God.

Another belief of the Gnostics was reincarnation, which was vehemently denounced by the Church. Reincarnation was a belief also supported by Jesus. According to various written works, Jesus also propagated the term karma. Part of the lost teachings of Jesus involves karma, past lives and right choices. People determine their own destinies. It is also a part of free will. If people do awful things to others, bad karma may knock at the doors of these individuals. These terrible things usually happen if people do not take responsibility for their actions and/or do not see their harmful actions as wrong.[49] Indian people coined the term "red road." One must do good things for all or one has fallen off the "red road." Falling off the right path can lead to bad things happening during the course of one's lifetime.

What would be the purpose of denouncing the concepts of reincarnation and karma? If someone was considered saved by accepting Christ as their savior at the 11th hour, a need did not exist to take full responsibility for one's actions and all individuals could be accepted into the kingdom of God no matter how horrible their actions. Were these beliefs propagated by the priests and others in power embraced and enforced to excuse their personal wrongdoings? If so, they truly fell off the "red road."

The Quakers, originally from England, came to the new world during the mid 1650s. Similarities existed between the spiritual practices of the Quakers and the Indian people. One of their beliefs purported that one did not have to be in a church to establish fellowship with others. Everyone has the light within them. Also, people who were repelled by the rules and rituals of religion discovered the Quaker views were more refreshing for the times. It was their philosophy that they had a responsibility to become friends with people of all races. The Quakers were known to be very respectful of the Indian people. They worked alongside the Indian people and did not try to change their form of spirituality. In 1681, William Penn met with the Indians under the great elm of Shackamason and made friends with the Indians.

Trees often serve as sacred meeting places for Indian people. Robert Hodgson, a Quaker missionary, was arrested, imprisoned and treated harshly because he was drawing a large crowd at his meetings. [50] The Quakers, Indian people and other groups such as the Gnostics were persecuted for their spiritual practices and beliefs because their beliefs differed from those who were self acclaimed Christians.

Despair relates to sin because it sets people up to be taken over by evil doers. Those with dark souls prey on individuals during their most vulnerable moments. Many of the children who attended the boarding and residential schools, while their parents were left to reside on reservations and reserves, were very vulnerable and lived in a constant state of despair. These children were often subjected to cruel and harsh treatment. The dark souls who perpetuated the abuse were feeding off the spirits of these innocent individuals like parasites. Many people have been seriously harmed when they were sexually abused by the priests, nuns, and others in authority.

Leon J. Podles described many scenes in which children were sexually abused at the hands of Catholic priests in his book entitled *Sacrilege: Sexual Abuse in the Catholic Church.* Only a portion of the sexual abuse was ever reported. Because this crime was committed in private, it was difficult to determine the actual number of victims. The number of alleged victims was 10,677 in the John Jay Report. This number was raised to 12,257 by later reports, and the number is most likely much higher than that; Podles estimated at least 100,000 fell victim to these pedophiles. As mentioned earlier, a number of sexual abuse cases were never reported, which may have resulted because of the shame experienced by the victims. Podles noted that the individuals who perpetrated the sexual abuse on these naïve children can be labeled as narcissistic, and this label was not only reserved for abusive priests. The diagnosis of narcissistic personality disorder was given to the Catholic bishops as well, because these bishops worked diligently to cover up the wrongful acts of the priests. It was all about appearances and not about the harm caused to the children. Podles also referred to these pedophiles as sociopathic. The priests were noted as having an indifferent conscience filled with apathy for the truth. They preached what they felt was the truth concerning the word of God and what best served their self serving wishes. Sadly, many of the staff members placed in charge of the boarding and residential school students did not differ from these reprehensible individuals.

  The abusive priests lacked the ability to assume social responsibility. If wrongful acts were brought to their attention, it would elicit an attitude of nonchalance. Although these narcissistic individuals were completely self-involved, they were skilled in the ways of social seduction, often with an air of dignity and confidence. They were proficient at deceiving others with clever persuasiveness. These abusive priests were skillful in enticing, coercing and tantalizing the needy and the naïve.

Those priests also possessed a pathological sense of entitlement. During the period of time when this country was being settled, the Euro-Americans also felt they had the right to take over anything that came across their paths simply because they were white and European. People who exhibit narcissistic personality disorder characteristics also express grandiosity through their obsessions with fantasies of success. They are convinced they are unique and in turn require excessive admiration and adulation. Several examples were given by Podles of occasions when pedophile priests would be given public recognition for their heroic acts of generosity and other forms of public service. At the same time, they were sexually abusing children. They were known to exploit others for their own ends, lack empathy for the feelings of others, could be envious of others, and were arrogant and became enraged when they felt frustrated or contradicted. They had to get their way.[51]

Attempts have been made to explain the existence of evil. It's been somewhat impossible to reconcile that God is good; God is all-powerful; and that terrible things can happen to good people, especially children. Christian Science correlates evil with an illusion of our mortal minds. It doesn't really exist. Buddhism equates evil to the bad karma one has created in a past life, especially concerning acts like the rape of a young child. That child must have carried to his or her current life a bad karma debt. Christianity doesn't offer any plausible explanation except that there is not an act so heinous that God cannot turn it into good. Concerning the three prepositions mentioned above, such as God is all-powerful; all three cannot be reconciled in the case of specific situations.[52] In turn, this dilemma has led many to challenge their faith when horrible things do happen.

Many of the boarding school employees mocked belittled and prohibited the Indian form of spirituality and denounced these ways as evil and savage. Moreover, if the children did not accept Christianity as it was forced upon them, they were told they would be doomed to hell. Hell meant the devil, his pitchforks and extreme heat that could melt the skin off their bodies. Those in authority who condemned others to hell considered those who were condemned as being unequal and worthless. A forced form of religion drew these children in, gave them hope, and then damned them for their perceived sins.

People who attended the Holy Childhood Boarding School reported they possessed a fear of the dark. One individual stated he believed he may become evil and dark if he did not convert to Christianity. These children were told they would be thrown in a deep dark hole if they did not change their ways and become Christianized. They were taught to despise their families' histories and that these histories had no value. Indian people working with the Aboriginal Healing Project in Canada referred to the losses of their culture that occurred at the residential schools as spiritual abuse. They were forced to reject their native tribal languages, and obey only those in authority at the boarding and residential schools. Their only viable future was a "white" future.

Those in authority at the boarding and residential schools taught the children about a false God, one who was merciless and cruel. The fear of God propagated by the Church caused further separation between individuals and their higher beings. It is difficult to determine when the fear of God was initiated and instilled as a part of Christian practices.

The Church and others who assumed authority began a quest to dominate women and later people of color over 2000 years ago. The Greek religion, from which much of Roman beliefs evolved, was one of dominance through acts of cruelty and barbarism, such as rapes of goddesses and mortal women. The Roman Empire followed suit. Women were listed as property in the Old Testament of the Bible 11 times. Women were not given the right to vote until 1920 in the U.S. and were treated with cruelty, including imprisonment and force feeding, when they marched to obtain that right. In current times, women continue to be portrayed in demeaning ways in the media as sex objects.

Jesus has been described as having the utmost respect for women and people of all races, and valued others' opinions and leadership abilities. He was open to learning about the various cultures. Jesus was known to have traveled with 72 women at one point. Mary of Magdalene was portrayed as a woman with seven devils and a woman with deep seated problems. She was referred to as a prostitute who washed the feet of Jesus with her tears and other disparaging accusations.[53] Other sources reveal that Jesus and Mary of Magdalene had a committed and intimate relationship and Mary was a gifted individual like Jesus and none of the derogatory descriptions applied. Some sources portray Jesus as a rabbi, meaning teacher. One of the most logical arguments for the relationship between Jesus and Mary was that Jesus would have been regarded with suspicion if he were not married. Rabbis were required to be married. Marshall referred to Jesus as a rabbi when he was describing events that led up to Jesus' crucifixion. [54]

Because of these prejudices against women the theologians and scholars justified the Salem Massachusetts witch trials that took place between 1692 and 1693. However, witch trials had also occurred in Europe from the 1300s to the end of the 1600s. Hundreds of thousands of people in Europe, predominantly women, were put to death. Joan of Arc, an astounding woman who assisted France in armed combat during the Hundred Year Wars, was charged with witchcraft and burned at the stake. These lethal witch hunts happened for many reasons and multiple theories were established to explain this phenomenon.

- The Church Oppression Theory involved the Church falsely inventing the concept of witches to eliminate opponents who threatened the Church's credibility and to gain wealth.
- The Greed Theory implicated the elites in their quest to seize the property of others.
- The mental health condition of the people involved in the hunts led to mass hysteria. The

- peasants became neurotic and psychotic, and in a group panic went after individuals believed to be witches.
- A Social Control Theory involved the desire to maintain control over the masses, and instill cultural uniformity. Administrative officials linked specific individuals to a dangerous conspiracy involving witchcraft.
- The Confessional Conflict Theory was associated with reformation and the conflict between the Protestants and Roman Catholics. Each group used witchcraft as an excuse to attack one another.
- The Pagan Religious Rebellion Theory is another reason why the witch hunts may have happened in Europe. Ancient spiritual practices were blamed by the Christians for causing disasters such as plagues, famines, and storms.[55]

Approximately 200 people, again mainly women, were killed in Salem. They were accused of practicing the devil's magic. The witch hunts occurred in Massachusetts as a result of a war that was started in 1689 by the English rulers William and Mary. The war of 1689 was fought against the French by the English and took place in the American colonies of upstate New York, Nova Scotia and Quebec. People in exile escaping the ravages of this war fled to the Salem area. These additions to the population of this area put a strain on the resources of the original inhabitants. Competition existed between the wealthy and the farmers over resources. The squabbling in the village was also considered the work of the devil. To rid the village of evil, those individuals who were associated with witchery were put to death, again mainly women.

Much speculation about these events occurred as a result of extensive modern studies. One of the theories associated with some recorded bizarre behaviors of accused individuals was linked to the fungus ergot found in rye, wheat and other cereal plants. This fungus can cause muscle spasms, vomiting, delusions and hallucinations. In later years, the colony came to the conclusion that those who were convicted were innocent and the colony compensated the families of those found guilty. [56] Although the witch hunts were terminated, discrimination against women continued.

Bishop John Selby Spong has attributed men's antagonism towards women as being linked to a primal fear, the fear of blood, which has not been addressed. He made reference to five places in the Bible relating to women and blood during menstruation and child birth. The blood of women during these times was considered unclean. Indian males also had a fear of blood because it was related to death. They were puzzled how a woman could bleed for four days and still be alive.

Indian people considered women's menstruation time a time when women were closest to the divine and were very powerful. Indian women had to sleep and live separately from their husbands during their menstruation time because of their perceived powers. They could not participate in ceremonies. Menstruation was referred to as a cleansing time for women, which enhanced their status even further within tribal communities. In the Bible it was stated there were restrictions placed on women as to when they could join others after childbirth or following menstruation. The period of time when women had to stay away from others was longer if a female child was born.

  Spong speculated that women were referred to as the weaker sex because of lack of bodily strength, their inability to protect their families as well as their male counterparts, and their vulnerability during the last month of pregnancy and while nursing. The connection mothers of newborns had with their offspring is associated with a form of weakness. The statement "women and children first" also depicts dependency. The interpretation of the story in Genesis in which woman was created from man has paved the way for the idea that men are superior and women are subservient.[57] During the earlier days of when the Roman Empire was in full swing, many Roman women became Christians because of the protection it provided them. Christians were considered to have a higher status; thus, were not as readily killed.[58] The Church has had a major influence on labels, definitions and role models of the underdogs in the modern world.

  When listening to a tribal drum group, take notice of the higher pitched voices of the men when they begin singing and then how their voices became deeper for the latter portion of the song. It was mentioned by an Indian singer and drummer that in order to seek balance; they celebrate their feminine side by singing in a higher voice for the first part of a song. Indian people who have managed to return to some of the traditional practices and have the ability to live in two worlds have found more of a sense of balance.

A vast number of similarities exist between the ancient Hebrew beliefs and that of the Native Americans prior to the arrival of the Europeans. According to ancient Hebrew beliefs, to practice Christianity in its true sense meant one needs to be modest, sensitive, loving, kind, empathetic and understanding, similar to the practices of traditional Indian people. The entity of Satan did not exist with the early Hebrew beliefs. Importance was placed on building a personal relationship with God independent from the community in which one resides. Native Americans fostered this same belief with their children at an early age.

First the interpretation of dreams was encouraged. Dreams symbolized the connection and communication between individuals and the Creator. Fasting and vision quests were another way in which Indian people would explore their relationship with the spirit world. Fasting is also mentioned in the Bible as a way of communing with God. Ancient Hebrew beliefs referred to sex as healthy, spiritual, and not sinful.[59] The union between man and woman, according to the beliefs of the Traditionalists, is not fraught with sin. It is considered natural, and there is an expectation that it will lead to creating life's most precious gift, children.

In the past, for those practicing their faith based Roman Catholic literalist standpoint, a stage of violence was set up against those who did not participate in their religious beliefs because the Roman Catholic literalists considered themselves superior to those who did not support their viewpoints. Today, this country is suffering from massive cultural divisions. Those who defend Christianity are out to impose their beliefs on others, and those who do not support Christianity are considered enemies of the truth. What has been created is an impasse, which can oftentimes be intense and unfriendly. Many Indian people have foregone the traditional spiritual practices of the past, taken up some other form of religion, or do not practice any form of religion or spirituality at all. When an individual lives without taking care of the spiritual self, one becomes lost in an abyss of doubt and uncertainty.

    Books describing religious beliefs are filled with religious ideas, symbols and attitudes primarily depicting the beliefs of the times in which they were written. A religious book is meant to be a canvas or a transparency.[60] The one viewing this work is suppose to develop their own perception about the meaning behind the images. The Bible was enforced as the word of God due to the authority of those who were behind its original inception and promotion. The word for Bible is derived from the Greek word *biblia,* or "the books," which is the plural term of *biblion,* a word taken from the Semitic *biblos,* meaning "papyrus," or scroll. Today, the term Bible symbolizes a collection of sacred texts that include: Torah, prophets, wisdom literature, Gospels, and epistles.[61] Christians predominantly believe the Bible contains all of God's messages about creation, His personal nature, desirable behaviors and sin, liberation and salvation. The purpose of the Gospels were to delineate Christ's life, his teachings and the sharing of good news about Jesus, concerning what he has done for all mankind.

The past as described in the old testament of the Bible has been laced with stories of destruction in the name of God. Indian people did not fight over religion or spirituality. The term religionistic has been used when describing organized religion. Religionistic practices include, but are not limited to, ritual, confinement, persecution, dogma, sins, rights and wrongs. Dogma is defined as a set of principles declared as truth without proof. The dogma portrayed as the fear of God has permeated throughout history to control people, and create a hierarchy between those preaching the word and the rest of the population. Personal interpretations of religious dogma rested on authority regarded as competent to decide and determine law based on the tenets of religion, and cannot be construed as the absolute truth. Traditionalists often wondered why Christians only participated in spiritual activities once a week. Traditional Indian forms of spirituality relate to a way of life and are ongoing.

Bart D. Ehrman in his book entitled *Jesus Interrupted, Revealing the Hidden Contradictions of the Bible,* stated that many reasons existed to serve as a rationale behind perceived forgeries based on personal interpretations, relating to the Bible and religious dogma. Forgeries, a term introduced by Ehrman to define biblical discrepancies, relate to the interpretations of biblical texts by individuals who were not qualified to do so, or did so under the pretext of hidden agendas. Those forgeries were put into place to oppose a particular point of view; to make a profit; to oppose an enemy; to defend one's own belief as divinely inspired; and/or to provide authority for one's own views. Keep in mind the fear of God was propagated to create a larger attendance for church services, and to exert control over another's spiritual beliefs. Another point to make as described by Marshall in his book *The Truth about Jesus and the Lost Gospels,* the Gospels in the Bible were not selected because they were better or based on truth. The Gospels were chosen to serve as a way to establish and secure the authority of male church leaders. [62]

Ehrman describes many contradictions and falsifications in the Bible. The Old Testament was written over six hundred years by dozens of authors and included 39 books. The New Testament consisted of 27 books written by 16 or 17 authors over a period of 70 years. The chance of there being a high level of ambiguity and differing viewpoints is quite high considering the vast amount of time and individuals who contributed to the writing of the Bible.[63] If one reads the books of Matthew, Mark and Luke from beginning to end, these books closely resemble one another with similar stories and similar words. Differences in the messages being portrayed start occurring with the book of John. [64] No writings exist dating from Jesus' actual lifetime or shortly after Jesus' death. The original sources that were put together long after his crucifixion no longer exist. Instead, what survived is renditions entitled the four gospels and other Christian writings, which have gone through many alterations over a long period of time. It would be a mistake to believe in the complete legitimacy of these written works.

In order for the Bible to be considered the absolute truth there needs to be consistency in the information being portrayed. It has been considered by many people that the Bible is a historically untrustworthy compilation of legends. During "the Jesus Seminar" a group of scholars stated that only approximately 20 percent of the Jesus sayings were correct. It was also reported that the accounts of Jesus' life were written many years after the events may have happened. These accounts cannot be considered remotely reliable.[65]

The Lost Teachings of Jesus by Mark and Elizabeth Prophet and the Gnostic gospels that were discovered in a cave near Nag Hammadi in Egypt could prove to be very interesting reading and may be closer to the truth. Some of the books in the Bible, like the legends passed down from generation to generation by the Traditionalists, are filled with life lessons that can provide guidance on how to live a life of goodness coupled with how to address problems as they arise. So much destruction has occurred at the hands of those who believed there was only one source of truth that many do not know where to hang their hat when it comes to seeking a form of spiritual and religious practices.

An on-line survey was conducted by *Parade Magazine* in October 2009 for a CBS News Sunday Morning program entitled "A Matter of Faith." The results of this survey were:
- Twenty-five percent of the respondents reported not being religious.
- Approximately seven out of ten believe in God.
- Half rarely attend religious services or they don't attend at all.
- Half practice the religion they grew up with.

However, the polls printed in the New York Times article dated April 27, 2009 stated that the number of atheists in the United States is steadily growing. During the last 50 years instability has been on the rise within many institutions including religious domains. The hidden agendas of these institutions are being exposed. The accuracy and authenticity of the massive amount of data that is made available today is in question. Christian dogma falls into this same category, which continues to be fully entrenched within many religious denominations. [66]

Traditionalists practiced a form of spirituality closely associated with a more meaningful relationship with their higher beings. Civilization can be renewed by once again introducing the importance of dreams, visions, and the feeling of connectedness promoted by Traditionalism and the original Christian beliefs, exploring the deeper meaning of the great mysteries. Fox promoted a pattern, which connected divine love and justice. All humans have within them the ability and promptings to do what is right for others and themselves. The community way of life in which everyone is treated the same and everyone looks after one another is strongly supported by Fox. Mother Earth and her children have suffered greatly and continue to suffer under patriarchal domination. There continues to be a need to move towards a spiritual vision that prays, celebrates and lives out the reality that there is a God and all humans are his children. According to Fox, He exists in living and nonliving entities of all shapes and sizes.

    The worshipping of a false god by seeking material goods, the addiction to alcohol, drugs and entertainment, all tie in with the vast emptiness many people feel. The missing connection is with the divine and not with those items that quickly lose their worth. The core of Christianity at its very beginnings was its sense of mystical practice and cosmic awareness. Mother Earth, the mystical brain in reference to dreams and visions, creativity, wisdom, youth, Traditionalism, and Mother Church are dying, according to Fox. [67]

    The boarding and residential school attendees' hair was cut, hair symbolizes power and other meanings denoted by various tribes and Native American men only cut their hair to show grief or shame. These Indian children were given Christian names and were forced to wear Euro-American clothing, and were also coerced to embrace patriotism for a country who did not respect their existence. A multitude of Indian people were lost in a world laced with a foreign form of religion coupled with abuse, homesickness and other disturbing feelings without the support and guidance of their parents and other loving caregivers.

The power and control exerted by patriarchal domination and the Church have continued to serve as catalysts for a massive amount of oppression that has been inflicted on Indian people, other people of color, and women. Validation for many of these harsh actions was derived from false interpretations of a book that needs to be examined for its authenticity, the Bible. Throughout history women have had to pay a high price for these faulty interpretations. Many of the Indian children, who were forced to attend the boarding and residential schools, were often too young to possess the ability to think abstractly. In other words, they could not formulate concretely the concept of what role the Creator or God occupied in their parents', and others' lives, or their own. As a result of various religious sanctions that have been carried out for thousands of years, many people are experiencing feelings of disconnectedness and imbalance because their spiritual needs have not been and are not being met.

Chapter VI
The Realization of Manifest Destiny
Manifest Destiny
The buffalo are few.
Land decimated by iron rails.
Indian communities torn apart.
Hear the engine puffing down the tracks.

Opiate smiles mask the pain.
Push westward, push westward,
Indian people moved about
from one useless plot of land to another.

America has been born
out of rebellion,
God's perceived given right,
the Realization of Manifest Destiny.

  The "Indian Problem" was a thorn in the sides of the European settlers and got in the way of pursuing the ideals set forth by "Manifest Destiny." Ignorance has often ruled, and is usually "handed down" in families. It continues today to dominate the overall consciousness of the Euro-Americans. Ignorance is based on fear. It is natural to be afraid of what is not understood. Prejudices and irrational hostilities are established against the misunderstood. Most settlers and political leaders feared and misunderstood the Indian people. Many tactics were utilized to solve the "Indian problem," and biological warfare was one of the destructive methods in a long line of historical abuses used against the Indian people.

Exposure to smallpox was used in biological warfare against a segment of the population unprepared to fight off its lethal properties. The unfortunate people who contracted this virus can expect to have two outcomes: death or blindness, along with grotesque scars. Once smallpox finds a host in a community, it rampantly takes off on its own. The virus can be easily transmitted through exposure to contaminated scabs or dried-out body secretions. Hernando Cortez introduced the first attack of smallpox genocide in 1519. Unsuspecting Aztecs were the victims. They were given blankets that were infected with the virus, and thousands died.

In 1763, the British provided the Odawa Indians in Michigan gifts of little insulated metal boxes. The British instructed them to not open the metal boxes until the Odawa returned from Montreal to their village near present day Petoskey, Michigan. Once the metal boxes were opened, smallpox virus ran rampant amongst the tribal people in the Odawa villages. Again, thousands lost their lives to the dreadful virus. The same year, British soldiers tried to spread the virus to the Indian people during Pontiac's Revolt in Ohio. In the dry-pus-form stored in insulated metal boxes, the virus can maintain its virulence for up to two years. Smallpox can be transferred to hosts through clothing and bedding, being exposed to cadavers who died from it, and inhaling the virus. Cremation is the only way to destroy the virus.

Livestock brought into this country by the European settlers are linked to many lethal diseases existing today. The diseases linked to these deaths are, but are not limited to, flu, tuberculosis, malaria, plague, measles, small pox and cholera. The history books defining the outcomes of any war portray the winners by the maneuvers of the generals and their weapons. However, many wars have been won by those who had the most horrible and destructive germs to spread to their foes. The Euro-American germs were so lethal that they decimated up to 95 percent of the Indian population.[68] Unintentional and intentional acts of genocide against the Indian people continued after the Declaration of Independence was signed in the effort to accomplish the goals of expansionism associated with "Manifest Destiny."

From 1775 to 1791 the Native Americans won 22 battles and smaller expeditions, such as the French Creek expedition, against the European and later on the Euro-American armies. Native American men were fearless fighters, and well disciplined strategists. The European and Euro-American armies made the mistake of thinking they were undisciplined, unknowledgeable "savages." An English general, named Braddock, fought against the Native Americans from 1755 to 1758 and lost fifty men to one lost by the Indian people. Indian warriors became valued, but not completely trusted, and were recruited to become allies for colonial and Euro-American armies as a part of the expansion endeavors. [69]

The Declaration of Independence was ratified on July 4th, 1776. The 13 United Colonies of North America declared their independence from the British Crown. One serious problem was still occurring during this restructuring period, the "Indian problem." Included in the Declaration of Independence were the provisions covering the "merciless Indian Savages." Indian warfare was equated to the obliteration of all Euro-American without concern for age, sex or condition, which painted a picture of Indian people being barbaric.[70] While some Indian warriors exhibited some extreme and harsh behaviors, generally speaking, Euro-American soldiers were far more brutal. Euro-American soldiers maimed women and children of all ages. Indian babies were even thrown to dogs as food, while they were still alive in front of their mothers. However, at the same time these atrocities were occurring, the American government continued to take steps to address the "Indian problem" under the pretenses that the Indians were solely at fault for all the problems the Euro-Americans were facing, such as the takeover of Indian land.

Treaties were mechanisms put into place as a formalized way of securing land holdings for Euro-Americans where Indian people used to reside. The first treaty was established in 1778 and the last was enacted in 1871. Over 400 treaties were established between Indian tribes and the United State government. Congress and the commissioners sent to secure these treaty documents secured with the tribes, who they invited to the table to review and sign these documents, were the conquered ones. These meetings were not based on equality, they exemplified expansionism. For example, the Treaty of Paris in 1783 took possession of Indian Territory from the Atlantic to the Mississippi.[71] Not all of the 550 federally recognized tribes established treaties with the federal government.[72]

George Washington was contacted by Henry Knox, Secretary of War, during the summer of 1789. Knox proposed to Washington that Indian policy needed further clarification and additional revisions. Indian policy was customarily under the Articles of Confederation. Knox proposed that Indian tribes be considered foreign nations. Under the Constitution, authorization was given to Congress to control all commerce with foreign nations, which caused even further alienation between the Euro-Americans and Indian people.[73]

During the 1790s, the United States government was faced with four alternatives concerning Indian policy. These options included extermination; re-located to small areas, while towns sprouted up around them; assimilation by transforming them into Christian farmers; or relocation to unsettled territories west of the Mississippi. President Thomas Jefferson supported assimilation as the only viable and humane process when he addressed the "Indian problem."

In 1793, Congress gave authorization to the President to provide tribes with domestic animals and farm tools. Agents were sent to demonstrate how to use these tools. However, policymakers were pessimistic about the possible outcomes of these acts of assimilation. They believed the Indian people would not accept the Euro-American culture and its value system. It was decided that a more efficient way of dealing with the Indian problem was to quarantine them.

President Jefferson's plan encompassed the transfer of the tribal people from the southern states to the northern states. Plantations were set up in the southern states and slaves were utilized to enhance prosperity for the Euro-Americans by expanding the goods produced by the wealthy landowners. The land in the south was divided into territories with a plan to establish states in the future. The lands vacated in the south by the Indians would be sold to help pay for part of the cost of Louisiana.

On July 5, 1803 Meriwether Lewis set off on the well-known Lewis and Clark expedition. William Clark joined Lewis in October of 1803 in the Indiana territory, across the Ohio River from Louisville, Kentucky. Jefferson's plan was that Lewis would inform the tribes about the election of the new "father" of the United States. The new father's hopes included tribal people embracing a commercial system, a system which had the potential to benefit anyone involved in this economic process. Jefferson wanted to establish peace and a trading domain in which the Indian people would stop their resistance and put down their weapons. [74]

Before the onset of European occupation of the newly discovered land, Indian Territory extended from the eastern shores to California. The natural boundary of the western portion of this country at the end of the American Revolution was the Mississippi River. In 1803, when Thomas Jefferson was president the boundary was expanded to the Rocky Mountains. By the 1840s the boundary reached the Pacific Ocean. Indian people were considered to be of heathen nature since they only possessed occupancy rights to the lands on which they were forced to reside. In other words, reservations served as a dumping ground for the Indian people. The population of these unfortunate people was numbered at only a few hundred thousand, reduced from millions when the Europeans first set foot on the Western Hemisphere.[75]

The Louisiana Purchase included all land west of the Mississippi River and east of the continental divide, which consisted of today's Louisiana, Arkansas, parts of northeastern Texas, Oklahoma, eastern Colorado and Minnesota. During the Lewis and Clark expedition, Lewis and Clark added Missouri, Kansas, Iowa, Nebraska, the Dakotas, Montana, Idaho, Washington, and Oregon as part of the Louisiana Purchase. Jefferson received fame and notoriety for his ingenuity and foresight leading to the Louisiana Purchase and the Lewis and Clark Expedition. Jefferson was relentless with ensuring that these portions of land did not become additions to the British colonies. The Louisiana Purchase and the Lewis and Clark Expedition served a prominent role in the forming of what is known as the United States and what would be later referred to as "Manifest Destiny."[76]

William Henry Harrison put into place an Indian Removal policy in 1809, because Indian people were thought to lack the capacity to live up to Euro-American standards. He negotiated the treaty of Fort Wayne in 1809, which ceded the majority of land in Indiana and Illinois to the Euro-American settlers. Harrison was not going to let a few "wretched savages" get in his way of populating an area that had the potential to support a large civilized population. He backed up his convictions with a large military garrison. Harrison became the governor of the Northwest Territories and then was elevated to one of the highest honors when he was elected as the 9th president of the United States.

Contrary to how Harrison despised the Indian people, he did recognize the power and respect held by the Shawnee leader, Tecumseh. He gave careful consideration to this fearless leader. Harrison paid this tribute to Tecumseh:

"The implicit obedience and respect which the followers of Tecumseh pay to him is really astonishing, and more than any other circumstance bespeaks him on those uncommon geniuses, which spring up occasionally to produce revolutions and overturn the established order of things. If it were not for the vicinity of the United States, he would, perhaps, be the founder of an empire that would rival in glory that of Mexico or Peru. No difficulties deter him. His activity and industry supply the want of letters. For four years he has been in constant motion. You see him today on the Wabash and in a short time you hear of him on the shores of Lake Erie or Michigan, or on the banks of the Mississippi, and wherever he goes he makes an impression favorable to his purposes."[77]

Despite Tecumseh's efforts and the efforts of other Indian warriors, the governmental military conquests were successful at reducing Indian land holdings east of the Mississippi. Congress passed a bill in 1819 to establish a "civilization fund." Ten thousand dollars was allocated for agricultural and literacy instruction of the Indian people. Those, who were in agreement with participating with this instruction, were provided assistance by missionaries. These missionaries served dual roles. First and foremost, they wanted to Christianize the Indian people. Secondly, they provided instruction to them about the proper customs required to obtain citizenship. Missionary sponsored farms and households were popping up in various locations in the country. These served as models of acceptable values and customs for Indian people to copy.

During the 1820s, Henry Schoolcraft visited the Ojibwe tribes and traveled with some of the men. He was impressed with the wisdom of these tribal people and the detailed pictographs left behind by them at each area visited. The Secretary of War, John C. Calhoun recommended Schoolcraft to the Michigan Territorial Governor, Lewis Cass, to assist with an expedition. The mission was to explore the land surrounding Lake Superior. Schoolcraft served as a geologist on the expedition.

Beginning in 1822, Schoolcraft conducted ethnological research while he was appointed the Indian agent at Sault Ste. Marie, Michigan. He learned the Ojibwe language from his wife, Jane Johnston, who happened to be of Ojibwe and Scottish/Irish descent. Schoolcraft's admiration for the native people quickly dissipated once he discovered that it would be more profitable to support the actions of Andrew Jackson. He began to take steps to obliterate the very same people who were connected to his wife's family, the Ojibwe people. One of the ways he did so was to take a portion of their written works and rewrote them to erase some of the Indian history. Schoolcraft also had strong desires to obtain notoriety for his written works. [78]

      The United States government has had long established mechanisms in place empowering those in authority to have control over the actions and resources of the general population. Public laws become enforced legislation through the actions of contradictory parties of a two party system, divergent priorities, and confrontational approaches. So keep in mind how the laws governing the masses come into enforced legislation. Oftentimes, laws are not based on sound logic and what is in the best interest of the people. However, the federal government strived to avoid the pitfalls of what happened in Europe with regards to land ownership and utilitarian form of leadership. Land in Europe was controlled by landlords. The giving of parcels of land to settlers created a country comprised of independent citizens.

      "All for the public good" were the politicians' claims in their effort to hide their and their supporters' self-serving agendas. When Andrew Jackson was elected president of the United States, he was supported by the wealthiest men in the south. The land in which the

Cherokee, Choctaw, and other tribes resided was targeted by wealthy entrepreneurs who wanted to expand their cotton plantations. [79] Jackson despised the Indian people and did not defend Indian rights. He openly rejected federal treaty obligations. President Jackson reinstated the Indian Removal Act, which was passed by Congress in 1830. This act gave the President the privilege of selecting the tribes to be removed and provided the financing for this removal. Seeds of greed and hatred fueled these acts of genocide and discrimination and the joint collaboration falsely justified the takeover of the Indian people's land.

Jackson's agents bribed, used deception and threatened individual Indian people and groups to accomplish the President's goals. Records were falsified. Tribal leaders for the Cherokee nation resisted their removal from their tribal lands at the state and federal level. In 1831, the tribe won their case due to their independent sovereign nation rights. Their victory was the result of Chief Justice John Marshall's legal expertise. However, Jackson was not going to let this setback deter him from his goal, he was determined to remove the Cherokees from their land.

The Choctaw nation was the first to be removed from their ancestral land in Mississippi during the winter of 1831. Several groups were pressed to travel through blizzards and subzero temperatures. Many of these individuals were without foot coverings and were malnourished from lack of food. One blanket was allotted to each family. The Creek nation was driven off their land in Alabama in 1836 in the same fashion, except many were in chains. 1837 marked the first year of the Cherokee ejection and the historic "Trail of Tears." In the same cruel way, the Cherokee nation lost approximately one-quarter to one-half of their tribal people during the deadly march to Oklahoma.[80]

In 1836, in support of President Jackson's efforts, Henry Schoolcraft resolved disputes over land with the Ojibwe. He employed tribal leadership to bring about the 1836 Treaty of Washington. The Ojibwe tribe surrendered to the United States government a considerable amount of land, more than 13 million acres, which was worth millions of dollars. Schoolcraft believed these native people would be better off learning how to farm. Government officials established a subsidy system through which they were given supplies during the transition period from hunting to farming.[81]

The mid 1840s was a turning point concerning the ideals of expansionism in the United States. Seeds were planted to adopt the principles of expansionism by John Adams and John C. Calhoun during the development of the original Constitution, after the war of 1812 and further propagated by John L. O'Sullivan. O'Sullivan went further and proposed the phrase "Manifest Destiny." "Manifest Destiny" involved the expansion of United States territory, which was considered prearranged by the divine, and descendents of European immigrants were to be the beneficiaries. These beliefs further justified the takeovers of Indian resources, such as water, land, timber, silver, gold and other valuable reserves. The expansion included a massive move westward to form a larger civilized land base for those who participated in the acts of freedom described by the federal government. "Manifest Destiny" made its public debut in the *Democratic Review* in the July and August 1845 issues. O'Sullivan founded the *Democratic Review* and was a co-founder of the *New York Morning News*. During this time period, he was considered a scholar, visionary, as well as a politician, adventurer, and literary artist. With popularity on his side, the concept he advocated took hold of the American public like a storm.

    The Euro-American infringement of tribal lands continued during the gold strikes of 1858, which offset the equilibrium of the Arapaho and Cheyenne tribes in Colorado. The government, in their effort to appease the white settlers, moved the two tribes to small reservations. These encroachments triggered the eruption of a bloody war that ensued until 1865. The white man's greed for gold led to even more threats to other tribal nations such as the Santee Sioux nation to the north. In 1867, Congress organized a Peace Commission to cease the Sioux War. [82]

    Geronimo, Red Cloud, Sitting Bull, Crazy Horse and thousands of their Indian comrades evaded and fought U.S. troops in the effort to hold onto their land and its resources. The U.S. Army continued to unwisely think that Indian people lacked the sophistication to be a threat. In 1866, an incident took place that came to be known as the Fetterman Massacre. Crazy Horse, Hump and Little Wolf were the leaders of a decoy group. They managed to trick the soldiers quite easily into following them. Several warriors ambushed and killed 81 troops.

In 1868, three years after the civil war, federal officials implemented a second Fort Laramie Treaty that established geographic boundaries for the Lakota reservation. This treaty ensured that encroachments would not occur within these boundaries. Ranchers, settlers, miners and others would be prevented from stepping foot on this land. However, the treaty was dismissed soon after its inception when miners wanted to tap into the "Black Hills gold." Cattle ranchers, railroad companies, and farmers followed suit and claimed additional parcels of land defined in the treaty as trust land.

The nation was starting to be interconnected by the construction of the transcontinental railroad in 1869. Before Lincoln's death he was the driving force behind this project. The building of the railroad was considered a pivotal accomplishment and the winning of the civil war was credited to it by many Euro-Americans. Government officials set up a system of military forts to provide security to the railroads and their associated municipalities. Before the completion of the railroads, railroad companies lobbied for free land with Congress. Congress endowed them with considerable expanses of tribal lands. Every acre of land that was given to these companies interfered with access to land, water, and game for the Indian people.

The transcontinental railroad stretched from Omaha, Nebraska, to Sacramento, California. The magnitude of resources necessary to construct this engineering marvel was tremendous. The skills were obtained in American colleges and perfected through the shackles of war. The industrious laborers worked with a fortitude developed by following orders during war time. Chinese men predominantly worked on the Central Pacific Railroad, and Irish men worked primarily on the Union Pacific. These immigrants numbered up to 15,000 at any given time during the construction of these railroads. Captive Indian men were also enlisted to work on the railroads.[83]

In 1871, Congress began the process of dismissing all federal treaties. Many of the tribal people were forced to live on useless arid plots, suffering slow agonizing deaths due to starvation. Related to the construction of the railroad and the development of reservations was the disappearance of bison herds. Bison served as the main source of sustenance for the Plains Indians and also furnished meat for the railroad builders. There was a market for bison hides. Eastern hunters and sportsmen from Europe visited the plains to hunt the bison before they became extinct. Before 1874, three main herds of bison were known to trek from Texas to Canada annually. By 1876 bison hunters contracted by the federal government had annihilated all three herds. The needless slaughter of bison destroyed the balance with nature the Indian people had maintained by taking only what was needed for food, clothing, and shelter. Starvation became unavoidable. This extreme suffering led to the surrender of the Lakota people, one of the most powerful tribes of the northern Great Plains, to the American military forces during the winter of 1877.

In 1885, the Major Crimes Act was enacted by Congress.

"...Sec.9. Then immediately upon and after the date of the passage of this act all Indians, committing against the person or property of another Indian or other person any of the following crimes, namely, murder, manslaughter, rape, assault with intent to kill, arson, burglary, larceny within any territory the United States, in either within or without an Indian reservation, shall be subject therefore to the laws of such territory relating to set crimes, and shall be tried therefore in the same courts in the same manner and shall be subject to the same penalties as are all other persons charged with the commission of set crimes, respectively; and the said courts are hereby given jurisdiction in all such cases; and all such Indians committing any of the above crimes against the person or property of another Indian or other person within the boundaries of any state of the United States, with the limits of any Indian reservation, shall be subject to the same laws, tried in the same courts and in the same manner, and subject to the same penalties as are all other persons committing any of the above crimes within the exclusive jurisdiction of the United States."

"To prevent a recurrence of cases like the murder of Spotted Tail by Crow dog, in which the murderer was set free because the federal courts had no jurisdiction over crimes committed by one Indian against another within Indian country, Congress declared that seven major crimes committed by Indians on reservations would fall under the jurisdiction of the United States courts. This was a major encroachment upon traditional tribal autonomy."[84]

In the past, Indian people doled out corrective actions for behaviors that were considered of a criminal nature against other tribal members and their property. The corrective actions were embraced as a deeply entrenched cultural practice that maintained order and peace within the tribal villages. For example, when someone was killed either intentionally or unintentionally, the family of the lost one made the determination of what was to happen to the one who committed the crime. Sometimes, the family would adopt the guilty party into their family to replace the person who was killed or the family would put the person to death to avenge their family member's death. It was the family's decision. When the federal government took over this responsibility, it caused many problems for the Indian people and threw off balance an organized system of governance. The authorities would often abuse these privileges by creating false accusations for crimes they didn't commit, or by being abusive to Indian people who were accused of committing crimes.

Along with the beginning of the boarding and residential school era, the year 1887 was another turning point for Native American people. Congress passed the General Allotment Act, also known as the Dawes Act, because Henry Dawes was its chief supporter. President Grover Cleveland signed this act.

"An act to provide for the allotment of land in severalty to Indians on the various reservations, and to extend the protection of the laws of the United States in the territories over the Indians, and for other purposes.

"Be it enacted by the Senate and House of Representatives of the United States of America in Congress assembled. That in all cases where any tribe or band of Indians has been, or shall hereinafter be, located upon any reservation created for their use, either by treaty stipulations are by virtue of an act of Congress or executive order setting apart the same for other for their use, the president of the United States be, and he thereby is, authorized, where whenever and his opinion any reservation or any part thereof of such Indians is at advantageous for agriculture and grazing purposes, to cause said reservation, or any part thereof, to be surveyed, or re-surveyed if necessary, and to allow the lands in said reservation in severalty to any Indian located thereon…"[85]

The General Allotment Act afforded the President the ability to distribute quarter sections (160 acres) of Indian reservation lands to each Indian person who was the head of a household. Bachelors over eighteen years of age received an eighth section. Those who accepted these allotments were required to live on their homesteads away from their fellow tribesmen. Another advantage to this initiative was to extend citizenship to the Native Americans as legal landowners.[86] Therefore, Indian land could be and was taxed.

The Dawes Act was strongly enforced in Michigan. Any reservation land that was not appropriated to Indian people went to the Euro-Americans. The Dawes Act was a part of the assimilation process that involved detribalization that caused Indian people to lose their tribal identities and thus, become American citizens. The "Indian problem" would fade away because Indian people would disappear into the fabric of American society and be a part of the large tapestry. The allotment process, which lasted two decades, caused long-lasting dependency and resentment by the Indian people and served as a catalyst for the accomplishment of the goals set forth by "Manifest Destiny."

Another historical event that has caused long lasting traumatic effects for the Lakota people occurred during the month of December in 1890, a few days after Christmas. A band of approximately 300 Lakota men, women and children were ordered to travel almost 150 miles through inclement weather without adequate food and clothing to the Pine Ridge Agency. After these unfortunate people were held captive by the American military upon reaching their destination, they were murdered in cold blood. The United States government awarded 18 of the soldiers, who participated in this mass slaughter, the Congressional Medal of Honor for shooting mostly children and women, some of the women were pregnant. This incident is known as the Wounded Knee Massacre. [87] Indian people continued to be plagued with additional hardships during the Twentieth Century.

Twentieth Century

For centuries federal laws have been affecting various sectors of the population in a variety of ways and have exerted control over the actions and resources of the entire population either directly or indirectly. Many governmental agencies put into place to serve the Indian population had a hand in various acts of discrimination, assimilation and genocide including the Bureau of Indian Affairs (BIA). During the early 1900s, the BIA worked on coercing tribal people to become peaceful farmers and adopting their white neighbor's morality and need for materialism. A BIA directive denounced the Sun Dance and other spiritual ceremonies. Strong spiritual connections were associated with these ceremonies and provided a balance within tribal communities. The ability to practice these sacred ceremonies was not legally reinstated until 1978.

Today, the BIA has under its command one hundred and eighty-five federally recognized tribal or Bureau managed schools. Congress has taken notice of the problems concerning the administration of BIA schools from the BIA itself, and has introduced amendments to address these issues. A public apology was issued by Kevin Gover, Head of the Federal Bureau of Indian Affairs, concerning the hardships caused by the insensitivity of the BIA officials towards the Indian population in the past. In 1924, Congress implemented the "Citizen Act." Indian people were made citizens of their own country. This act came with high costs such as the taxes that were imposed at a later date and led to the loss of tribal land. During the next three decades, the BIA continued to break up parcels of communally held land and allot it to Euro-Americans. Euro-American businessmen repeating the behavior of "Manifest Destiny" fanatics, took advantage of unsuspecting tribal people and leased or bought approximately two million acres per year.[88]

By 1928, most Indian people were living in poverty. That same year, Lewis Meriam conducted his historical study. His report indicated the vast majority of Indian people suffered from a lack of health care and educational opportunities. The Euro- American economic and social standards were of no benefit to them. The "Great Depression" was another hardship. Policy makers continued to ignore the needs of tribal people even after the Meriam report was publicized.

During the late 1940s, the government decided to continue to coerce the tribal people from their lands and communities for various reasons. One reason was the costs allotted to provide financial support for Indian people. Another reason involved the clearing of reservations for purposes of mining. The overarching reason was to continue the process of assimilation.

In spite of these acts of discrimination, Indian men continued to "fight the white man's wars." "According to John Collier, then Commissioner of Indian Affairs, there were 7,500 American Indians in the armed forces as of June 1942, less than six months after the attack on Pearl Harbor. By October of that year, another observer reported that the number of Native Americans in the military had risen to well over 10,000. By 1944 almost 22,000, not counting those who had become officers, were part of the United States armed forces. At the war's end, there were over 25,000 Native Americans scattered throughout the military services, with the bulk of them in the U.S. Army." These numbers represented a larger proportion than any other ethnic group in the U.S. [89] Native Americans primarily fought in the wars because they linked being a warrior with honor, and because they felt they were upholding what they promised in treaties; however, the Euro-Americans did not honor their treaty obligations.

During the 1950s and early 1960s, a massive termination effort was conducted, which was reflected by governmental policies. During this time, 13 tribes lost their federal recognition status. Loss of status involved the disappearance of federal protections and services along with their trust status. The Menominee tribe in Wisconsin and Klamath in Oregon were the largest tribes to fall prey to this calamity. When tribes lost their trust status, it meant that these tribal entities had to pay taxes. In order to pay these taxes, they had to start selling off their land. Their reserved land bases shrunk immensely, which continued to support the goals set forth by "Manifest Destiny." [90]

Beginning in 1952, federal policymakers passed legislation that allowed the storing of highly radioactive waste by-products from the mining of uranium primarily in reservation areas. Mining was also conducted in reservation areas in spite of massive amounts of ore deposits located in other locations. Maximization of profits for energy corporations served as the motive for these mining practices. The Navajo, Lugunas and other tribal communities were exposed to highly carcinogenic/mutagenic agents as a result of these mining maneuvers. The storage of nuclear waste has continued to occur on reservations such as the Mescalero Apaches in New Mexico, in the Yucca Mountain area, and the Navajo treaty land base of the Western Shoshoni.

The American Indian Movement (AIM) was created in Minneapolis, Minnesota in 1968 as a means of protecting the rights of the Indian people. This movement replaced an anti-poverty program based in Minneapolis. AIM was originally referred to as Concerned Indian Americans until members recognized the comparison of titles to the Central Intelligence Agency. The initial goals of AIM included the improvement of economic and educational conditions for Indian people.

Many Vietnam veterans returned to the United States and found an unbearable situation and became members of AIM. The majority of Indian people were living in poverty. Vietnam veterans who experienced "cognitive dissonance" as a result of fighting in that war turned their psychological distress into political activism. The term "cognitive dissonance" refers to when people's values and beliefs turn out to be drastically different from the realities he or she is going through.

Many Indian men fought in wars because they felt they were upholding requirements set forth by treaties between their tribes and the U.S. government. "Why was I fighting to uphold a U.S. treaty commitment halfway around the world when the United States was violating its treaty commitments to my own people and about 300 other Indian nations?...I was fighting the wrong people, pure and simple…"[91]

According to the Indian activists, the government was continuing to instill policies associated with sadistic national colonialism. Native Americans were openly questioning termination, and relocation as a result of the extreme levels of poverty and other serious issues that existed on the reservations. AIM became a part of a crusade process that strived to restore treaty rights, and change the educational system. Under the educational system, Indian people were taught self-hatred, and the goal of AIM was to reestablish and safeguard tribal identity.

In 1969, more than 300 Native Americans took over Alcatraz Island in San Francisco Bay. "…Indians occupied and claimed the abandoned federal property on the presumed stipulation put in an Indian treaty that said abandoned federal lands would revert to Indian ownership… A Sioux treaty of 1868 did indeed contain a provision stating that abandoned American forts would revert to Indian ownership, but only a few of the activists were Sioux and none were duly elected tribal officials who could take administrative control of the property in the name of the tribe. Still, the takeovers continued, if for no other reason than to publicize the revival of Indian activism and notify whites that Indians were going to assert tribal rights wherever and whenever possible."[92]

In September 1971 approximately 60 Indian people, led by Russell Means, descended upon the BIA's Washington office to confront Wilma Victor, a past headmistress of the Intermountain Boarding School near Brigham City, Utah. She previously served as Deputy BIA Commissioner, and her new role was considered a conflict of interest. AIM representatives felt she may not support the needs of the Native Americans.[93]

"In 1972, Indian activists organized a massive march on Washington, D.C., known as the Trail of Broken Treaties. The caravan was to form on the West Coast and wind its way across the nation picking up followers as it went. It was to arrive in Washington during the final week of the presidential campaign. Indians poured into the city. The bulk of them assembled at the Bureau of Indian Affairs building to await word regarding where they were to be housed during their stay in the capital. Eventually they were told that they were to be housed in the Department auditorium. As they were leaving the BIA, guards began to push a number of people out the door. The young protesters turned on the guards and seized the building. The occupation of the BIA lasted for nearly a week before the Indians agreed to leave. In return, the federal government agreed not to prosecute the protesters." [94] For many years federal agents conducted secret missions to discredit and eventually put behind bars the entire leadership of the American Indian Movement. Today, AIM is still an active advocate for Native American rights.

In the 1970s an organization called the Indian Health Service (IHS) was established to provide services to Indian people. The same IHS program implemented sterilization services for Indian women. This program resulted in involuntary and oftentimes uninformed sterilization of 42 percent of all Indian women of childbearing age, in an attempt to decrease the Indian population and as part of the genocide efforts. The program was ceased in 1976. During the same time period, approximately 13,000 Navajos residing in the Big Mountain region in Arizona were removed from this land base to make way for the Peabody Coal Company.[95]

The Indian Child Welfare Act (ICWA) was passed by Congress on November 8, 1978 and was signed by President Carter after numerous hearings were held in the Senate to cover all issues regarding the status of Indian people in the United States. The most significant discovery from these hearings was the high percentage of Indian families that were disrupted by the removal of their children by private and public agencies. The purpose of this act was to protect the best interests of Indian children and support the permanence of tribal communities and families. However, child abuse and neglect continues to occur at higher rates for tribal children than for the rest of the population.

During the 1980s, Inuit children residing on the oil rich North Slope in Alaska served as guinea pigs for field testing hepatitis vaccines, which happened to be banned by the World Health Organization (WHO) from international distribution due to a possible link to the transmission of Human-immunodeficiency (HIV) microbes. When Alaskan parents refused to allow further inoculation, the field tests were transferred to the lower 48 states, and the unfortunate targets were reservation children. The profits of two major pharmaceutical corporations were connected to this study.[96]

In order for tribal people to access services, such as medical care and food subsidies provided by the federal government, they need to present identification cards to prove their tribal lineage. This created another dilemma faced by many Indian people. A definition needed to be developed by the various tribal and governmental entities in order to determine who would share the benefits of tribal membership. Blood quantum issues have created dissention amongst Native Americans. To define what it meant to be Indian, not only predicated biological factors, but a cultural sense and feeling of belonging to a distinct tribal nation. Historically, Indian people welcomed anyone into their tribal community who wished to participate in their cultural practices. This interference by governmental officials created further alienation within tribal communities, due to preserving and securing tribal benefits as a means of survival. The idea of blood quantum has been based on the quantitative approach to determining tribal membership that dates from the early nineteenth century. The determination of tribal identification, loss of tribal lands and other cruel and harsh treatment continues to cause many problems for Indian people.

The introduction of "Manifest Destiny" supported the Euro-American belief that they had the divine right and privilege to pursue the takeover of all land and resources between the Atlantic and Pacific Oceans. As a result, tribal people throughout the United States and Canada have had to work diligently to rebuild their tribal governments and begin to regain a sense of balance after they have been victimized over and over again by acts of discrimination, assimilation, and genocide. In spite of the social welfare programs put into place to address the problems Indian people are facing, many still experience the social ills of domestic violence, substance abuse, child abuse and neglect more than any other segment of the population.

Chapter VII
Eagle and Coyote Infiltrate
the Holy Childhood Boarding School

A Place of Death

The halls whisper the horrors
experienced by the victims.
Sexual, spiritual, emotional, and physical abuse abound.
Held hostage by boarding and residential school
legislation.
What happened to the children's souls?
Inadequate amounts of food, long spoiled.
Days spent in arduous labor,
washing floors, tending livestock and crops.
Young minds being molded to believe
they are savages, heathens, less than human.

Homesickness, many children died due to illness,
these places associated with death,
the boarding and residential schools.
Parents in the depths of despair on reservations,
while their children parish.

Silence maintained through censored correspondence.
Demonstration of love forbidden.
Children building strong alliances,
through acts of camaraderie.
Only the strong survived through steadfast resiliency.

The Origin of Residential and Boarding Schools

Total control of the Indian children's education was viewed as the most feasible option to achieve total assimilation and the adaptation of a civilized lifestyle for Native Americans. The government, with assistance from church entities, began implementation of the boarding and residential school systems. For the children, separation from their families would reduce their families' influence and further the assimilation process. Some Indian people have managed to survive with little to no repercussions. However for the majority of Indian people, the boarding and residential school initiative made more of a negative impact than all other efforts to destroy the Indian people either intentionally or unintentionally, including armed forces, starvation, disease, loss of land, and Christianity. The outcome of this legislation was a vulnerable population laced with disease, death, poverty, and other social ills, such as domestic violence, alcoholism, child abuse and neglect.[97]

In 1875 Richard Henry Pratt was given responsibility of 72 Indian men charged with murder and rapine at Fort Marion in St. Augustine, Florida. Rapine is the act of seizing property by force. During their stay at the prison, these prisoners served as slave labor to offset the cost of running the prison. Pratt rehabilitated these men. They lost the appearance of being savage and adopted the characteristics of the Euro-American population. The Indian men were placed in jobs without guards. Following this, in 1879, the Carlisle Indian Boarding School was established by Pratt with support of the federal government. The boarding schools were fashioned after the same rehabilitative principles, which included the school attendants serving as slave labor to offset costs.[98]

Two boarding schools and one orphanage opened in Michigan. The Catholic Church opened the orphanage in Baraga in 1887, and Indian children were the primary occupants. Holy Childhood boarding school in Harbor Springs opened in 1889. The federal government opened the boarding school in Mt. Pleasant in 1893. Numerous other boarding schools opened in the United States and the Canadian government followed suit modeling the residential schools after the American boarding schools.

Boarding and residential schools were run like military camps. Indian children were stringently taught how to follow orders. The children had to fall into formation, march in a straight line, and oftentimes wore military clothing and shoes. During the weekdays, the children attended school. They were taught English, math, history, and geography usually by Euro-American teachers. Some of the teachers tried to be kind and helpful, but others were cruel. On average, only a few hours a day were spent in the classroom, and the other portion was spent doing chores. The children received minimal care and education. Students constituted the majority of the labor pool and did most of the meal preparation, building repairs, gardening, caring for livestock, and cleaning.

Learning how to accomplish these tasks would help prepare them for adulthood in the white man's world because an only viable future was a white future. Girls were prepared to work as servants or to become homemakers. Boys were trained in the areas of gardening, repair and maintenance of homes and farms, the running of farms, printing presses, and the building of houses and furniture. Many of the children participated in an outing program in which they were placed in Euro-American homes and expected to perform tasks for their room and board. They were forced to change the way they look and forget their language, customs, and religion. Their loss of identity formed mixed messages about their heritage and about themselves, resulting in contempt for those in power as well as their parents and elders. [99]

Harold, a former student who attended the Shenwauk residential school in Ontario, Canada, reported, "It was really awful because at the residential school you didn't have a name. They put that number on your shirt." Again, being treated as an inanimate object released those in authority from any guilt for their wrongdoings. This can be reaffirmed by the pictures displayed on the walls at Algoma University in Sault Ste. Marie, Ontario, Canada. Children were shown in the pictures wearing numbers on their clothing. In the Native American tribal way of life one was not permitted to own anything that was provided to them by the Creator. The land, food and other necessities were bestowed to them to use and must be appreciated. The only thing that could be owned was their given names. Only one person in a community could have a specific name, and this name was derived by spiritual means such as visions, dreams and naming ceremonies. Names provided their identity throughout their lifetime. When English names were given to the children in the boarding schools as a part of the assimilation process, it led to identity confusion, which has also created a host of problems.

Children who attended the boarding and residential schools suffered from various types of abuse. Concerning sexual abuse, Harold stated "I'm glad I wasn't a big boy." The bigger boys were the ones who were hauled off during the evening hours by the nuns and priests at the Shenwauk Residential School in Canada.[100] One woman reported she spent years in therapy until she finally grasped the fact she had been a victim. The shame and guilt she experienced as a result of the sexual abuse she was forced to endure at the hands of a priest at the Holy Childhood Boarding School caused her chronic emotional stress into adulthood.

Nuns would maintain relationships with young boys and these boys would become confidants for these women. Mentally healthy women in their 30s or 40s do not fall in love with boys who are 10, 11 or 12 years of age. Pedophiles work in a way that does not permit children to refuse. It is cunning, measured, and done under the pretext of fondness. These children were used as sexual outlets. Once the deviant person tires of the current victim, they dump them and prey on other unsuspecting children. Victims then often feel abandoned. Children could not escape because these institutions became their prison. There were held captive. [101]

Another report involved nuns at the Holy Childhood Boarding School who began their seduction by kissing the younger boys good night. One of the abusive nuns was in her 20s, rather plain and chubby. The favored boys would get kissed on the lips and she would tickle them. Jerry stated that a few years went by for him until the kisses started getting longer and longer, and then he was taken to her bedroom. Usually when the boys became older around 12 years of age, they were taken to the nuns' bedrooms. One day, after Jerry was pulled off the playground and had been forced to perform sexual acts, they were caught in a compromising position by other nuns, yet the perpetrator did not receive any retribution.[102] The children were habitually exposed to "institutionalized pedophilia" and "sexual terrorism." The pedophiles included, but are not limited to, priests, nuns, and protestant clergy.[103]

      The religious instruction that was provided added to the confusion and degradation of many participants. Oftentimes, they were abused in various ways by the very same people who were providing religious instruction. Children who demonstrated resistance to the teaching practices and the regimented authority were subjected to humiliation and harsh punishments. They suffered whippings and unusual torture such as standing on their tiptoes with arms outstretched while their hands were hit with wooden boards and rulers. The treatment of boys was typically more severe than that of girls. Harsh punishments occurred when children tried to run away, although this did not deter many from attempting to do so.

      The boarding and residential school environments are referred to as deviant subcultures within the Euro-

American culture. Very little instruction was provided to prepare the boarding and residential school employees for their employment. It was common practice to hire the dregs of society who could not obtain employment elsewhere to work in these institutions. There were some good people who filled these positions, but their efforts were overshadowed by the harm others did.

Three former students who attended the Holy Childhood boarding school reported about some of the harsh treatments that occurred at that school. An excessive amount of emotional abuse was inflicted on these children. Jennifer was beaten with a rubber hose when she wet the bed or was forced to wear the urine soaked sheets in front of her peers.[104] Tim reported that he was called a "dirty savage" by staff at the Holy Childhood boarding school, which led to problems concerning the understanding of his own identity and as a result he struggled with self esteem issues. [105] Kent had seen children at the Holy Childhood boarding school who were beaten if they spoke their native language.[106]

When the children first arrived at the school, they felt lonely and isolated. The harsh policies concerning the highly regulated family visits caused children to suffer from homesickness. Most children who attended these institutions were separated from their family before they were developmentally mature. Sheila, a former student of the Shenwauk residential school in Canada reported that her sister was only three years old when she was left to be taken care of by the staff at the residential school. She could not have contact with Sheila. Currently, both sisters are in their late fifties. The younger sister requires medical attention continuously. Her medical needs seem excessive and appears to be a way in which she garners attention. Sheila transports her sister to her medical appointments. [107]

Indian children were sent away from home from one hour or even further to attend the schools. Before 1957, Indian children who lived in St. Ignace, Michigan had to be taken across Lake Huron on a barge and then transported by car to Harbor Springs, Michigan. The Mackinac Bridge was built in 1957, which eliminated the use of the barge system. The expense of travel such as this was more than most Indian families could afford, which deterred them from visiting their children. In 1924, the Native American per capita annual income was approximately $81. [108]

Prior to the 1920s, boarding school officials would have to seek preapproval from the local reservation superintendent or an Indian agent before permission could be granted for children to go home, even for severe hardship, such as deaths in the family and sick relatives. Indian parents learned to get around these sanctions by stating that their children were needed to assist with farming. Since farming was a part of the assimilation process, it served as a more worthy excuse. When John Collier filled the position as Commissioner of Indian Affairs in 1933, these policies took a turn for the better. Students were permitted to go home for the summer months and usually for family hardships.

Indian children developed alliances with each other and looked after one another while attending these institutions. Many of these children had never met Indian people from other tribes. They also practiced pan-Indianism, which involved the learning and adopting of portions of languages and cultures from other tribal communities. Friendships were often formed, some lasting the extent of their lives. They made fun of the teachers and gave them names the students felt best suited their personalities. On occasion, they snuck out at night together and did things they knew they were not supposed to do, such as breaking into buildings on and off school property. Sports, choirs, bands, and dances were other ways long lasting friendships were developed and ways in which the children maintained their sanity. Sharing the common experiences of attending boarding and residential schools was another way in which life long bonds were established.

When a child was sent to bed without a meal, the other children would often sneak them food. The children experienced what could be referred to as slow, agonizing starvation. School officials were allotted very limited funding, which served as a strong indication of the lack of importance of Indian children. During the 1930s, the Meriam report included the lack of fresh food and milk for boarding school residents in the United States. The average per capita food allowance was 11 cents per day. As a result, students suffered from malnutrition because of the shortage of food. The Meriam report suggested 35 cents per day for each student. This would ensure proper nutrition and food supply.[109] The recommendations put forth by those who conducted the Meriam study were often ignored. On another note, during the time the Meriam team was observing some of the boarding schools, they made notice of the extreme levels of quietness. Episodes of intermingling and comfortable conversations were non-existent.

Disease also ran rampant in the boarding and residential schools with tuberculosis being one of the most serious. Measles, mumps, influenza, and trachoma were other health maladies. Trachoma is a disease that inflicts the eyes. Often, the parents were often not informed about their children's illnesses. Children with these diseases and healthy students were kept together at the schools. Overcrowding was another issue. These schools were often filled to capacity and beyond. Due to the lack of special services and poor diets, the children often died as a result of contracting these diseases. Neglect is another form of oppression in which a person is deprived of love, care, nurturance, support, or other pertinent assistance, as well as basic material needs such as food, shelter, and clothing. The children were provided shelter and clothing; however, their other needs were grossly neglected. They often experienced failure to thrive. As a result, many Indian people associated these institutions with death and despair.

The boarding and residential school experience did prepare children to communicate with the English speaking population. A high percentage of the attendees had a difficult time returning to their home of origin.

Their difficulty fitting in with their families was a result of biased instruction they received at the school, as well as the lack of bonding because of their long absence. Much of the native language was lost, along with many of the traditional customs. Many boarding and residential school attendees did not return to the tribal communities. Instead, they joined the white population and were acculturated into their way of life. They worked at jobs on farms or in towns. Some moved to the urban areas and others were hired by the boarding and residential schools as teachers, cooks, and caretakers.

Some of the students were grateful for learning trades taught at the schools. Jeff, a former student who attended the federal boarding school in Mt. Pleasant, Michigan, learned how to be barber while he was attending the school, which brought him money when he was in the armed service. He was hired by his peers while serving his country to cut their hair. The school gave him the confidence to tackle things like serving as a meteorologist, which was also a part of his career path. Jeff still carried resentments towards his father for letting him down as a child, because his father had a drinking problem. According to Jeff, he was also not a good provider. His family was forced to move to the reservation and the housing was substandard.

And Jeff did not like the "outing program," as he referred to it. The outing program was when he was forced to live with a family and work for them for room and board after he left the school. Jeff wanted to go to school instead of being forced to work. On the other hand, he stated he believes his attendance at the boarding school paved the way for a better life for him and he was more than happy to leave the disappointment behind, his family of origin. His family's poverty due to his father's alcoholism and additional poor conditions, such as substandard housing, was difficult for Jeff to endure during his childhood. The school afforded better housing, regular meals, and future job opportunities. [110]

     A vast number of Indian children were released from the boarding and residential schools when they were ready to attend high school. After spending years of following the stringent rules at the schools, they had to try and fit in with their families and the outside world. They were not taught how to think for themselves. Teenagers often have difficulty making smart choices. During the late teens, the brain begins to develop its prefrontal cortex and inferior cortex, the areas that supervise judgment and self-control. This process is not completed until the mid-twenties. As a result, teenagers and young adults are subject to making bad judgments, lack inhibitory control, and have a likelihood of developing addictive behaviors. However; these susceptibilities can be lessened if they receive caring support.[111]

     Most of the teenagers who left these institutions were not welcomed by their families. The years of separation and the vast differences these attendees had with their families caused them to feel alienated and the needed support and guidance was nonexistent. A large number of Native American people are living with regrets that resulted from making poor choices when they were teenagers and young adults. Many Indian people married individuals that mirrored the caregivers at these institutions and ended up in loveless relationships or divorce. The negative impact of these harsh environments resonate throughout tribal communities today.

Eagle and Coyote explore the inner workings of the Holy Childhood boarding school during the early 1940s to assist the reader with an understanding of boarding school life. They do so by infiltrating the spirits of two boarding school participants. Trial and tribulations are revealed as they learn about this subculture. It was discovered that the children become unified in their endeavors as a method of survival to battle loneliness and the drastic changes that occurred to their lifestyles.

Eagle and Coyote Visit the Holy Childhood Boarding School in 1943

The Holy Childhood Boarding School is located in the scenic village of Harbor Springs, Michigan. Children were enjoying their one-half hour of freedom during a recess period by playing and talking with one another. Handmade stick figures and rocks served as toys for the children. An elderly matron stood scrutinizing their activities. Her eyes were squinted and her lips were pressed tightly together as a look of contempt crossed her face. Ragged oversized clothing was the attire for the majority of these children. The villagers and charitable organizations donated clothes. The school was run on a shoestring. The priests and nuns ran the boarding school with their limited resources in their attempt to fulfill the school's mission of civilizing the children, and they felt that they were on a divine mission to save these children from the demons of the wretched pagan ways of their families.

****

"Listen Coyote, I have to select the spirit I am going to blend with so quit joking around. I have to concentrate," said Eagle adamantly, as she stared down from the oak tree in the schoolyard.

"Oh, let me ask you one more riddle," replied Coyote.

"Okay. Just one more and that's it," stammered Eagle.

"Why did the chicken cross the road?" asked Coyote, smiling coyly at Eagle.

"To get to the other side. That's easy," responded Eagle.

"No, that's not the answer."

"It's not?" replied Eagle with a surprised look on her face.

"No, it's not. Give up?" asked Coyote, smirking at Eagle.

"Yes, I give up," sighed Eagle.

"To show the skunks and porcupines that it could be done," said Coyote. He laughed at Eagle's expression.

"Let's get down to business. I can't believe I'm having so much trouble making this decision," said Eagle as her talon scratched the branch she was sitting on.

"I got an idea. Do you want to hear it?" asked Coyote.

"Sure."

"The Creator told us he wanted to learn as much as possible. So I thought we could enter the spirits of two older children, a boy and a girl. We could watch how they work with the younger children and perhaps they will reminisce about their days at the boarding school. Plus, we can see what it's like for them to return to their own family," said Coyote.

"I think you are on to something. Perhaps we can find older children who are going home for good," said Eagle.

"Hey, look at those kids over there," said Coyote as he pointed his nose in the direction he wanted Eagle to look.

A tall boy, who appeared to be in his teens, was leaning against a pole in the yard. A group of girls in their teens were standing in a circle saying things to each other and looking towards the boys who were standing nearby. The girls were giggling and pointing.

"I choose the girl with short dark hair tied back with the dark green ribbon. The one with the green dress," said Eagle.

"I choose the boy leaning against the pole," said Coyote. "He really seems to be full of himself."

The recess bell rang loudly, and all the children ran into the school building.

"Let's find some place to leave our bodies where they can be safe," suggested Eagle as she started thinking about their vessels' safety.

"How about we place our bodies on the roof of the school? It's such a large building. I bet nobody goes up there," said Coyote.

"You're just full of good ideas. Aren't you?"

"I guess I'm on a roll."

"I would like to prepare a place for us to sleep. You can take some leaves and branches so we can build a shelter to keep our bodies out of the weather," said Eagle.

"Why don't we fly up to the roof and see what's up there first?"

"Okay. The children just went inside, so the chances of us being spotted are practically nonexistent," said Eagle.

The roof was covered in tarpaper and well sealed. A small enclosure with a door was at the far end. Eagle and Coyote went to check it out. Coyote was turning the doorknob with his mouth when they heard heavy footsteps coming up the stairs to the door. Eagle grabbed Coyote and they flew to the nearest tree to hide.

"Gosh, we made it just in time. Look at that kid. How old do you think he is?" inquired Eagle. She barely got the words out when the boy was joined by another boy who looked older.

"What are those boys up to?" asked Eagle.

"It's hard to say."

The boys were huddled together, sitting against the wall of the enclosure. A third boy, who pulled two white bed sheets from under his shirt, joined them. The other boys followed suit by pulling bed sheets from under their shirts. They all quickly tied the sheets together.

One end was secured to a metal pole that was situated near the enclosure. The other end was slung over the roof and reached to almost eight feet from the ground. The oldest boy started climbing down the sheets and was followed by the other two. The smallest one landed on his rump with a thump. He stood up quickly, rubbing his backside. The three boys ran quickly to the nearby woods and were soon out of sight.

"Did you see that? They ran away," exclaimed Eagle as she tried to maintain her composure.

"Yes. We need to find a safe place and prepare for our spirit travel pronto."

"I agree. We need to get to the bottom of why those boys ran away and what else is going on at this school," replied Eagle.

"Look. There is an abandoned nest over there. Let's check it out," said Eagle.

"It looks big enough for the two of us."

"Yes, I think it's an osprey nest," said Eagle.

"I am not sure I am looking forward to this adventure, Coyote."

"I feel the same way. But we have to abide by what the Creator has requested of us," responded Coyote.

A spell was placed around their bodies, and their spirits left them to inhabit the two children they selected earlier. Eagle and Coyote's spirits sought permission from the children's souls before fusing with them.

The girl, who was selected by Eagle, was in the kitchen washing tin cups. There were three large trays stacked high with dishes and spoons. The metal cups were piled high. The girls were bent over the sinks, washing one plate and cup at a time, while their backs throbbed with dull pain and their minds tried to focus on anything, but the mundane task at hand. Other girls were rinsing, drying, and putting away the tableware. A nun sat on a stool and supervised the girls as they toiled in the kitchen. She had a ruler in her hand and tapped it gently on her other hand to remind the girls of what would happen if they failed in any way.

"Sarah," said another girl, calling to the girl whose spirit Eagle inhabited.

"What?" asked Sarah.

"Can you hand me that stack of dirty plates?"

"Yes, Mary," replied Sarah, as she stopped what she was doing to retrieve the stack of dishes and hand them to Mary.

Coyote selected a boy named George. He was busy cleaning the boys' bathroom. George and another boy were talking about the boys who ran away.

"I wish I had the guts to do what Percy, Sam and Henry did. Right now they are on their way home," said George.

"I wonder if they'll make it. It would give me hope if we try to make a run for it," said the other boy.

"Yeah, I want to go home so bad. I should be used to this place. I've been here six years, but it never gets any easier," said George.

"I hear you," replied the other boy.

"Fred, I know it looks like I am favored by some of the nuns, but you would not want to be me," stated George as he tried to fight back the tears.

"Yeah, why is that?" asked Fred.

"Did you ever wonder where I go when that nun comes and gets me at night?" asked George.

"No. I guess I'm sleeping when that happens," replied Fred.

"Lucky you. When I turned 12, that nun called Sister Synester, and the other one called Sister Black, decided it was high time to turn me into a man," said George.

"What do you mean George?" asked Fred.

"I don't want to talk about it anymore," replied George, as he turned his attention towards a younger boy.

George grabbed the boy because he was speaking the Ojibway language. "If you are caught, the nuns and priests will beat you because you are only supposed to speak English here."

"I have to tell you something. Can you hear me, Eagle?" asked Coyote telepathically.

"Yes, I read you loud and clear, Coyote."

"Some of the nuns are using the boys at this school in terrible ways."

"You're kidding!"

"I wish I were," said Coyote sadly.

"George, the boy whose spirit I fused with, talked about the boys who ran away. I wonder if they were being subjected to the same things George has to go through."

"Oh. I hope not."

"You already found out a lot, Coyote. My girl, Sarah, has been facing drudgery on a daily basis, and the nuns watch their every move."

"It's back to work. I hope we find out there are good things happening at this school and not only bad things," said Eagle.

****

The boys were huddled around a tree in the woods. They were cold, and nighttime was quickly approaching.

"We need to find food soon. I'm starving," said Henry.

"Let's sneak into town and see what we can get when it gets dark," replied Percy.

"I think we might find something to eat at one of the cafes," said Henry.

"I could eat just about anything," said Sam.

"After eating the mush at that hell hole all year, somebody else's leftovers will be more than welcome," said Percy.

"This is the first time I wished it was dark," said Henry.

"Yes, I know what you mean. I think the demons come out at night at that school," said Percy.

"I'm just glad I'm small for my age. My size seems to protect me," said Sam.

"Yeah, we're lucky. I feel they don't like me because I'm so dark," said Percy.

"There is a bigger boy, and I think his name is Francis. He gets pulled out of his bed almost every night," said Henry.

"Remember when we tried to talk to him about why he left at night with the nuns and sometimes a priest? He would not talk to us. He got this funny look on his face," said Henry.

"Hey look, the sun is finally going down. Let's start heading to town," said Percy.

****

"Betty, it's Sunday. We need to make sure we don't put on our Sunday best. I have torn stockings and a tattered dress. Those nuns care way too much about how we look. We need to get back at the nuns. I want to embarrass them," said Sarah.

"It's always about how we make them look," said Betty.

The girls dressed in clothes that were in poor condition. They walked into the sanctuary in single file. The nuns glared at them. Another part of the plan was to sing the hymns in their worse singing voices, using the wrong words while they sang. They were in public and felt safe, at least temporarily, from any form of retribution for their acts of rebellion. Acts of comradeship were ways in which they brought some fun to their lives.

"Sarah, the girl I am visiting, just did something interesting Coyote. She went against some of the nun's expectations."

"You mean she was rebellious?"

"Yeah, you could say that, Coyote. They dressed in clothes that were in the worse shape and did not sing the songs correctly at church. They did this right in front of the nuns and the parishioners who attend this church. You could tell some of the nuns were infuriated."

"They do find ways to have fun, don't they?"

"I just hope they don't pay for it later."

"What are you finding out, Coyote?"

"George experienced things last night that would make your toes curl. He was taken from the sleeping chamber and was used in ways that made my stomach turn."

"His spirit is being so beaten up, isn't it Coyote?"

"When those horrible acts were happening to him, it was like he was above his body, watching what was going on, and not really in his own body. He learned to remove himself and just go through the motions to protect himself."

"That boy is going to have some major problems later on."

"You can say that again."

****

Sister Sylvester was one of the kinder nuns. She provided comfort to the children who were punished severely by the other nuns. Joan, a six year old who had a bedwetting problem, was forced to wear the urine soaked sheets on top of her head and was beaten with a rubber hose in front of her peers. Sister Sylvester's heart went out to Joan and she would caress Joan's head and reassure her that she was going to be okay. Sister Sylvester followed through with that promise. She witnessed Joan's sister changing and hiding the sheets to protect Joan from retribution. Sister Sylvester never told a soul. Joan never received another beating for wetting the bed.

****

In one of the classrooms, a child was having difficulty with an assignment.

"You filthy heathen, you are going to go to hell if you don't pay attention to your lesson," said Sister Synester.

"I don't know how to do this problem," said Peter as he trembled in his seat.

"You would understand if you weren't raised by filthy heathens just like you," said Sister Synester.

"I'm trying. Really, I am," pleaded Peter.

Another student was tapping a pencil eraser on his desk while the nun was berating Peter. It was a very quiet way of informing Peter that he was being supported by his peers. Peter did not feel alone and found comfort in the support he received. Talking to one another was not permitted while they were attending instructional sessions or participating in any other activities, such as religious instruction and meal time. The students were forced to stare straight ahead and could not look at their peers.

At the same time, Sarah was providing support to another student in a different classroom by tapping her pencil eraser on the top of her desk. Susan was trying to solve a math problem at the front of the classroom on a blackboard. Sister Black was yelling and calling her a stupid Indian. The students' ability to hear was very keen. The students, after a very short time at the school, developed a sense of hyper-vigilance. Their survival often depended on their awareness of their surroundings at all times, which in turn heightened their senses.

"I don't know how to do the problem," said Susan.

"It was part of your homework. Why didn't you ask someone to help you?" demanded Sister Black.

"I'm sorry. I did not have time last night. We had to clean the floors," responded Susan as she pleaded with Sister Black.

"That's no excuse. I want you to do this problem right now," screamed Sister Black.

Susan made another attempt, but could not figure out how to do the math problem.

Sister Black grabbed a handful of hair on the left side of Susan's head and jerked her head from side to side managing to pull out a chunk of hair from Susan's head. Susan decided the year before she would never cry again when the nuns were abusive to her. She would not let them get the better of her, and not crying was the one thing that was in her control. Susan's hair ended up being thinner on the left side of her head for the rest of her life.

"Go back to your seat, you stupid Indian. Your pathetic parents did not teach you anything, did they? They are as useless as you are," said Sister Black, as she crossed her arms.

"Issabel get up here and show this stupid Indian how to do the problem," demanded Sister Black.

Issabel quietly walked to the front of the room and worked out the math problem to Sister Black's satisfaction. She was so glad she had caught on to this assignment. She was usually one of Sister Black's targets for abuse.

When they passed in the halls or other areas of the school, they would use their eyes to relay messages. In addition to tapping, this form of communication was also learned by the students. They could relay entire sentences with the use of their eyes.

"I am sending you to bed without supper," screamed Sister Black at an older girl named Ellen. Ellen supposedly did not sweep the hallway as Sister Black liked it.

An older girl passed Sarah and told her that she needed to bring food to Ellen by the use of her eyes. Sarah responded with her eyes that she understood and would do so.

The students at the school suffered continuously from being hungry, near starvation. Most of the time, the rations of food the students were provided were not adequate. Their meager portions did not meet the necessary nutritional requirements, and the harsh labor forced upon them caused them to burn more calories than they were ingesting.

"Most of the adults are so abusive to the children here," sighed Coyote.

"It must be so confusing to them. You know, to be taught about the Bible and how to be kind to your neighbors and all the other things the Bible teaches, while at the same time they are being abused in every way possible."

"You got a point, Eagle."

"I want to share something else I witnessed with Sarah. Sarah and other girls her age have the ability to communicate by using eye contact."

"That's interesting. Tell me more, Eagle."

"A girl was sent to bed without supper. Another girl told Sarah with her eyes that it was her turn to bring food to the girl who was being punished."

"Sarah understood her?"

"Yes, she did."

"That's phenomenal!"

"We can talk to one another telepathically, Coyote. They can talk to one another by using eye contact. I think living here has gotten them in touch with some of the gifts their ancestors possessed."

"You know Coyote, humans have lost the use of many of these gifts. These children had to dig deep into their psyches to find ways to survive in this harsh environment."

****

The next day the three boys who ran away from the boarding school were digging through a garbage can behind a local café.

"What are you boys doing?" asked a police officer.

"We're looking for food," replied Percy.

"Why aren't you at school?" asked the officer.

"What school? We are on our way home," responded Percy.

"You're those Indian kids who are staying at the boarding school," stated the Police Officer adamantly.

"No, we're not. We are on our way home," said Henry.

"Get in the car," ordered the police officer.

The boys started running. They were in the woods before the police officer got to his car.

"I had the boys within my grasp, but there were three of them and they ran off into the woods. I know those kids are from Holy Childhood. We got to go looking for them," said Edward, the police officer who talked to the boys.

"We should go to the school and see if they are missing some kids," responded Floyd, another officer who was at the police station when Edward arrived to seek assistance.

"They were Indians. I'd stake my life on it. Not the usual white kids you see hanging out around here. The Indian kids are usually with those nuns from that school. These kids were alone," said Edward as he put his hat and coat on.

"I know you are probably right, but it would be helpful if we knew their names. We have to act fast. We can't trust those damn Indian kids for one minute running amuck in our town," said Floyd.

****

Edward knocked at the front door of the boarding school. Sister Brown answered.

"Good evening Sister," said Edward as he awkwardly took off his hat. Edward was not a religious man, and he felt a little uncomfortable being in the presence of the nun.

"Yes, it is," responded Sister Brown curtly.

"We spotted three boys rummaging through some garbage cans behind the café."
Are you missing any children?" asked Edward.

"Three boys did run away, because the lazy louts didn't want to do their chores," said Sister Brown. Then she added under her breath, "ungrateful heathens."

"What are their names? It would make it easier for us to catch them if we knew their names," inquired Edward as he took out a small pad of paper and a pencil.

"Their names are Henry, Sam, and Percy. I think Percy put them up to this. He's the biggest of the three," replied Sister Brown as a smirk crossed her face.

She felt she was going to get back at Percy for bringing embarrassment to the boarding school. She was hopeful the police officers would treat Percy more harshly. Sister Brown also knew the boys' punishment for running away once they were returned to the school was going to be severe.

****

Sister Synester ordered the students in her classroom to take out a pencil and a sheet of paper.

"It's letter writing day. First, I want you to tell your parents you are learning a lot at school and like it here. Then tell them about movie night," demanded Sister Synester.

George had a flashback to the time he was pushed down the stairs of the basement and was forced to sit in the dark while the rest of the students were watching a movie. He was only eight years old. George swore when he was down there he could hear ghosts and goblins trying to get at him. He was terrified. George developed a fear of the dark because of that situation. He held onto that fear for most of his life. He knows he couldn't put that incident or any other horrible incident that he went through at the school in the letters to his parents. George could only write what the nuns told him he could write.

    Other children developed a fear of the dark because they were taught to fear the devil and what they would be subjected to if they did not follow the lessons of the Bible. Since they were considered heathens, they already had a link to the dark forces, which was told to them repeatedly.

****

    June finally arrived. The children were being sent home to spend the summer months with their parents or other caregivers such as grandparents. Some of the Indian parents worked at the school during the summer months. They painted and did some repairs. Even if the parents were at the school, the children could not stay with them. It was school policy. Some of the children's parents could not care for their children, because their lives were such a mess. There were high levels of substance abuse and domestic violence. Many of the parents had attended the very same school during their youthful years.

    "I can't wait to sleep in my own bed," said George to Floyd, one of the friends he made while at the school.

"Me either. We are going to be home for good. We have served our time," responded Floyd.

"Yes, we have definitely served our time."

"I wonder what's happening in Swinging Iggy," inquired Sam. (St. Ignace Michigan is referred to as Swinging Iggy.)

"I don't know, but I can't wait to find out," replied George.

At the same time, Sarah was packing her meager belongings. *I cannot wait to see my mom and dad. I bet they can't wait to see me,* thought Sarah.

"Ellen, do you need any help?" asked Sarah.

"No, thanks anyways," replied Ellen one of Sarah's peers.

"I can't wait to get home. This is it. We have graduated from this hell hole," stated Sarah.

"Yes, we have," added Mary, another one of Sarah's friends.

****

Sarah was greeted by her mother and father. She sensed some reluctance when her family first saw her. Sarah's younger siblings were excited she was home. When the family would go on outings, often Sarah was not invited to go along with them. Her parents explained to her that she was older and they thought she would not be interested in what they were doing. Sarah could sense there was more to it than that.

"Ellen, I am really confused about how my family is treating me," said Sarah, when she met Ellen in the park.

"You mean the feeling like you are not welcome?"

"Yes. They have these conversations without me, and then when I walk into the room, they become quiet very quickly."

"The very same thing is happening to me at my house," stated Ellen as she wiped a tear from her eye.

"Are they sneaking out of the house without you, Ellen?" asked Sarah.

"Yes, they are."

"What do you think that is all about?" asked Sarah.

"I overheard my mom and two of my aunts talking about me. They were talking about how snooty I was now that I have all this education. You know, my mom went to the same school. Why is she doing this to me?" asked Ellen with a quiver in her voice. Another tear slid down her cheek, a hurt look crossed her face.

"My family is doing the same things to me," whispered Sarah. "It is as if I am a stranger to them. I'm thinking about moving to my grandparents' house. That's where I used to stay during the summer months."

"I might do the same thing," said Ellen.

****

"Tell me about your time at school. How was it for you, son?" inquired George's father, John.

"It was horrible dad. I could not tell you what was going on because those damn nuns dictated what we could write to you in our letters. I never had the opportunity to tell you what was really going on," said George. He was turning red in the face.

"Calm down son. Tell me what happened at school."

"The nuns put me down in the basement when I was eight because I wouldn't give up my seat to one of their favorite students."

"Then they told me how I could be a favorite, and they did these awful things to me," said George.

"What did they do to you son? You can talk to me about it."

"They made me do horrible things with them at night. Yeah, I became one of their favorites, but it was horrible dad," replied George, as he started crying.

"Oh my God, I never imagined anybody else ever had to suffer those terrible things, especially you, George. I buried those terrible experiences and forced myself to pretend they didn't happen. I am so sorry, son," said John as he wiped tears from his eye. "Those were terrible things done by horrible people. We didn't deserve to be treated that way," said John, as he stood up and hugged his son.

"They made us work so hard. The food was nasty, and I was always hungry. I never got used to being hungry. We used to sneak downstairs and steal food at night," said George.

"I used to do the same thing."

"You know," John said, "when I pass people on the street, and I don't even know them, we look at each other, and we can tell we have spent time in that hell hole. We secretly know it is something we have in common.

That place changed me into someone I didn't like most of the time."

"I did make some really good friends there, dad. We used to do things for one another to get by like bring food to each other if we were sent to bed without supper," said George.

"Yeah, I did that too. I think I will look up some of my old pals, sit a spell, and shoot the breeze," said John, as he appeared to drift off for a moment while he was thinking about his old friends.

"We used to sneak out at night and break into some buildings at the school. It was fun when we did things like that. It was like we didn't have any problems for little while," said John.

"Wow, dad. We have a lot in common," said George as he managed to smile weakly at his father.

They stood and hugged for a minute, then left the house to go and meet with their friends. They spent the entire afternoon shooting the breeze and downing a six pack or two to numb their pain. George was only 15 years old and he was quickly turning to alcohol to deaden his pain.

****

"Hardly anything good has come out of that school except their friendships Eagle."

"Do not forget about the gifts they were able to use such as eye contact and pencil tapping in lieu of communicating verbally as a part of their survival mechanisms. They were definitely resilient."

"Yes, but look at the costs. Those poor children. Let's go meet with the Creator and find out what our next assignment is. And then let's take a little time off. You know a little R and R."

"I hear you Eagle. I am very tired and in need of a little escape from reality."

Eagle and Coyote removed the spell surrounding their bodies. Their spirits reentered their own bodies, and they flew off into the horizon.

Chapter VIII
Life on the Rez

This chapter is about the trials and tribulations of Indian people who reside on modern day tribal reservations in Michigan and other states. The information for this chapter is based on research, personal experience and interviews. A hunter and gatherer society was forced to reside on a plot of land chosen by outsiders causing much angst for the Indian people. Reservations were allotted to the tribal people when they were forced to vacate their homelands as a result of legislation, such as the Indian Removal Act of 1830. There is a question in the Ojibwe language *enjibaayan* meaning where someone was born or where was one's spirit from. When an Indian person formally introduces him or herself, they often give the area in which they were born as part of the introduction. Umbilical cords were often buried in the area in which a child was born.

"Since 1492, European military traditions have twisted around and through American Indian lives like a corkscrew. Tribes not only fought traditional enemies but also every imperial power that came to the North American shores. And every imperial power eventually sought Native American allies in their struggle to wrest the land from its indigenous owners. Native confederacies were formed to fight the European interlopers and their tribal allies. Many of these confederacies were formed primarily for military purposes. The long conflict with the Euro-Americans turned several tribes into virtual military states, always under the threat of attack and annihilation. When many of the tribal nations came into the reservations, they lived under what amounted to martial law."[112] As a result of this unyielding rule and constant conflict, the Indian people ended up feeling exhausted and lived in a state of unrest.

    On the east coast reservations were establish during the 1600s, and later on, reservations were established on the western portion of the country during the 1800s. These reservations were situated in areas in which the land was not suitable for agriculture. The land was oftentimes arid, rocky and/or sandy. Additionally, hunting and fishing were not always adequate options for providing food for the tribal families on these reservations. The game and fish in many of these locations was scarce. As a result, the people living on the reservations had to rely on the government for food. Having an area in which a number of people are forced to live, mostly due to their lower social economic status, can lead to an underclass mentality. This mentality is drawn from self-fulfilling prophesies associated with negative stereotypes, such as "drunken Indians." [113] Reservations continue to be a breeding ground for many societal ills, and the blame is often placed on the victims.

    The first reservation was developed by the Puritans in 1638 near new Haven, Connecticut. A treaty was signed during that same year in November between the British government and the Quinnipiac tribe concerning land holdings. In 1666, the Mashantucket Pequot Indian Reservation was instituted by the Connecticut Colony located by the Thames River in New

London County near the town of Ledyard in Connecticut. The first reservation is still in existence today.[114] Reservations were established all over the country. Given the longevity of reservations, it appears they may be around for some time in the future.

During the 1860s, it was decided the best way to end Indian resistance was to develop smaller reservations, proceed with the assimilation process, and make the Indian people farmers. Two reservations were established, one in the Black Hills country of the Dakota Territory and one further west in Oklahoma Indian Territory. One hundred and forty thousand Indians were moved to these reservations from a multitude of tribes with different cultures and languages. Many may have served as allies for either the British or Euro-Americans. After that point in time, more and more reservations were established all over the United States.

Housing on the reservations was substandard until the Department of Housing and Urban Development began providing funding for the building of housing units. Associated to the funding were standards to which the homes were to be built including quality windows, roofing, insulation and other requirements. These homes were provided to the Indian families on a sliding fee scale; the lower a family's income, the lower the rent payment.

When the Europeans first came to this country, money was a foreign concept for the Native Americans. Today, many tribal people still have difficulty managing their money. Poverty has been commonplace in the past and still continues to be a problem for many Indian people today. The Pine Ridge reservation, for example, was noted by President Clinton as resembling a third world country. Indian people who came across more money than they were used to would often over spend as a result of going without for so long. To this day, many Native Americans do not possess budgeting skills and fall behind on their bills.

The job market and educational opportunities are usually scarce due to the rural locations of many of the reservations. In order to pursue a degree from a college or university, tribal members usually have to travel to another community. Transportation is another issue. Without adequate transportation it is difficult for these individuals to seek advancement of any kind. Welfare to work programs have existed on the reservations such as Temporary Assistance for Needy Families (TANF); however, resources need to be readily accessible.

Domestic violence, substance abuse, child abuse and neglect serve as constant reminders of unresolved issues from the past. The Indian Child Welfare Act was put into place in 1978 because Native American children were being removed from their parents' care and placed with Euro-American people. Unfortunately, many children are still being removed as result of child abuse and neglect. The inability of parents to give up their addictions to alcohol and/or drugs is the most common reason for the termination of parental rights.

Eagle and Coyote explore life on a fictional reservation somewhere in Michigan. They are faced with budgeting problems and are exposed to domestic violence, child abuse, and substance abuse. These problems are widespread on today's reservations resulting from unmet needs associated with historical trauma. This chapter is going to bring to the table an interesting turn of events by having Eagle and Coyote test the waters to see what it would be like if families were provided support. They exercise creative approaches to solving some of the problems that arise during their visit to a reservation.

****

Upper Michigan in the 1990s:

"Are we almost there?" asked Coyote.

"Yes. I think it is past that small group of trees," replied Eagle.

"Remember, we are new tenants. We moved in yesterday and are not even settled in yet," reminded Eagle.

"I wonder what this experience is going to be like," inquired Eagle.

"It can't be any worse than traveling with Columbus. We can only go up after that horrible experience."

"You're right, Coyote. That was a lousy time."

"Our visit to the French settlement wasn't all that bad," stated Coyote.

"I liked visiting the Ojibway village. They were so nice and accommodating. We learned a lot from the elders during our visit," retorted Eagle.

"I liked it too."

"This time we are going to be a couple of tribal elders who are down on our luck. This is definitely a switch," stated Coyote.

"Yes. Remember we lost our home because of a fire and we didn't have insurance," replied Eagle.

"I am so glad we were prepped by the Creator about modern day elders," stated Eagle.

"I am too."

"Look at those homes. They really don't seem to be in bad shape. This assignment may not be too difficult after all," said Eagle as she carefully landed in the woods close to the housing site.

"The Creator told us he would leave a trunk of clothes near a large maple tree. There are several maple trees over there," stated a concerned Eagle as she looked towards the trees.

"It's over here," yelled Coyote as he located the trunk.

"Quiet. We don't want the people who are living here to hear us."

"I'm glad it's a smaller trunk. I was afraid that we were going to be left with this heavy trunk to carry. We have this image to uphold of being elders, and we shouldn't be seen carrying something really large," stated Eagle.

"Again, everything is going to be fine. It always is," replied Coyote as he began the process of shape shifting.

Coyote shape shifted into an elderly man who was approximately five and a half feet tall. He was of slim build. His back had a slight downward curvature at his shoulders. Gray hair covered his head. His hair had one long braid tied with a tan leather strip. Coyote quickly donned his boxer shorts and finished dressing, which consisted of a yellowed white t-shirt, covered by a red plaid shirt, blue jeans, suspenders, dingy white socks and scuffed work boots.

Eagle was shape shifting into a stout elderly Indian woman while Coyote was dressing. Eagle quickly pulled her long slip over her head and then donned her long patchwork skirt and baggy, faded turquoise blouse. She laced her tennis shoes over ankle socks that covered thick ankles. Her long, gray hair was tied back with a single braid. Their weathered faces were covered with wrinkles and had a leather texture to the touch. Both had dark eyes, which were deeply set.

"The Creator told us the back of our house would be facing these woods. We would have to walk about 50 yards with the trunk of clothes to a pale yellow house with brown shutters. There will be green curtains in the back windows," said Eagle.

"I appreciate your attention to detail Eagle. It comes in handy."

"Thanks, Coyote."

"We need to use our assigned names, Francis."

"You're right, Stella," replied Coyote.

The house was filled with older furniture and all the walls were painted a cream color. An old tapestry was hanging on the wall in the living room. It was a picture of a lake and meadow with horses. An older television was located in one corner on a square wooden table. There was one easy chair and a couch with gold and brown flowers.   Their bedroom contained a full size bed, two end tables and a tall dresser. Knobs were missing from some of the dresser drawers, and the drawers had numerous scuff marks. A bathroom was situated in the hall between their bedroom and the kitchen. The bathroom sink was chipped, and the faucet was tarnished. The floor was covered with off white linoleum speckled with gold. The bathtub faucet was also tarnished, and the bathtub itself was a faded pale green. Surrounding the bathtub were black and white ceramic tiles.

  There was a small bedroom at the end of the hall. A twin mattress was lying on the floor. A tattered dark blue sleeping bag and pillow were strewn on the mattress. This room was reserved for company should they ever have any. Cardboard boxes were stacked along one of the walls.

  The kitchen sported an old wooden table with four chairs situated in the center of the room and a file cabinet located by the backdoor. The appliances had seen better days. The electric stove had a high back with large white enamel knobs. The large sink and dish drain were located at the opposite end. The cupboards were painted white, and the refrigerator was gold and did not match the white stove.

****

  After their long journey to the reservation, Eagle and Coyote settled down rather early in hopes of getting a good night's sleep.

"Wake up Francis, I think I hear someone in our house," said an alarmed Stella as she nudged Francis frantically.

Francis sprang to his feet, grabbed a fly swatter off the wall and headed into the living room with Stella following suit.

"What are you going to do with that fly swatter? Swat the intruder to death?" whispered Stella as she muffled a laugh.

A young man in a dark hooded sweatshirt and jeans was caught going through the medicine cabinet in their bathroom.

"Call 911, Stella, while I teach this young man a lesson," ordered Francis. Francis had no idea how he knew about the 911 number.

Stella picked up the phone and dialed.

The young man said in a shaking voice, "Don't worry old man. I am not going to hurt you. I just want to take some of your drugs."

"Why do you want our drugs?" asked Francis.

"I want to get high, dude," replied the young man.

"You have no right breaking into our home. Now get out of here right now," ordered Francis.

The young man, not wanting to comply, pulled out a switch blade and moved towards Francis. Francis possessed the strength and agility of an athlete. He kicked the switch blade out of the young man's hands and turned him around. He pulled the man's arms behind his back and pushed him out to the living room. Stella was waiting for them. She had a large cast iron frying pan in her hands, anxiously waiting to see if she would need to use it. The young man was astounded at the circumstances he found himself in and appeared to be looking for a way to escape. Francis shoved him down on the easy chair and stood in front of him daring him to make a move. The young man tried to stand up, and he was pushed back down. He tried a second time, and then gave up.

A tribal police officer knocked at the door and said, "This is the police! We received a call from this residence. Please open the door."

"I'll be right there," responded Stella as she shuffled to the door and opened it.

"Officers, this man assaulted me," said the young man.

"You have got to be kidding me. How old are you?" asked one of the police officers as he turned his attention to Francis.

"I just turned 70 last week," replied Francis.

"What are you on, Billy? Are you having hallucinations, buddy? This man could not take you on," said the police officer.

"I'm not lying," said Billy adamantly.

"Okay. Whatever you say," said the officer as he winked at Francis.

"What were you doing in their house Billy? It's 3:00 in the morning," asked the other police officer.

"We caught him digging in our medicine cabinet," stated Francis.

"Francis managed to knock the knife out of his hand and between the two of us we got him out to this chair," stated Stella.

The police officers frowned and looked at the two of them.

To cover their tracks, Stella said, "We took defense classes, so we could protect ourselves if we need to and we get exercise. My old man is in good shape, and I have my weight to back me up."

The police officers shook their heads at the same time and then one of them said, "Perhaps you can give lessons to the rest of the residents here."

The other police officer said, "Let's go, Billy, and get you behind bars for the night to keep you out of trouble." He grabbed Billy's arm and moved him towards the front door.

"Let's check the doors and windows so we can figure out how he got in," said Francis as he followed them to the front door to make sure it was locked.

"Look at that window. Billy cut the screen and broke the glass. Would you go get the hammer and nails, Stella. I'll get the small piece of plywood I saw lying on the ground under the front window," said Francis.

"He must have really wanted the drugs. I didn't know those drugs were in our medicine cabinet," said Stella.

"The Creator thinks of everything. Let's go check out these drugs."

"There's aspirin, Celebrex, Zoloft, and Xanax," stated Stella.

"We can look up what these drugs are used for. I think we will need to visit the library in town. The Creator also told us we have ailments older people get, but we actually won't feel the symptoms. That's probably why we have the medications. I would like to take the bus to town tomorrow and stop at the grocery store on the way home. We don't have any food in this house," said Francis.

"The Creator told us we have food stamps, and we were given the amount people in our situation would get," said Stella.

"We are also given a check each month. I think the Creator referred to this as social security," said Francis.

"I don't know about this money stuff. I hope we can figure it out," replied Stella.

"I think we will get the hang of it."

****

"Francis, don't get carried away. I don't think we have enough money to buy all this meat."

"Look how great it looks. It's all red and calling out my name," replied Francis.

The cart was heaped with chicken, steaks, pork, fish and vegetables. Francis is beaming with anticipation about the feast he would partake in when he returned home.

The woman at the checkout counter started ringing up the purchases. The total of the purchases was $280. Stella handed the woman her food stamp card. The woman frowned and ran the card through the machine.

"You have overspent according to the amount on this card. You are $80 over. You are going to have to put some of these items back, then return to the checkout," stated the sales clerk as she was trying to hide her frustration.

"How embarrassing! We are so sorry. Francis come on let's go put some of these groceries back," ordered Stella.

"I just remembered. We got these checks. Can you put these toward our purchases?" asked Francis.

"You will have to go across the street and cash them at the bank," replied the sales clerk.

"Honey, why don't you go to the bank, and I will stay with the groceries," said Stella.

"Okay. I will be right back," replied Francis.

The bank teller asked Francis for some identification, and he told her that he left his wallet at home. He had to provide his address and phone number in order to get the check cashed, then the groceries were paid for, and they had the store manager call a cab to transport them and the groceries home.

After the groceries were put away and they ate a hardy meal of steak and salad greens, they sat down on the sofa together to discuss what they learned when they went to the library.

"One of those drugs is used for pain. We must have hurt ourselves. Or maybe it's our age and pain is what happens when you get older. We were both prescribed drugs for depression. I wonder if this is common for tribal people to be prescribed these drugs," asked Stella as she scratched her head.

"I don't know, but that young man expected to find drugs when he broke into our home," replied Francis.

"Look, we got mail. It looks like the phone company wants to contact us and welcome us as new customers," reported Stella as she was flipping through the envelopes and opening the mail.

"It looks like they are asking us for money. We owe them $40 for this month. They say we owe an installation fee," said Francis.

"How much money do we have left from our checks?" asked Stella.

"I have $100 left from my check, and you have $180 left over from your check," replied Francis.

"I think we have enough money to get by," said Stella.

They heard a soft knock at the door. A woman was standing on the other side and asked if she could collect the rent. The rent they owed was $80.

Stella calculated the amount they had left and she was satisfied they still had $200 to last until they received their next checks and food stamps. They sat down to start reading the books that were left in the home about the area and tribe they were visiting when the room suddenly turned dark. Francis found the circuit box and reset the main switch. Nothing happened.

"I wonder if that letter we got from the electric company was a bill, and they want money from us too," inquired Stella.

After feeling their way to the kitchen, they opened the closet door and managed to find some candles and matches. The candles were lit and they began shuffling through the mail to see if they owed any more money for utilities and other expenses. They discovered they owed $90 for electricity, which was two months overdue from their last residence. The heating bill was due. The amount of that bill was $120. It was May and they decided they would give a partial payment towards that bill.

"It looks like our bills are following us from some place we supposedly lived before we moved here," retorted Francis.

"The Creator goes all out when the stage is set for these excursions," replied Stella.

"We'll use more blankets if necessary. I am not worried about freezing this time of year," said Stella.

"If my calculations are correct, after we pay the electric bill, we will only have $110," replied Francis.

"We better put some of the meat we purchased in the freezer to preserve it for later," said Stella regretfully. She was looking forward to a huge feast and had difficulty concealing her disappointment.

"You're probably right," replied Francis as he shared Stella's disappointment.

"Let's call the electric company first to get our electricity turned back on," stated Stella as she looked up the phone number.

"I think we need to read over the information about what services are available. Perhaps we can get some help with getting more food or help paying some of our bills," said Stella.

They started reading about the demographics of the tribe and the services that were available. A food distribution program was available to tribal members who meet the income eligibility requirements. Francis located their tribal identification cards and their income verification statements.

"We will try the tribal social service department first and see what they can do for us," said Stella.

****

Francis and Stella began walking to the social service department, which was located a mile from the reservation. On their way to the agency, they witnessed a disturbing scene.

Stella and Francis heard crying and looked in a large living room window and saw a girl and a woman being abused by a man who looked extremely angry.

"Did you see that? That man hit his daughter and knocked her down. Her mother tried to save her and she was struck also," said Stella stunned, as she tried to hold her composure.

"Let's knock on the door and see if we can provide a distraction. I don't like what I am seeing and I want it stopped," said Stella.

Francis knocked on the door loudly.

The man answered the door. He was wearing a white t-shirt with a few small holes in it and a baggy pair of denim shorts. Francis could see the woman and girl sitting on the couch. The woman was hugging the girl to comfort her. The man demanded to know what Stella and Francis wanted.

To get inside the home, Stella decided to say, "We are having problems paying our bills and we would like to know if you could tell us where to go to get help."

The man stood aside and addressed the woman, "Mary, where did you go to get us help with our electricity and rent?"

Francis used this as his cue to step inside with Stella following suit.

"We need to talk to you about something else," said Stella.

"We saw you hit your daughter and your wife. That is not acceptable," said Stella as she crossed her arms and looked sternly at the man.

"Let me get things straight right here and now. My family is my business and it's none of your business how I handle my family," said the man as he inched his way closer to Francis.

"You really don't want to threaten me, young man," replied Francis and he planted his feet firmly on the floor.

"You're lucky I have respect for my elders," said the man as he backed away from Francis.

"We would like to speak to you calmly about your options," said Stella.

"What options are you talking about?" replied the man.

"You can participate in services and learn how to control your anger, or we will report what we saw," said Stella.

"Yes. We were going over a handbook about the tribal services and learned that the social service department provides lots of services," said Francis.

"I don't want them snooping around our house again. They barged in and accused us of all kinds of things and said we were going to lose our kids if we didn't shape up," said the man as he looked at his wife to get her support for what he said.

"Yes. They did threaten us," she replied.

Francis had an idea and suggested, "Why don't you contact that agency and ask to be signed up for services? If you volunteer to do these things and whatever else your family needs, this may make you look really good."

"What's it going to be? Do you want us to report what we saw or are you going to volunteer to get help on your own?" demanded Stella.

The man stood staring at them with his arms crossed. Still wanting the upper hand, the man responded by saying, "I'll think about it. My dad treated me a lot worse than I treat my kids. He was a mean drunk."

"That doesn't mean you have the right to hurt anyone in your family. What your dad did to you was wrong. You deserved better than that. Now the ball is in your court and you can stop this cycle of abuse here and now," replied Stella.

"We understand raising a family and just life in general is stressful, but there are better ways of handling your stress," said Francis with stern sincerity.

"We are willing to be there for your family if you are willing to get help," said Stella.

The man would not give Francis and Stella an answer about what he was going to do. Francis and Stella left feeling their hands were tied. They followed through and filed a report of domestic violence and child abuse to the social service department. The social worker stated this was the third report of suspected child abuse and the agency would investigate the situation.

Francis and Stella met the man, who they learned later was named Roger, and his wife, Mary, entering the social service department entrance. Francis informed them that they had to file a complaint about what they saw. Roger was not upset. He told Francis and Stella he decided to volunteer to partake in parenting sessions and see what he could do about his uncontrolled anger.

"I always told myself I would give my kids a better life than I had. I am not happy with myself. I became my father, that mean S.O.B. I hated that man, and I do want better for my kids. Thanks for setting me straight," said Roger, and he extended his hand to Francis for a handshake.

"We meant what we said. We will be there for you. We just moved into the neighborhood, and we don't really know too many people yet. You would be doing us a favor if your family could take an older couple under their wings," stated Stella.

Roger and Mary looked at Francis and Stella in disbelief. They both came from poor families and were viewed as "those people from the reservation." All their lives they were scrutinized and looked upon unfavorably. Both couples began to spend a lot of time supporting one another. Mary and Roger had two children, a six year old daughter named Susan, and Sam, their four year old son. Francis and Stella helped them care for their children by providing free childcare so they could get out and do things together, such as going to the tribal exercise facility. They were considered their adopted grandparents.

Roger and Mary helped Stella and Francis get assistance with their utility bills. This freed up more money for additional food and other expenses. They also aided Stella and Francis with budgeting. Stella and Francis discovered they were not eligible for the USDA food distribution because they received food stamps. Roger provided them with transportation to their various appointments.

****

Eagle and Coyote left the reservation after spending almost a year there. They had much to share with the Creator.

"All and all, we had a nice visit on the reservation. Didn't we?" asked Eagle.

"Yes, we did. We found out life on the reservation is not easy. It is full of despair and heartache," reiterated Coyote, and he added, "remember Billy who was so desperate for our drugs, poor kid."

"We didn't get off to a good start with budgeting and the other problems we ran into," retorted Eagle.

"It's our fault. We didn't do our homework about how to use money. That paper stuff was foreign to me. The Creator told us to read what we needed to know about surviving in the modern world. I am glad we met that family. Things ended up pretty good with that situation," said Eagle.

"I don't know about you, but I learned a lot from my mistakes," said Coyote.

"You mean our mistakes," said Eagle.

Chapter IX
Eagle and Coyote's Day in Tribal Court

After generations, as one of the nation's poorest and most neglected segment of the population, Indian people are still facing the aftermath of historical trauma. They have gone through devastating experiences for hundreds of years. The more Native American people were told they lack worth, the more this belief was instilled in their self-concept. They have internalized the current and past acts of oppression. Although Indian people represent a small segment of the population in the United States, they have had a proportionally large number of challenges. The results of the 2000 census indicated that there were 2,476,000 people identified solely as American Indians or Alaska Natives with 562 federally recognized tribes.

Some of the difficulties faced by Indian people today involve acts of violence. Indian women suffer from higher rates of domestic violence than any other sector of the female population in the United States. Indian women are 2.5 times more likely to be victims of domestic violence than women from other ethnic groups. According to the results of the Amnesty Report, 86% of assaults against Indian women are by non-indigenous men. These men are rarely caught or charged with a crime.[115] Studies have been conducted to review why this is occurring. It was determined these higher rates of acts of violence are associated with displacement, colonization, and a lack of resources, such as educational opportunities to assist tribal women with these difficult and harmful circumstances. Associated with these disparities are these women's lack of confidence and fear of retaliation.[116]

Concerning child abuse and neglect, American Indian or Alaska Native children had the highest rates of victimization, which were 14.0 per 1,000 compared to 9.1 per 1,000 for white children. Many of these circumstances involve substance abuse and other mental health issues. Death rates due to alcoholism are more than seven times the national average for Indian people. And to top things off, the government has continued to inflict acts of discrimination.[117]

The Bureau of Indian Affairs (BIA) mishandled potentially billions of dollars in Indian money. The corruption continues to run rampant. The acts of corruption depicted in the movie *Thunder Heart* are still a reality. This movie provided a rendition of how the area of a Badlands reservation in South Dakota and surrounding areas were under close surveillance by the Federal Bureau of Investigation. Acts of greed and other forms of corruption were happening at the hands of corrupt governmental officials and powerful companies working on supporting their own financial interests at the expense of the inhabitants residing on the reservations.

The mining of uranium and other minerals along with the dumping of toxic waste products has been an ongoing threat to the lives of tribal people in the wEsthern states for many years. The area represented in the movie was being mined for uranium, which caused contamination of the water supply for the residents. Interested parties who were close to exposing the corruption were either prosecuted for crimes they didn't commit or were murdered. A consistent reality persists for Indian people, which involves being forced to endure severe injustices for hundreds of years.

    Boarding and residential schools and the Indian Removal and Dawes Act are some of the ways the government propagated acts of discrimination and genocide against this disenfranchised group of people. Unfair policies and discrimination practices have had a hand in the destruction of the self-esteem of the Indian people and have led to many of the problems the Indian people are confronting today. Travel through time with Eagle and Coyote as they explore what is happening to a tribal family as a result of unresolved past trauma. They join forces at the tribal court level to get to the bottom of the problems the White family is facing.

****

The year is 2007 in a small town in Upper Michigan.

    Eagle and Coyote were requested to visit this community by the Creator and were assigned the roles of tribal prosecuting attorney and caseworker. Coyote decided he wanted to fill the position of caseworker and was given the name Henry Glassman. Eagle gladly accepted the role of prosecuting attorney and was given the name Sally Martin. The Creator laid the groundwork so they would fit into this community without a hitch by altering the memories of the community members. The Creator felt the best way to obtain information was to be an integral part of the action.

The White family has been experiencing several serious challenges, such as child abuse and neglect, alcoholism, and domestic violence. The grandparents of these children faced similar issues and were a part of the social welfare system when their children were younger. The family resides on the reservation. The atmosphere of the reservation is filled with violence and a general unhappiness for the residents. The societal ills of alcoholism, substance abuse, domestic violence and poverty run rampant.

George and Sarah White have four children: Macy, four years old; Kevin, five; Steven, seven; and Mary, nine. It looked as if Mary was taking care of her younger siblings when Henry, the caseworker for the tribe, arrived at the home. George was sleeping on the couch and Sarah was at work. The police have been trying to get the social service program involved with the family on several occasions. The family happened to be closely related to the tribal chairperson, so the social service department was hesitant to intervene. This would be considered a high profile case for the tribe. The case had everybody involved, fearful of retribution. Sally Martin and Henry Glassman were recently hired by the tribe. Thus, they were lacking of seniority, so they were assigned the case.

****

"Please state your name, position and tell us about the services you provided the White family for the last three months. Also, inform the court about the progress that has been made by the family," requested Sally Martin, the tribal prosecuting attorney.

"My name is Henry Glassman. I am a caseworker for the Tribal Social Service Program. I have arranged several services for the White family," stated Henry.

"Please list in detail the services you have provided to the family," ordered Sally.

"Sarah and the children have been provided mental health services and continue to participate in these services. Our program has tried to get George to participate in substance abuse services and complete a mental health assessment," replied Henry.

"Can you inform the court about the progress the Whites have demonstrated concerning services?"

"Progress was slow at first for Sarah. However, she has participated in all the services for the past three months. She has attended all mental health and substance abuse sessions. It has been reported by the counselors that Sarah has made significant progress. Sarah completed the parenting classes that were a part of the parent/agency agreement. I have been very impressed with Sarah's progress, and I recommend that the children be released to Sarah with supervision by our program," reported Henry.

"What about George? What progress has George made regarding services?" inquired Sally.

"That's a different story," reported Henry.

"That's a pile of crap. I'm sick of you guys sticking your nose in my business," said George as he stood up and pointed a finger at Henry. George was wearing an orange jail jumpsuit. His ankles were locked together with shackles, and he had handcuffs restraining his wrists. George has demonstrated a tendency to resort to violence if he didn't get his way. He caused serious harm to a guard and an inmate during his short stay at the local jail.

The police officer who was standing in the courtroom was joined by another. They grabbed George and sat him back down on the chair.

"One more outburst out of you, and I will charge you with contempt," said the judge sternly as he pointed the gavel at George.

George scowled at the judge and then looked towards Sally to see if he could intimidate her. Sally returned his gaze with a cold steady look that would assure almost anyone except George she meant business. An evil smile crossed his lips as he continued to taunt Sally. Sally looked down at her notepad and started writing notes.

"*That stupid broad is mine*" thought George smugly.

Court was adjourned until the following day.

****

Sally approached Henry telepathically to relay her thoughts about the chilling episode she just experienced.

"*Henry, George is playing a game of cat and mouse with me. He is trying to see if he can control me like he does his wife. I admit his gaze is chilling. However, I cannot let him begin to believe he is in the driver's seat.*"

"You're right Sally. I would be curious to find out what his background is. We need to explore this further to get a better understanding. I will let you know what I find out."

"Thanks Henry".

"In the meantime Sally, try not to let him get to you. You give people like this an inch, they take a mile. I am behind you 100%. Do not forget that!"

"Thanks for reminding me. With your support, I can handle just about anything."

"Keep in mind he is going to come after me first because I was the one who alerted the authorities."

"Lucky you! I will say prayers for you."

"Thanks, Sally."

****

Henry opened the file cabinet in the storage room and located the White file for the time period when George was placed in foster care. He sat down at a small table located in one of the corners of the room. The White family was provided a host of services ranging from mental health counseling, anger management and substance abuse services. Frank, George's father, did not complete the requirements set forth by the parent/agency agreement established between the social service department and the parents. Frank participated in one outpatient and two in-patient treatment programs without success. He left the second in-patient treatment program before he was scheduled to be released.

The police were called to their home on several occasions due to domestic violence. George's mother,

Helena, was rushed to the hospital on two of those occasions with broken ribs and a broken arm, and serious lacerations to her face and torso. One of the domestic violence reports indicated that Helena was punched repeatedly and then shoved down the stairs. Helena's brother, Ethan, was a witness to Frank pushing her down the stairs. Helena ended up with a broken arm and lots of bruising. Frank was stopped in his tracks when his oldest child, George, hit him over the head with a chair. The police arrived. When Frank regained consciousness, he jumped one of the police officers and knocked him down. He was arrested for assaulting a police officer along with the additional counts of domestic violence assault concerning Helena.

    There were four children, George 12, Esther 10, Brenda 8, and Lilly 6. When Helena received mental health counseling, she was diagnosed with clinical depression. Some days Helena was able to get out of bed and take care of business and other days she would be found sitting on the couch staring blankly. On those days, she was unable to handle the smallest of household chores. Frank was known to work long hours as an auto mechanic. It was reported that George and Esther were put in charge of their younger siblings' care when they were not attending school. When the caseworker visited the home, there was very little food for the children. Helena reported that Frank would spend his entire paycheck in the bars and there would not be anything left for household expenses.

Wow, this family was a mess. I have to read further to uncover the mystery behind George's violent behaviors.

The caseworker report was extensive. A note was included with one of the reports to her supervisor, fearing the children would be in danger if they were placed in Frank's care.

The allegations that were made against the parents were as follows: both parents were charged with neglect; the mother was charged with failure to protect; the father was charged with physical abuse and exposing his children to domestic violence. George and Esther, the older children, appeared to be Frank's scapegoats. They reported that they took the beatings, so the younger children would be spared.

The school reports indicated George had a lot of difficulty in school. He was expelled on three occasions for beating up his classmates. He was considered one of the class bullies. George did not respect his teachers and his grades were below average. On the other hand, Esther was reported as being a model citizen in the classroom, completing all her assignments and her grades were above average, mostly B's.

That's interesting. It appears George was not as resilient as Esther. On the other hand, was she better at covering up her horrible home life? I will need to explore this further.

Reading a bit further, Henry discovered that Esther had experienced some health problems, mostly unexplained stomach and headaches.

The children were removed from the home and the rights of their parents were terminated due to the lack of cooperation of both parents. Various aunts and uncles adopted the children. George's father died when he was in his early 40s from cirrhosis of the liver and their mother ended up moving in with one of her sisters who adopted two of her children. Helena appeared to get her life together. She obtained a nursing degree at the local university and works as a nurse.

I want to find out what happened to Frank and why he turned out the way he did. What made him so angry? It is more understandable why George is angry and definitely has some unresolved issues. I think I will try to locate George's mother and see what she has to say. Perhaps there are also other relatives that can shed some light on this puzzle. I have my work cut out for me.

An adoptive home study was completed for George's grandparents, so they could adopt the children. It was in the children's current file. The name listed for the grandmother was Alice White. The Child Welfare Commission turned down the home study because the grandmother was caring for the children and she asked the agency to remove the children immediately. They were driving her crazy. Alice was given another opportunity and again asked the agency to remove the children. Then she was charged with her third driving under the influence (DUI) violation and had to serve a month in jail. The children were removed for the last time from her home to another foster care home.

This family's problems run deep.

****

Henry decided to contact Alice White to set up a meeting with her.

"Hi, Mrs. White. My name is Henry Glassman.

"What can I do for you Henry?" asked Alice.

"I would like to set up a meeting with you to discuss your grandchildren, George's children. When would be a good time to meet?"

It was obvious Alice was caught off guard, but felt an obligation to give in to Henry's request. There was a pause and then she said, "How about tomorrow?"

"What time would be convenient for you?"

"How about I meet with you at 2:00 p.m.?"

Henry pretended to be looking at his calendar and then responded by saying, "2:00 it is."

"Where do you want to meet?" asked Henry.

"Could you come to my home?" asked Alice.

"Yes, that would be fine. Can you give me your address," asked Henry.

Her current address was given, and they said their goodbyes.

****

Henry drove to Alice's home the next day to meet with her.

"Hello Mrs. White," said Henry as he extended his hand.

Alice ignored the gesture and opened the door further, so he could enter.

Alice led Henry into the living room. She sat down on a high back chair and motioned to Henry to sit on the sofa.

The living room contained older furniture that was kept in good condition. Catalogs and magazines were lined in a neat row on top of the coffee table. A clock chimed two o'clock in the corner. The walls of the living room were covered with a dark wood paneling. A large screen television was tuned to a soap opera. Porcelain dolls were lined up on a shelf above the television.

Alice was of medium height and body frame with black hair. Considering her age, her hair must have been colored to cover the gray. She wore a jean skirt that was just above her knees and a red shirt that fit snugly against her slim waist.

This woman has worked very hard to hide her age.

"What's this about?" asked Alice as she sat down and rung her hands together.

"Well, I want to find out what kind of father Frank was. I want to know if you could shed any light on what is going on with the family right now."

To lighten the topic slightly Henry added, "What was George like when he was a child?"

"George was a good kid. He was helpful around the house. You know, he took real good care of those younger kids," said Alice as she rearranged her skirt and tried to appear calm and relaxed.

"Frank, on the other hand was a bad kid. Ever since he got out of that boarding school, he was not the same. He would walk around the house hitting his siblings and snarling," reported Alice.

"Why do you think he was like that? Did he ever tell you why he was so angry?"

Alice shifted in her seat and looked down at the floor and said, "Frank told me one time that the nuns were having their way with him. I didn't believe him at the time. You know, when I look back to when he told me, I think he may have been telling me the truth. I heard about some really bad stuff happening at that school. I learned that years after Frank attended. I wish I would have listened to him when he tried to tell me about what happened to him. I could not believe at the time that nuns could do such a thing. I just thought he didn't want to be there," said Alice as she tried to maintain her composure.

Henry nodded and tried to engage Alice to provide her reassurance.

Alice kept staring at the floor.

"Frank got into some real bad trouble when he was a teenager and ended up in jail."

"What did he do to end up in jail?" asked Henry.

"He hit someone with a pool cue and broke open the man's skull. It was awful. The man was a son of one of our neighbors. These neighbors helped us when we were down on our luck on a few occasions. It was a shame what Frank did to Gary," stated Alice.

"That's too bad. What happened after that," asked Henry.

"Frank did some rehabilitation in the joint. Then they thought he learned his lesson and released him," reported Alice.

"Tell me about his relationship with Helena," inquired Henry.

"That was not a marriage made in heaven."

"Why's that?"

"Helena was always doing something that would make Frank angry and then he would get in trouble. It was a vicious cycle," said Alice.

"So let me get this right. Helena would make Frank angry," said Henry.

"Yes. She was such a whiny thing. Helena, you could never make her happy. Anyways, that's what Frank used to say," said Alice.

"Can we change the subject for a moment?" asked Henry.

"Sure."

"What was Frank like as a Father?'

"I thought he was a little harsh sometimes, but it was none of my business."

"What do you mean by harsh?"

"He would slap them around and yell at them. Frank didn't seem to have a lot of patience when it came to his kids," replied Alice.

"Can you tell me about Frank's father? What was he like?" asked Henry.

"You know, I was one of those popular girls back then. I met Frank's father in passing and he really was not in the picture if you know what I mean. Back then, they didn't push to get to know who the fathers were. They just gave us that ADC," said Alice.

"What is ADC?" asked Henry.

"I think it was aid to children or something like that," responded Alice.

"How many children did you have?"

"I had four children. I ended up marrying the man that fathered my last two," said Alice.

"So this man served as the father for Frank and his siblings," asked Henry.

"Yes. He didn't much care for the two older children, which was why I put them in that boarding school to avoid trouble."

"What do you mean by trouble?" asked Henry.

"Hank would get real mad at Frank and Rose if they didn't do exactly what Hank told them to do."

"What would he do to them when he got angry?"

"He would beat them real good with a belt or whatever he got his hands on."

"How did he treat the younger siblings?"

"He treated them real good since they were his kids," replied Alice as she looked down at her hands.

"I thought I was doing a good thing. Putting them in that school to protect them," said Alice as she wiped a tear from her eye.

Alice went on to explain, "They were going to stop my ADC and make me go to work. I didn't have any skills, so I decided to find someone to marry me. I had to pay the bills, you know. Hank was a good man and all. He had a real good job. Hank was a plumber."

In order to avoid appearing as if he was passing judgment Henry decided to reassure her and told her that she did what she had to do.

"Can you tell me about your childhood?"

"I had a pretty good childhood up until I was about 8 years old and then my parents put me in the same boarding school that Frank and Rose went to. It wasn't so bad for me. I was one of the favored children. You see, my parents had a little money and they gave the school things like clothes that my siblings and I outgrew. I had the nicest clothes in my class and didn't have to use the clothes that were donated to the school," said Alice.

"So you were never abused at the school?"

"No I wasn't. I heard some rumors when I attended that boarding school that some of the girls in my sleeping quarters were taken away at night by some of the nuns and priests. These girls would not talk about what happened to them. I don't know why I didn't believe Frank. I guess I had other things to tend to." Alice stopped and straightened her skirt. She avoided making eye contact with Henry.

She went on to say, "I saw some girls get their hair pulled. Some of the kids who wet the bed would have to wear their wet sheets on top of their heads to teach them a lesson. Sometimes they would be beaten with a rubber hose if they were repeat offenders," said Alice.

"That didn't bother you when they were hit or their hair was pulled?"

"No. I kept to my own. It wasn't happening to me so why should it bother me."

I remember what I learned about children who were overindulged, and favoritism is a form of overindulgence. They become extremely self-involved, lack empathy, and can be immature for their age. Alice definitely portrays these symptoms. She did not seem to care at all about the other kids who were being abused. No wonder she did not stand up for her own children.

"You know what I found difficult when I got out of that school?"

"What's that?"

"I got out when I was fourteen. My younger siblings were not sent to the school. It was only my older sister and me. My family treated me like I was a stranger. They wouldn't invite me on outings most of the time. It made me feel bad. I thought they would be so happy I was home," said Alice as she wiped another tear from her eye.

"I am sorry to hear that," replied Henry.

"Because at the school they had our days mapped out so much. We had to get up at 6:00 a.m. Stand in line for breakfast and do chores before and after school. Things were set up at certain times and they told us what to do all the time. We had to follow all their rules and there were a lot of them. We didn't learn how to think for ourselves and with my family not wanting me around most of the time, I started getting into trouble," said Alice.

"What kind of trouble?"

"I started partying and fooling around. I liked the attention I got from all the young men," said Alice as she smiled sheepishly.

"You probably needed to feel like you belonged somewhere."

"Yes. I did. I know now that it was not the smartest thing to do. You know, the parties and all the boyfriends, but it made me forget all my problems."

They discussed more details about the family, such as her daughter Rose and other details about the family's past. It was reported that Rose became a nurse at the local hospital and she was just diagnosed with cancer. Alice's sister keeps her informed about what is happening with Rose. Henry thanked Alice for sharing so much with him and left her home. While driving to the tribal court building, he pondered everything he learned from Alice and the family's files.

****

Meanwhile, Sally was meeting with George's defense lawyer, Edward Shipment, and Lauren Spuds, the guardian ad litem for the children, to discuss an action plan for the White family. After careful deliberation, it was determined that George could not have custody of his children. It was not in the best interest of the children.

To back up the children not being released into George's custody, Lauren went on to explain, "George has been offered a lot of services and he has refused to comply."

"Can you explain further? What services was George offered?" inquired Sally.

"Before George was incarcerated he was provided substance abuse services with the First Hope Services and tribal social services. There were an extensive amount of no shows for scheduled appointments," reported Lauren.

"What do you consider an extensive amount of no shows?" asked Edward.

"He missed more than half of the scheduled appointments, according to Henry, the family's caseworker. George mentioned he didn't like the counselor at the First Hope program, so Henry arranged for George to participate in services with tribal substance abuse services," stated Lauren.

"Why didn't he attend the tribal services from the beginning?" asked Edward.

"George told Henry he didn't want anything to do with the Indians, so Henry felt his hands were tied and he needed to set up services outside the tribe," replied Lauren.

"She's right," said Henry as he entered the room where they were meeting. He was slightly out of breath from running from his car to the tribal court building.

"I would like to share with you what I learned from digging into the archives and going back three generations. Plus, I met with George's grandmother and discovered some interesting information that can possibly shed some light on the problems this family is facing," said Henry as he looked around the room at everybody in hopes that they would be interested in what he wanted to share.

"Tell us what you found out," requested Sally.

"Yes, I am curious about why George is so angry," said Edward.

"I met with Alice White, George's grandmother, to find out what I could about the history of George's family of origin. Frank, George's father, had a terrible childhood. Frank's father was not involved in his life at all. Frank was the result of a one-night stand according to Alice. She claimed she was very popular in those days. Frank and his sister Rose have different fathers. Alice married a man named Hank and Hank did not like Rose or Frank, so they were placed in a boarding school. Alice said she did it to protect them. Hank would beat Frank and Rose if he thought they got out of line. He would hit them with a belt or whatever else he could get his hands on," said Henry.

"Frank's childhood sounds horrible," retorted Edward.

"There's more," said Henry.

"Please go on," requested Sally.

"Frank told Alice that he was sexually abused by the nuns when he was attending the boarding school."

"What did Alice do about that?" asked Sally.

"She didn't believe him when he told her at the time. Now she thinks he was telling the truth," reported Henry.

"Why's that?" asked Gloria Steinworth, Sarah's defense lawyer who walked in with Henry to join the meeting.

"Alice told me she heard and read about the horrible things that happened at that boarding school," responded Henry.

"Alice appeared to demonstrate some remorse because she didn't believe him. She told me Frank got into a lot of trouble after he was released from the boarding school," said Henry.

"What kind of trouble," asked Sally?

"He hit a young man with a pool cue," responded Henry.

"He was incarcerated for that?" asked Sally.

"Yes, he broke open the man's head. He spent a couple of years in prison and participated in rehabilitative services," replied Henry.

"I have more to tell you," said Henry.

"Plcase go on," replied Sally.

"Alice reported that George was a good kid. He was put in charge of his younger siblings along with his sister Esther. He pretty much ran the household when Frank was at work. It appeared that Helena, George's mother, suffered from major depression. She could hardly move or do anything at all. Alice reported that Frank would get mad at Helena and it sounded like there was domestic violence. Alice reported that Frank would slap and yell at the kids. My thoughts were if he did those things in public what did he do behind closed doors?"

"What happened to George's parents?" asked Edward.

"Frank died due to alcoholism when George was in his teens and Helena got her life together after Frank's death. She obtained a degree in nursing and has been doing well," reported Henry.

"Almost sounds like a happy ending," stated Gloria.

"Not quite," said Henry.

"George and Sarah's marriage was anything but healthy. There have been several reports of domestic violence. Sarah has reneged on filing charges against George every time. I know this sounds like a stretch, but I think Frank's past has seriously affected George and made him what he is today," said Henry.

Surprisingly, Lauren said in George's defense, "I don't think it's a stretch. It has been reported by Kevin and Steven's teachers that these children have gotten into several fights at school. Steven has been suspended on three separate occasions due to his aggressive behaviors. Kevin's behaviors have not been as severe as Steven's. I think that is because of Kevin's age. He is only six years old. Kevin's teacher told me that she was not sure if Kevin started the fights, or if he was being picked on. She is trying to get a handle on this," reported Lauren.

"These children have been exposed to domestic violence. There have been substantiated neglect charges. Not to mention the physical abuse that may have occurred," said Henry.

"These children have been exposed to so much," Lauren reiterated.

"The police informed me that Mary called 911 concerning the last domestic violence episode. She told the police that she was afraid her dad was going to kill her mother," said Lauren

"My heart goes out to these children," said Sally.

"May I remind you that we need to make decisions based on what is in the best interest of the children," reminded Lauren as she looked at everyone in the room.

"Normally, we don't delve into the history of families. Decisions are made based on current behaviors that are demonstrated by the parents," said Henry.

"What's your point, Henry?" asked Sally.

"The other case workers reported to me that so many of these cases end up with the termination of parental rights and the children being raised by other family members or strangers," said Henry.

"That's a shame," retorted Lauren.

"The best scenario would be the parents getting their acts together because you know children blame themselves. They often think their parents did not consider them important enough to do what they needed to do to keep them. And, as a result, they feel abandoned and oftentimes repeat the same mistakes their parents made," retorted Henry.

Henry went on to explain," I met with some of the Child Welfare Commission members. Some of them have served on the commission since the 1980s. The problems that cause families to be in the child welfare system have been occurring from one generation to the next. We are not even putting a band-aid on the problems. I seriously recommend to this court to try other methods instead of terminating the rights of these parents."

"What do you suggest Henry?" asked Sally.

"I want to see George participate in mental health counseling until all the unresolved issues are dealt with. George was only self-medicating when he used alcohol to deal with his problems," replied Henry.

"Frank, George's father, was not loved and nurtured like children need to be. He certainly did not learn how to parent properly while he was at the boarding school. His mother only cared about what was in her best interest and not the best interest of her children. It appeared that Rose and Frank served as a source of income for Alice until she married Hank, and the boarding school probably wielded harsh treatment on them also," added Henry.

"Were you able to meet with Rose, Frank's sister?" asked Edward.

"No. Alice did not know how to reach her. They haven't been on speaking terms for the past ten years," reported Henry.

"Did she explain what caused the estrangement," asked Lauren.

"Alice told me that Rose wasn't speaking to her because of some silly reason like the favoritism that Rose accused her of concerning Rose's younger siblings," responded Henry.

"I can understand Rose's frustration with that situation. It appears that Rose went through so much and her younger siblings did not have to go to the boarding school and were treated more favorably by her stepdad and possibly Alice," said Lauren.

"Let's get back to George's childhood. George lost his childhood because he was given the responsibility of caring for his younger siblings. He was forced to put up with his father's abuse and was witness to the abuse that was inflicted on his mother. His mother was emotionally absent. Love and nurturance was absent during George's upbringing also. I can see why George is so angry. We need to find a therapist that can address unresolved childhood trauma. I think he is dealing with severe shame issues and may possibly have post traumatic stress disorder," said Henry.

"Explain these shame issues Henry," requested Sally.

"I did some research on the subject. Shame can manifest itself in many ways including behaviors that mirror individuals who have been diagnosed with narcissistic personality disorder and a host of other disorders. A symptom of some of these disorders is uncontrolled rage. Given George's past, I feel he has every right to be angry and may have an issue with control. The system failed Frank's family, and it is failing George's family too. Instead of getting upset with George because of his aggressive behaviors and lack of cooperation, we need to take a less punitive approach of understanding."

"I think you're right Henry," said Sally.

"I believe if we get to the bottom of what is causing George's inappropriate behaviors, we can make some positive changes for the family," said Henry.

"What about the children? What services are they being provided?" asked Lauren.

"They are all in mental health counseling. I will look into how those services are going and see if there are other services the children could benefit from. Sarah has already been attending mental health services," replied Henry.

"It sounds like you are doing a great job with the family," stated Edward.

"Thanks."

"Making mental health services a requirement ordered by the court after George has been provided so many other services to no avail is definitely a different approach. He has been so uncooperative to this point. However, if he is self-medicating then substance abuse services would not be the answer. We do need to find the underlying cause. How would we feel if the only way we can get through life is going to be taken away? Alcohol is George's source of comfort. I would fight to keep alcohol in my life too if I was in George's position," stated Lauren.

"All children love their parents and want their parents to care for them," added Lauren.

"I know. We have had children burned with cigarettes by their parents and they still want to be with them," replied Henry.

"I hope the judge accepts these recommendations," said Sally.

****

Henry and Sally switched back to their Eagle and Coyote beings and were discussing what they discovered.

"Eagle, I think we found out a lot. The court system can be so punitive and quick to pass judgment."

"You did your research Coyote. I was so impressed."

"I think the favoritism Alice was shown while she attended the boarding school led to her self-involvement among other things," stated Eagle.

"Alice didn't seem to be concerned about what happened to the other children at the boarding school. She used Rose and Frank as a source of income and then freely sent them to the boarding school due to her husband's behaviors instead of putting her children first. Of course, both Alice and Frank did not learn how to be appropriate parents when they attended the boarding school either," stated Coyote.

"The coldness and treatment of the children who were forced to go to those institutions usually created a bond between those who attended," said Eagle.

"Alice seemed to lack that. She didn't mention any connections to the students at the boarding school she attended."

"Frank self-medicated himself to the point at which it caused his death," said Coyote.

"George abuses alcohol and is very aggressive like his father," said Eagle.

"We know through our research and experience that the boarding schools were laced with abuse of every form. I wonder how many people who attended these institutions suffer from alcoholism," inquired Coyote.

"I don't think we can exclude the other acts of assimilation and discrimination, such as the establishment of the reservations," replied Eagle.

"The Anishanaabeg have been the most exploited and abused group of people we have ever encountered," said Coyote.

"It's amazing they exist today considering the hardships they and their ancestors were forced to endure," replied Eagle.

Chapter X
Remnants of a Shattered Past

Lost in the folds of deception
laced with faulty perceptions,
avoidance of responsibility,
no praise for amazing resiliency.
The use of substances to numb the pain,
slipping quietly into the rain.

Depression is only part of the solution.
Desperation not leading to resolution.
Facing the angst of despair,
caseworkers try to repair,
the damage done by the unaware.

Oppression forced one to pick a side,
while others were along for the ride.
Post Traumatic Stress Disorder, Shame and
   Malignant Trauma
are a large part of this unresolved drama.

Who's willing to step up to the plate
for those who cannot afford to wait.
Historical trauma has taken its toll,
while Indian people were forced into
   a subservient role.

Oppression represents financial gain
for Euro-Americans avoiding distain.
Establishment of another poor working class,
many more ceilings made of glass.
The use of substances to numb the pain,
slipping quietly into the rain.

The purpose of this chapter is to address the outcomes of the boarding and residential school legislation and other acts of discrimination, genocide and assimilation. The negative outcomes of historical trauma have caused serious dysfunction in the lives of a great number of Native American people. Historical trauma represents the collective and cumulative wounding occurring across generations resulting from catastrophic events. The trauma is held personally and spread from one generation to the next. Family members who have not directly experienced the traumatic event(s) can feel the effects of the event generations later. Many Native American families continue to suffer problems involving domestic violence, child abuse and neglect, coupled with substance abuse and other serious problems that tear at the worn fabric of Indian families.

Today the government agencies providing support to Indian communities have been giving top priority concerning assessing and treating the high rate of suicides among tribal youth. Suicide rates are more than twice the national average for this sector of the population. Economic hardship, a lack of health insurance, and a shortage of mental health care providers are some of the reasons associated with the high suicide and violent crime rates. Indian children happen to be twice as likely to die from accidents, violent deaths, homicides or suicides. These circumstances are accountable for 75% of all deaths among tribal people.[118]

A loss of the Native American's cultural heritage is another reason behind this dilemma. Intentional annihilation of cultures has been known to create a situation resembling a slow, agonizing death. A culture's demise cannot be taken lightly. Healthy cultures are essential for providing significant meaning to anyone's life. People affected by cultural eradication can become disoriented and develop feelings of hopelessness, and the damaging effects of the disruption of the cultural identities of many Indian people still resonate.[119]

"The 'marginal man or woman' is acculturated or assimilated by the dominant group, but only to a certain extent. The individual is trapped on the periphery of both societies, because he or she is neither exactly the same as the rest of the subordinate group nor completely accepted as a full-fledged member of the dominant group. Change in a subordinate group seems to imply that the group is being acculturated to the dominant group's customs, behavior, dress, economic practices, and/or religion. It is also assumed that the marginal persona who undergoes acculturation attaches the same meaning and usages to the technologies, practices, and patterns that he or she has adopted in the effort to adjust to the dominant group." [120] What happens to the people who have been marginalized and do not feel as if they belong anywhere? The lack of feeling a sense of belongingness has caused a whole host of problems.

Historic Traumatic Transmission or intergenerational stress is related to the cumulative emotional and psychological damage that has existed across generations. Psychological baggage has been passed from Indian parents to their children, in addition to the trauma and grief experienced in this lifetime. These aftereffects play out in today's Indian households. Studies have been conducted linking the experiences of Holocaust survivors and men who have gone to war with how these traumatic experiences have affected their offspring. Warren Petoskey, in his book entitled *Dancing My Dream*, portrayed how his father's rage, alcoholism and emotional distance colored his own worldview. Unresolved historical trauma will continue to impact the people of Indian descent until it has been addressed mentally, spiritually, emotionally, physically, and economically.

Colonization led to the violation and takeover of tribal land bases when the Indian people were forced to move. Thus, they lost their way of providing for their own families along with the loss of their homelands. These displaced Indian people had to renegotiate their way of living to appease the dominant culture, which in turn endangered their own sense of identity. [121]A land of opportunity for the Europeans soon became a land of oppression for the Indian people.

Pedagogy of the Oppressors

The term "pedagogy" refers to the art and science of teaching. Acts of oppression have caused harm to people of all races. Many lessons can be learned by looking at past and present acts of oppression. Oppression is defined as self-serving acts that are harmful to others coupled with the loss or lack of empathy. Oppression represents the enforcement of something that is undesirable or harmful to a person or group of people, causing deprivation of something that is needed, wanted, and/or helpful. To be oppressive means the actions intimidate or devastate an individual's or group of people's mental or physical health, well-being, or coping ability. Racism and oppression go hand and hand.

Acts of racism and genocide were clearly portrayed when the Euro-American population was increased to a staggering amount while the number of tribal people was greatly depleted. The Indian population reached an all time low in 1890 of less than 250,000 in the United States. Currently, the number is at approximately 2.5 million, which is still drastically low compared to what the population was when the first Europeans arrived in this country.[122] The Euro-Americans maintained their control through advanced weapons and other methods to exert power and control. The Indian people put up a good fight, but the vast numbers and technological advances of the Euro-Americans eventually won out. Unfortunately, history often repeats itself.

Historically, many dominant cultures have placed status as the vital premise behind their social interactions. Status and supremacy also go hand and hand. Through the acts of self obtained status, a person or group may possess the right to feel justified in ridiculing and/or stereotyping members of other groups. Racism and prejudice can be driven by a need to raise one's self-esteem, an unfulfilled quest to feel better than or superior to others. As a result, the privileged persons feel they are superior, and more entitled than those who are considered lower on the social ladder, regardless of their merit.

For example, the first Pilgrims who came to this country would have all perished if the Indian people did not lend them a hand. The native people showed the Pilgrims how to farm, hunt, and survive the harsh climate. When the Pilgrims and other Europeans became heartier and their numbers grew as a result of the assistance provided by the Indian people, many Indian villages were wiped out completely by the European settlers.

The desire to obtain power has a propensity to compromise one's integrity. Power is defined as an act or acts in the context of control that wield influence for the oppressor and serve as an exertion of force. The need and obtainment of power tends to corrupt individuals who possess it, and absolute power results in absolute corruption. Think back to the ideals set forth by Columbus with his domination of the native people of the Caribbean, those in authority at the boarding and residential schools, and the governmental officials such as President Andrew Jackson when he enforced the "Indian Removal Act." Power and control did lead to total domination and a lack of freedom for those who were subjugated. Acts of supremacy fed by the drive for superiority or perfection are defined in legislation and by the dominant culture as their divine right.

For fear of retribution, the Indian people could not openly oppose the control inflicted on them by the Euro-Americans after years of exploitation, which is correlated with the "culture of silence" delineated by Paulo Freire.[123]

The acts of oppression also led to a lack of cultural authenticity. The oppressors defined and controlled the subjugated Indian people, their identities, and what the perceived roles the Indian people were suppose to adopt as a way of silencing them, carried out through education and other legislative actions. Many Indian people were coerced into adopting the Euro-American culture, and at the same time weakening their ties to their own cultural heritage. An insistence on conformity leads to the stereotypical thinking that is prominent with individuals who practice racism to justify their acts of domination.

The Euro-Americans studied the tribal people to the extent necessary to gain an understanding of what the Native American people valued, such as their spiritual practices and their children. This, in turn, paved the way for the Euro-Americans to dominate them more effectively by either threatening to take away or have taken away what the Native American people held dear to their hearts. Traditional spiritual practices were outlawed in Canada and the United States from the late 1800s into the 1970s. Children were considered a precious gift bestowed upon them by the Creator. Native American children were removed and placed in boarding and residential schools. Whole tribes were forced to move from their homelands and placed on reservations. They were not permitted to be hunters and gatherers. These losses created voids and an imbalance with Indian people. These voids and the resulting imbalance concerning the well-being of many Indian people still exist today.

The Euro-Americans also lost a great deal as a result of these acts of oppression. They suffered from a loss of their cultural identity when they left their homelands, they lost a knowledge base by not allowing themselves to learn valuable lessons from the Native American population, and now many Euro-Americans are struggling with the destructive acts that either they or their predecessors inflicted on the Indian people. Some Euro-Americans have said that they feel guilty when they consider what their race has done to the Native American people.

To counteract these acts of oppression, the Indian people, while trying to feign off total domination, would develop a perception of the dominant culture's moods, customs, habits, attitudes, and idiosyncrasies to survive. Perception is referred to as exercising the powers of awareness, recognition, and knowledge. It is the ability to see beyond appearances and examine situations thoroughly. For example, a tyrannical employer may try to pass himself/herself as a compassionate, giving person, and in turn the employees view this as self-deception. A battered wife becomes hypersensitive to the attitudes, moods, and behaviors of her husband to avoid further violence. As a result, the oppressed become more knowledgeable about the oppressor, than the oppressors are of themselves.

Freire explained the implications of oppression for the oppressor. Both oppressors and the oppressed are completely caught up in the act of oppression, and both are greatly influenced by these acts of violence. These acts of violence are usually perpetuated from one generation to the next. A possessive consciousness is established in which everything in one's path becomes something to be dominated, which has included, but is not limited to, land, people, and the manufacture of goods. People and material items are objectified. The oppressed have no function except what is imposed on them by the oppressors. The oppressors cannot begin to understand their drive for control, because it has taken over their lives. They begin to believe that in order to exist in this world they must abide by their strong possessive instincts. They are reduced to establishing a sense of identity by the amount of animate and inanimate beings and things in their possession. Objectifying the animate, humans and animals, often leads to cruelty.

Complete domination over another person is in itself a hallmark of cruelty.[124] "The pleasure in complete domination over another person (or other animate creature) is the very essence of the sadistic drive. Another way of formulating the same thought is to say that the aim of sadism is to transform a man into a thing, something animate into something inanimate, since by complete and absolute control the living loses one essential quality of life, freedom." [125]

Paula Gunn Allen uses the term "white-think," delineating another way the harm those who were in the dominant group have caused themselves and others. Allen addresses individuals who view only a small fraction of a person and think this is the totality of their being. At the same time this individual is preoccupied with their own missing segments of personal identity. One of the questions that depicts this dilemma is "What do you do?" Meaning what is the person's career. People are more than their careers. However, this is a common question and it is rare that someone truly cares enough to want to know a person in depth. While that question is being asked, the inquiring person is asking themselves what is missing in their own life.

    White-think is almost devoid of consciousness and is anonymous. It serves as a blockade to genuine communication with all cultures. It is a pertinent technique for survival and expansion for the white culture, due to the detrimental effect it can have on those not under any form of protection. White-think can lead to the death of one's psyche and spirituality. For example, Indian people believed medicinal herbs induced healing. Medical doctors replaced these beliefs by acquiring the power of healing. These transformations changed the entire balance of specific belief systems. Allen goes further to explain that the oppressive actions and their results made the Euro-Americans feel safer. [126] However, they must not be excused from taking responsibility for their oppressive actions.

    A proud people, who provided for themselves and their families, were forced onto reservations and had to become beggars for food and other necessities. Hence, they lost the status they held within their tribal communities. Many tribal people succumbed to alcohol to deaden the pain while they watched their children hauled away to boarding and residential schools, many experiencing deep seated despair. Many Indian people today are faced with the ramifications of shame and Post Traumatic Stress Disorder as the result of historical trauma.

The Impact of Shame and Post Traumatic Stress Disorder

Shame and Post Traumatic Stress Disorder (PTSD) can have long-lasting and devastating consequences. Shame can include these facets: a feeling of dishonor, unworthiness, embarrassment and regret. Persons who bear the ill effects of PTSD vacillate between avoidance and denial, coupled with a psychic numbness. They can experience serious reactions to triggers tied with past trauma. These reactions may include, but are not limited to, disassociation, fears, phobias, insomnia, and intrusions in the form of chronic or acute intense emotions and thoughts. Shame and PTSD can lead to the impairment of everyday functioning.

Individuals who are suffering from PTSD can also experience a feeling of detachment; lose interest in life, daydream, and display a constricted effect and oftentimes abuse drugs and/or alcohol. The constricted effect involves an individual not letting anyone get close to them and having difficulty with intimacy. These individuals become hyper vigilant, on edge, and are usually exposed involuntarily to intrusive mental images and thoughts. Inability to concentrate and/or sleep may befall these individuals. They may obsess about the stressor, cry with little or no provocation, and can be startled or aroused negatively by the slightest reminder of the trauma. They have difficulty distinguishing feelings of guilt, shame and anger, and often go through stages associated with grief without resolution. The severity of the disorder is lessened if the trauma was caused by nature. Intentionally imposed human traumas are considered to be the most damaging.

Many Indian people have been inflicted with intentional acts of violence and abuse as adults and children. The boarding and residential schools were laced with episodes of such harmful acts. Harold said he was glad he was not a big boy. The larger boys were often hauled off during the night to satisfy the lustful urges of the caregivers at the residential school he attended in Canada. Sexual abuse can have long lasting devastating effects on one's psyche. Indian people were referred to as "dirty savages." They were perceived as being less than human, deserving of no respect or kindness.

During a tour of the Algoma University Site, formerly the site of the Shenwauk Residential School in Sault Ste. Marie, Ontario, it was reported that children who lost peers to illness or other causes were required to haul the bodies of their dead peers to the grave site. Children were beaten and punished severely in front of their peers at the residential and boarding schools. Yulanda stated the hair on one side of her head is thinner, because she was not good at math and was severely punished by having her hair pulled in front of the class for not knowing how to solve problems correctly at the blackboard. Yulanda has refused promotions within the tribe that she is employed at because she would have been expected to manage budgets. Anything to do with math has caused Yulanda concern and she refuses to place herself in positions in which she may be expected to work with math problems of any kind.

Other causes related to PTSD include additional intentional human actions such as combat; witnessing physical, emotional and sexual abuse; a hostage situation; terrorism; witnessing a homicide; participating in violence/atrocities; death threats; witnessing parents' fear reactions; and criminal assault. Other sources of stress are related to unintentional accidents and disasters, such as fires, explosions, nuclear disasters, and building collapses. Acts of nature and natural disasters can also be a cause of PTSD.

Shame can produce many of the same characteristics as PTSD and some dissimilar symptoms.

Shame is not a natural state and is a representation of moral conflict strongly associated to fear. Remaining in a constant influx of fear deters one from moving past the moral dilemmas he or she may be facing. Circumstances such as when someone feels as if they have behaved immorally or are deficient as a human being can lead to feelings of shame, which sets the stage for fear. Facing fears can be scary, to say the least, and most people would rather avoid those unpleasant feelings.

Kent reported he was locked in the basement at Holy Childhood Boarding School when he got into a scuffle over a chair. It was Saturday evening and the children were about to watch a movie. A child, who was favored by one of the nuns, wanted a specific chair, and

Kent wanted to sit on the same chair. Ultimately, the favored child got his wishes met, and Kent was sent to sit on the basement stairs alone in the dark while the others watched the movie. This event had a twofold outcome, not only associated with his fears, but also contributing to his sense of worth. Because he was not the favored one, he considered himself worth less than the other child. Additionally, he stated he now has a fear of the dark and attributes this fear to the basement incident and being forced to sit in the dark.

Kent has developed his sense of self through his experiences at the boarding school, as well as time spent with his grandparents when he was released from school for the summer. He somehow managed to keep a foothold in two worlds, the traditional and the Euro-American worlds. Other individuals were not as able to hold onto part of their Native American culture and developed false identities to appease the dominant culture.

A great number of individuals struggle daily with feeling something vital is missing from their lives, and they just cannot put their finger on it. The children who attended the boarding and residential schools were issued uniforms or wore donated clothing. This created a sense of sameness. They lost the individuality they possessed when they resided with their parents and other tribal caregivers, who fostered their individuality. They lost their given names and were given Euro-American names. Their hair was cut short because long hair was considered to belong to savages. Eventually, they lost all semblance of who they were before entering the boarding and residential schools. They became strangers to themselves, without any hope of a bright future. Individuals develop false identities when they change themselves to what they think others want or have forced them to be. They define themselves by the roles and positions in their lives. The children who were placed in these schools were forced to live under the care of strangers, some very cold and cruel. The role and purpose of many Indian people was determined by the Euro-Americans. How the individual has chosen to adjust to the losses affects the redefinition of their lives.[127]

      Some people believe that many individuals use the past as a crutch and an excuse to associate problems such as alcoholism to the hardships they have faced and continue to face today. However, contrary to that belief, these substances have been used as a means of dealing with the pain surfacing in their lives as a result of past trauma experienced by them and their predecessors. Oftentimes, substance abuse and PTSD go hand in hand.

      One common denominator exists in regards to addictive behaviors. Addictions are used to achieve detachment from feelings. Detachment lessens the feelings of pain. In other words, individuals were and continue to be self-medicating. With the progression of their addictions, individuals feel more and more detached from their feelings of shame and other uncomfortable feelings. The use of alcohol and other substances suppresses their anxiety.

      PTSD rates have revealed a strong correlation to health and social problems, which permeates both tribal and other veteran groups. The number of Indian people suffering from substance abuse was vastly similar to other veteran populations. Alcoholism rates in tribal communities can be consistently related to the level of combat experience of tribal people. During recent studies, it was confirmed that at least 60 percent of all Vietnam combat veterans suffer from a variety of symptoms of PTSD to some extent. Vietnam veterans have reported that they have had frequent headaches with no explainable reason, acute and/or chronic bouts of depression, extreme nervousness, anger and rage, heightened startle responses, sleep intrusions and flashbacks of traumatic events. [128]

Problems associated with their combat experience have manifested in antisocial behaviors, substance abuse, and an inability to sustain close personal relationships with friends, spouses, or family. Divorce and suicide rates associated with Vietnam veterans are above average in comparison to the same age group of nonveterans. During the Vietnam War, two percent of the troops who served in Vietnam were Native Americans. At that time, Native Americans encompassed less than one percent of the entire U.S. population. The number of Native American veterans in combat doubled the number of the general population. Enlistment rates for tribal members who have resided on the reservations have proven to be twice the national average, and these recruits have often served on the front lines. [129]

"Being a warrior in Vietnam involved performing a large number of duties, as well as numbing oneself to the overwhelming fatigue, the drudgery, the almost unbelievable filth of living in the bush, the shock of seeing horrible wounds and looking upon dead bodies, and one's own fear of becoming a casualty… Their ancestors had been correct in viewing warfare as a mysterious disruption in the natural order and that without proper spiritual preparation, the horrors of war would certainly scar their very souls forever… Military training had not really prepared them for the total experience of Vietnam."[130] As a result, many tribal men who fought in Vietnam are suffering from PTSD.

PTSD can lead to strong feelings of anxiety, which can be reactivated by external and internal triggers associated with overwhelming events. The overwhelming event will be played out in restless sleep patterns, irritability, outbursts of anger, difficulty concentrating, memory deficits, hyper- vigilance, feelings of vulnerability, fear of repetition of harmful events, looking over one's shoulder due to the anticipation of disaster, and being overprotective of loved ones and oneself.

Along with these symptoms, the person suffering from PTSD may also demonstrate avoidance techniques to escape all reminders of the trauma. Impaired social and occupational functioning may occur as a result of avoiding people, specific situations, or by bouts of anger. These symptoms can lead to physical ailments, such as elevated blood pressure, sweating, cold and sweaty hands, and elevated heart rate, which can take its toll on an overly sensitive nervous system.

Treatment of PTSD may include systematic desensitization involving gradual exposure to the terrifying event or item. Other methods involve the development of positive coping strategies, cognitive/behavioral treatment, psychodynamic psychotherapy, hypnosis, pharmacotherapy, group and various forms of individual therapy, in-patient treatment, psycho-social rehabilitation techniques and creative art therapies. A host of treatments for PTSD exist, and many of these can be provided with results occurring within six to 12 weeks. The first order of business is to recognize and bring to the forefront the possibility that many Indian people may be experiencing untreated PTSD and shame issues. The issues tied with PTSD and shame are often overlooked and go untreated.

Individuals living in a state of imbalance must get to the bottom of things to address any unresolved issues. For example, worth may have been determined by how much a person does for others. Often this belief was instilled by parents and was passed down from one generation to the next. Hence, the individuals inflicted with shame issues do not see themselves as worthy unless they are doing something for others, and as a result they seriously neglect taking care of themselves in the process. Once these individuals get to the bottom of why they feel unworthy most of the time, they can heal from the shame these faulty beliefs have caused. A massive amount of tribal people have been exposed to or have experienced sexual, physical, and emotional abuse. The long-lasting negative consequences of shame and PTSD can lead to an inability to carry out everyday activities.

The Long-lasting Effects of Sexual Abuse

Many children who attended the boarding and residential schools were either victims of sexual abuse and/or witnessed their peers being hauled off in the middle of the night to satisfy the sexual desires of the employees. For the lucky children who were raised in healthy surroundings, their emotions and feelings were regarded. However, that was not the case for the children whose upbringing was filled with sexual abuse and other abuses and neglect. When they were sad, angry, or fearful, their parents or caregivers did not acknowledge their feelings, provide a safe environment for their personal expression, or offer comfort. Children in supportive homes are told they are permitted to feel what they are feeling. They are given license to express their feelings. With support children can learn that feelings are not unsafe or hazardous. As a result, they build up a tolerance to difficult feelings and emotions.

Sexually abused children rarely got this support and without this reinforcement, they develop the mindset that they cannot experience the full depth of their anger, rage, sadness, shame, pain, and fear. They believe the anguish of these feelings would be unbearable. These children believe they could not hold their heads up and participate with their peers in school or on the playground if they fully acknowledged their pain and grief. The outcome of "stuffing their feelings" is the inability to trust their own feelings. The caregivers in the lives of these children were often out of control, and their feelings often led to violence.[131]

Many survivors of sexual abuse are prone to:

- Suffering from depression and despair.
- Experiencing anxiety and panic attacks.
- Alternating between overwhelming anxiety, fear, rage, to being completely numb (major depression).
- Feeling agitated and experience hypervigilance.
- Experiencing frequent nightmares and have difficulty with sleeping.
- Fearing their emotions.
- Concerns about going crazy.
- Having difficulty experiencing pleasure, relaxation, and/or joy.
- Harming self by abusing their bodies.
- Misusing or developing an addiction to alcohol or drugs.
- Contracting eating disorders.
- Having physical illnesses that may be result of the abuse.
- Experiencing difficulty with identifying personal needs.
- Possessing a fear of success.
- Not completing things they started and having trouble with getting motivated.
- Feeling different from others and if people got to know them, they would leave them.
- Experiencing self-destructive feelings and/or thoughts of suicide.
- Feeling bad, dirty, and are shame based, and not feeling at home in their bodies.

- Feeling powerlessness and helplessness.
- Sometimes experiencing out of body experiences.
- Startle easily and have a hard time returning to a more peaceful state.
- Having difficult trusting others and making close friends.
- Experiencing trouble with establishing and maintaining healthy relationships.
- Having difficulty giving and receiving nurturance, being affectionate and setting healthy boundaries is extremely difficulty. [132]

A vast amount of survivors of sexual abuse were too busy surviving to pay attention to the ways in which they were harmed. The long-term effects of sexual abuse can be so elusive that it is hard to identify how the abuse affected those who were harmed. Sexual abuse can permeate all areas of one's life: sense of self; intimate relationships; sexuality; parenting; employment; and one's sanity.[133] If one is treated like an inanimate object, one's sense of self is seriously threatened. A lack of trust can negatively affect any relationship and can certainly impede the establishment of intimacy. The stuffing of feelings such as rage, anger, sadness and a lack of trust of one's own feelings can certainly obstruct the development of proper parenting and employment skills. Confidence is vital for both the parenting and employment roles. Feelings of depression, helplessness, anger, generalized confusion because of not feeling a connection to one's own body, isolation, and the feeling of being dead inside can lead one to question their sanity. Healing cannot occur until the pain caused by these harmful conditions is recognized and fully addressed.

Many children who attended the boarding and residential schools were forced to be subjected to acts of violence against their bodies, souls, and minds. They were either witnesses or victims of the abuse. The children were forced to watch their peers as they were subjected to abuse or they were the ones being abused. Some children were actually hauled off during the day to perform heinous acts for the pedophiles. The shame and degradation these children were forced to endure had long-lasting negative effects. Today, Indian people suffer from higher rates of alcoholism, domestic violence, child abuse and neglect than other sectors of the population. The unresolved anger, rage, shame, depression and other mental health issues must seem insurmountable for many Native American people.

Residential and Boarding School Syndromes

Participants in the Aboriginal Healing Project have established a term for those who attended the residential schools in Canada, which is "residential school syndrome" and in the United States it is referred to as "boarding school syndrome." The Residential and Boarding School Syndromes were terms coined to describe what happened when a governmental system separated children from their families and communities and prevented them from speaking their language and adhering to their cultural heritage. These syndromes consist of the appalling effects many Indian people suffer as a result of their experiences. Children removed from their home and subjected to abuse in these institutions often developed serious personal distress. They experienced a disconnection physically, mentally, emotionally and spiritually.

 These syndromes have been linked to problems with self-concept, lowered or diminished self-esteem, emotional numbing tied with inability to form lasting healthy bonds with others, somatic disorder, chronic depression, anxiety, phobias, insomnia, nightmares, dissociation, paranoia, sexual dysfunction, heightened irritability, tendency to fly into rages, alcoholism and drug addiction, and increased chance of taking one's life due to feelings of desperation and hopelessness.[134] These symptoms are also similar to those delineated earlier for Post Traumatic Stress Disorder and shame.

 Yulanda stated, "There was a girl who went to the school and knew not a word of English. They beat her if she would talk in her language." Jennifer relayed she was beaten with a rubber hose for wetting the bed. The majority of the staff at these institutions were proficient in the use of violence and degradation to wield control over the children. These practices were introduced during crucial developmental periods of the children's lives.

 Modeling can lead to the adaptation of learned behaviors while observing others. Observation can result in the acquisition of new patterns of behaviors. Many children either witnessed and/or were victims of child abuse in many forms while attending the residential and boarding schools. Children can be trained to follow directions by reinforcing behaviors through rewards and/or punishment. When children were beaten for speaking their native language, they began to believe their safety was far more important than their cultural heritage. Sometimes children were given gifts when they learned some of the Euro-American ways being taught in the boarding and residential schools. Through a variety of methodologies, the employees of these institutions coerced the children to adopt the ways of the Euro-Americans.

The children who attended these institutions suffered spiritual disconnections when they were forced to practice a religion not their own and told they would suffer the wrath of God if they didn't follow a foreign form of religion. They must have been confused when the same people who told them they were worthless savages because of their traditional beliefs were abusing them in every way possible.

Warren Petoskey described his father's symptoms and how these were associated with his father's boarding school experience in his book *Dancing My Dream*. His father attended the Carlisle Boarding School in Florida. Warren remembers sitting across from his father at the dinner table while he was gnashing his teeth and breathing hard, and would go into fits of rage at the slightest provocation. His father was also an alcoholic. Warren's father was extremely critical of everything Warren did. He would have to sit or stand by his father's chair for hours at a time without speaking or moving. One evening Warren's mother was the focal point of his father's rage. When Warren stepped between his parents to protect his mother, his father threatened to kill him while he was wielding a baseball bat, but he was too drunk to catch him. Warren believes his father's deep immense pain and harsh behaviors stemmed from his childhood experiences, particularly his father's boarding school experience. [135]

      The children's development was thwarted because they suffered from being forced to form primary attachments to providers who were prejudiced and oftentimes dangerous. Sometimes they did not bond to any adult caregiver, which has been known to lead children to develop attachment disorders. Traumatic events encouraged bonding with those they may never have considered safe before. Children would build these unbreakable alliances with other children as a survival mechanism, which enhanced their resiliency. The atmospheres of the boarding and residential schools were often unsafe and unpredictable, with rarely a safe person to go to for comfort and solace. These unsettling environments have also been linked to the development of malignant trauma.

Malignant Trauma

      Some of the unsettling results of unsafe environments may be the onslaught of malignant trauma. Malignant trauma can occur as the result of the non-responsive behaviors by those who were obligated to care for the children. The children's needs and their cries for help were ignored or met with punishment. The victims experienced a sense of helplessness and hopelessness, which existed over long periods of time. Children are programmed to test the waters by crying out during the night as young infants and children, and if their cries are responded to, they develop a sense that they carry a certain level of importance.

Having needs met can lead to the development of trust. Consider the children who were forced to stay in the schools, lying in bed at night, feeling lonely and fearful. They required reassurance that they were going to be all right and needed nurturance from a caring adult caregiver. They would lie on their beds crying, and nobody came to their aid. They realized at a very young age that the only people they could count on were themselves. These children became more and more silent as they lived their lives in quiet stillness, swallowed up by the darkness.

Malignant trauma may result in five losses: (a) helplessness associated with the loss of the expectation of help; (b) loss of control over one's body and psychological integrity; (c) loss in the belief that the other is obligated to respond to a cry out for help and reassurance; (d) the loss of the obligated other's relatively continuous, constant, and appropriate recognitions of and responses to cries and needs, which is tied to a loss of trust; and (e) the loss of one's commitment to recognize, respect, and respond to his or her desires and needs. [136] The chances of overcoming these losses are minimal to nonexistent.

Martha stated she felt sorry for the children who were so young and were forced to attend the residential school. Martha attended the Spanish Residential School in Spanish, Ontario. These young children would lie in their beds sobbing at night, and no one came to their rescue or provided them with any comfort. The older siblings could not associate with their younger brothers and sisters at any time during their stay at the school. Siblings were housed in separate sleeping quarters and attended instructional lessons in different classrooms. Martha said the hardest thing was when she was sick and did not have the kindness of her mother during those times.

      What happened to the children who were hauled out of their beds to satisfy the lust of the nuns, priests or other caregivers in the boarding and residential schools? The same individuals who preached about the evils of their traditional ways were violating these children's innocence and right to keep their bodies safe from harm. The boundaries of a person's body can be considered the boundary of the self. The surface of the skin provides a shield against the external forces. [137] The children were forced to grow up with the premise that their bodies were not theirs and belonged to their abusers. Any hope of developing a positive self image was virtually extinguished long before its possible inception.

      Children need to be cared for by an obligated, responsible and faithful other. These necessary experiences cannot be duplicated in adulthood to erase the harm caused to the child during the formative years. Somehow these individuals must find ways, through the help of caring professionals, to organize their fragmented mindset concerning trust and fidelity for themselves and others. This skewed mindset has led to many forms of unresolved stress, including ethnostress.

Ethnostress

Ethnostress has been linked to the maintenance of feelings of self worth. Historically, Indian people have been forced to continually renegotiate their environments, including the communities in which they resided. Therefore, the effects of these negotiations led to other problems that can be defined by the term "ethnostress." Ethnostress is caused by a disruption in the development of cultural beliefs and personal identity. Stereotypes can carry a lot of weight in relationship to self-perceptions. They may influence social relationships through the creation of an illusion of reality.

Today, many people have the freedom to express their cultural identity and move beyond past oppression. Many Native Americans have fallen into a trap of internalizing the stereotypes, such as filthy and/or drunken Indians, that have been placed on their parents and grandparents. As a result of these false perceptions, Native American people of the United States and Canada have had and continue to have the highest rates of suicide, alcoholism, family breakdown, and other family and individual difficulties than any other cultural and/or ethnic group. These points are being repeated over and over again; however, they are important points that need to be addressed.

"Response patterns" associated with ethnostress include feelings of hopelessness and powerlessness caused by an act or acts committed by the people in power. Interactions with people from their own culture and interactions with people from other cultures are negatively influenced by ethnostress. One of every two tribal adults has personally dealt with alcoholism during the twentieth century. Researchers have not conducted studies exploring the correlation between the high rates of alcoholism with the attendance of the residential and boarding schools.

Indian people were forced onto reservations and their livelihoods were taken away, which exacerbated confusion about their own identities. Thus, they became reliant on the government to provide for some of their basic needs, such as clothing, food, and shelter. However, other basic needs were neglected and pushed aside. For example, the voices and concerns of the Indian people were not heard, and only the need to conform was considered paramount by the dominant culture. As a result, these needs were not met:

- Being heard in communication.
- Being seen.
- Knowing their communication is accepted and believed.
- Knowing that others have faith and trust in them.
- Being allowed to take a place of honor in the world.
- Feeling secure about, and at peace with one's self.

- Feeling that one's existence is not detrimental, but beneficial to the important people in one's life.[138]

It is important to consider the differences between wants versus needs, and the magnitude in which the desire to place wants before needs has caused a vast amount of damage. Wants are usually short lived in their importance. Needs are essential for survival throughout the course of one's lifetime. Trauma can seriously damage an individual's psychological and emotional well-being and, in turn, can negatively impact survival. The unmet needs, such as feeling a connection to others, have impeded a vast amount of people of all races of securing feelings of a healthy emotional well-being. In order to address the problems caused by historical trauma, communication between all parties must be established.

Loss of Communication Skills

Many people do not possess the communication skills that may lead to a meaningful connection to others, which deters their ability to sustain healthy and satisfying relationships. "White think" was addressed in the *Pedagogy of the Oppressors* section of this chapter that addressed people being referenced by only what they do for a living and the lack of interest in what is going on in others' lives. Other factors are also involved in the loss of communication skills. Listening intently and concentrating on the real meaning behind what someone else is saying usually does not occur. The listener is thinking about how what is being said relates to something in his or her life or what they are going to say next. As a result, most of what was said was not truly heard. Technology has replaced a lot of face to face conversations. A multitude of people would rather text a message via their cell phone than make a phone call. The commercial demonstrating the text and tweeter capabilities of a cell phone package while a family is sitting at the dinner table is an excellent example of the loss of communication skills.

Many of the Indian children who attended the boarding and residential schools came from different tribal entities. However, they were placed in these institutions and treated like they were all the same. Many of these children came from distinctly different cultures. Sometimes they were from competing tribal groups. Oftentimes, they did not even share the same native language. This created barriers to establishing a sense of connectedness. Language in itself is a very important means of communication with others. The ability to communicate in one's own language as well as the shared commonality of cultural practices was taken away from a multitude of Native American people.

The past of Indian children involved censored and restricted communication while they attended the residential and boarding schools. The children were forced to remain quiet and stare straight ahead while they were in the classrooms. They developed a method of communicating with their eyes when outside of the classroom. They could speak volumes with eye contact amongst their fellow peers. These children were punished, often severely, if they spoke their native language. Speaking became a privilege which could not be practiced for much of the day and into the evening, when they were working on their homework or completing chores. Their communication with their parents through letters was censored.

    If these children were forced to attend the boarding schools for long periods of time, they discovered that communication with their families of origin was difficult to impossible when they were finally permitted to return to their homes. Trust was one of the main reasons. Their parents and other siblings who did not have the misfortune of attending these institutions were worlds apart. These children spoke differently, and often their appearance was dissimilar from the rest of their family. They soon discovered they did not fit with their families of origin, usually shortly after moving back home.

    In the effort to fit in, they would take part in activities that were not always in their best interest. Sarah reported during an interview that her family would take off and go on family outings, and she was not invited to go with them. Other times her family would stop talking when she entered the room. She felt as if she was a stranger in her own home. Sarah began participating in activities she later regretted with anyone who would allow her to hang out with them. Many Indian people are still paying today for the mistakes they made as teenagers and young adults.

    The abuses inflicted on the Indian people for centuries have caused long-lasting negative effects. The end result of historical trauma has been a variety of hardships experienced by people of all races, especially Indian people. The outcomes of the various acts of oppression have harmed both the oppressors and the oppressed. The oppressors became a slave to power, control and the ownership of the inanimate and animate, while the oppressed lost their precious freedom. They have been plagued with Post Traumatic Stress Disorder, shame, malignant trauma, ethnostress, and residential and boarding school syndromes, with minimal hope of a better tomorrow.

Chapter XI
A Journey's End

In the past, tribal parents raised their children within the context of the family and their immediate communities. Ongoing cultural oppression, health disparities and a lack of access to services and economic opportunity coupled with chronic poverty, have depleted hope for many tribal families. The cumulative effects of intergenerational historical trauma and chronic stress only add to the problems Indian families are still facing. The combination of chronic situational stress and unresolved historical trauma has led to an increased risk of developing psychological and behavioral disorders as adults.[139] However, Indian people have demonstrated amazing resiliency and many are able to return to some of the cultural beliefs of the past. There is a dim light at the end of the tunnel that many Indian people have managed to see and work towards. And some of them need to be shown the light.

Eagle and Coyote discuss the journeys they have taken through time to find what is behind the problems many people face today and why some have managed to survive through generations of historical trauma. The Creator requested them to visit an early Ojibwe village, join Columbus's first journey, visit an early French settlement in New France, infiltrate a boarding school, visit a modern day reservation, participate in tribal court activities, and other activities throughout many centuries.

They surmise what was learned to prepare for a final report to present to the Creator.

****

"Rise and shine sleepy head," said Coyote as he nudged Eagle.

"Where am I?" murmured Eagle as she stretched her wings.

"You're on top of Mt. Rushmore in South Dakota. Remember those huge carvings of famous presidents? They were so important that their faces were carved out of the rock on the side of a cliff. Some people risked their lives to do those massive carvings, simply amazing."

"I remember about one of the men who had their face carved on that wall. He was known as Jefferson and he was considered an important president because of how much land he acquired," replied Eagle.

"Okay, smarty pants. How did Jefferson do that?"

"He developed this proposal called the Louisiana Purchase, which not only included the state that is referred to as Louisiana today, it also included a lot of land west of the Mississippi," replied Eagle.

"Interesting; however, we have to focus on the task at hand. We have to discuss why the state of this country is in such a mess. People cannot get over some of the terrible things they and their families of origin have gone through. Those who appear to be in power don't seem to be happy either. Look at all those divorces. What about those teenagers? They are glued to those electrical devices. They don't talk to each other or their families ," stated Coyote.

"Yeah, things do appear to be a mess," replied Eagle.

"I think I want to rehash what we have experienced and go from there," said Coyote.

"Let's do that."

"We've been traveling through time together for quite a while and have seen so much. This isn't going to be a small task," said Coyote.

"I know. Let's start from the very beginning when we met those cave people, and they were fighting to stay alive because of the dinosaurs," said Eagle.

"I don't think we have to go back that far. Let's start with that Ojibwe village we visited in the Americas before the Europeans came to their land. I liked what I learned from that experience. One of the things that stood out for me was the way they were so respectful of one another," stated Coyote.

"I know. The Ojibwe existed in a peaceful manner and everyone pulled their own weight. There wasn't a job that was beneath them. The villagers took pride in everything they did. The Ojibwe worked and played hard. Listening to the drum and watching them dance was so moving. Every time the men began beating the drum, a tear would come to my eye. It was so touching. I could feel the heartbeat the drum represented to them," said Eagle trying to hold back her tears.

"Story time around the fire at night was very enlightening. I learned so much from those stories, Eagle. If I remember right, I think they were called legends," said Coyote ignoring Eagle's tearfulness from remembering the meaningfulness of the drumming experiences.

"You're right. The stories were called legends."

"Let's get back to the task at hand," stated Eagle, as she scratched the ground with her talon.

"The Creator told us about prophesies that were told concerning the Anishannabeg. All of these seem to have come true. People did come across the big waters and feigned the brother face at first, until they took over the unsuspecting native people. They were told to move westward; however, how far westward would the native people had to move to escape the ravages of the land hungry Europeans?" asked Coyote.

"It never mattered how far they moved. No matter where the Indian people lived, the European settlers either wanted their resources, or they did things to kill the Indian people, such as dumping toxic waste near where they lived. I think the takeover was eminent. The battles between the Muslim people and Europeans set the stage for what happened to the Indian people," replied Eagle.

"I also remember that women and men were treated equally at the Anishanaabeg villages. The Europeans were not practicing this form of equality in Europe before and after they arrived in the Americas. In fact, the Ojibwe women owned the property. What I mean by property was the wigwams, along with the things inside and outside of the wigwams," said Coyote.

"That's right. Equality does not exist for women today. I also recall how happy the children were as they played alongside the adults copying what they were seeing the adults do. This was one of the ways they prepared for adulthood. The game of lacrosse and other games they played brought so much joy to them," stated Eagle, smiling in remembrance.

"The type of leadership they used really worked for them. The clan system was represented by various birds and animals. They had so much admiration and appreciation for these creatures. Each creature was believed to possess special strengths and gifts. It was amazing how these gifts were represented in their leadership. They believed each person possessed these animal and bird gifts, giving them the strength and the abilities to carry out their roles specific to the needs of the entire village," said Coyote.

"I think appreciation is one of the things that seem to be missing today. Often people don't seem to be grateful for anything. It seems they take a lot of things for granted and aren't pleased about the things they do have."

"I think you are on to something, Eagle. I like the way you can analyze something, then come up with a solution to the most difficult situations," offered Coyote.

"I value your gifts, too, Coyote, like the way you sum up a situation so quickly and react with such speed and accuracy," said Eagle.

"I know sometimes I get on your nerves, but at the same time I know you respect me. We work well together as a team," said Coyote.

Both were silent for a moment and then Eagle asked, "What did you think about the way the children were raised in the Ojibwe village?"

"You mean, all the adults being responsible for raising the children?" responded Coyote.

"Yes."

"That really worked well. Everyone looked after the children in the village. The elders taught the children valuable lessons through the telling of legends, and stories and demonstrated skills like basket weaving. The children were so respectful of the elders, and all the adults for that matter, even their parents. What happened to the children today? The adults make so many excuses for children's disrespect. You hear parents say things like they are teens; what do you expect? It's surprising how they treat their parents and at the same time they don't pull their weight around the house. It's just plain awful," retorted Coyote.

"I think it's terrible, too. Teenagers, as they refer to them these days, seem to be more a liability than a gift. They sit on their behinds, eat the food their parents buy, and then have the gall to talk to their parents disrespectfully."

"All I can say is that Creator isn't happy with the way things are now," replied Coyote.

"I don't blame the Creator for feeling that way."

"We can't forget things weren't always rosy. The Ojibwe fought some nasty battles with the Iroquois and other tribes over land and its resources," said Coyote.

"Yes. They were doing that as a way to protect the future of their children. But when they weren't at war, the communities were peaceful. Everyone got along with one another. There wasn't this competition, and come to think about it, a hatred or loathing between members in the communities as we see today. They're fighting over jobs, money, status, and things. Over things, mind you, such as who has the best car. Who has the best anything? Why do they even care? It's so sad," said Eagle."

"Those expensive cars come with big price tags. They are saddled with these high payments. Who is controlling who?" asked Coyote.

"We're jumping ahead a bit. Let's think back and explore the time we spent with Columbus," said Eagle.

"We learned how this western continent was discovered. Others were here before Columbus, but he was the first one to institute European leadership. I use the word loosely, the word 'leadership,'" said Coyote.

Eagle agreed with Coyote and added, "You got that right. There wasn't much in the way of leadership."

"At least when they were on the ships, the work was distributed equitably. Columbus had his quota of chores, as did the other sailors. You do have a point. He abducted the native people and put them at the bottom of the ship, where they huddled together for the entire trip. They were barely fed, were given very little water, and nearly half of them died. They were fed the sailors' scraps," said Coyote.

"Parts of that adventure I erased from my mind. What happened to those people was so horrible. Those who didn't cooperate were slaughtered. Some were slaughtered just to set an example. This happened to villagers of all ages, babies and all," said Eagle, as she looked away with tears streaming down her face.

"They were living peacefully in a Caribbean paradise, and suddenly one day their world was turned completely upside down," said Coyote, as he tried to hold back the anger he was feeling.

"It didn't even appear that Columbus or the other sailors were at all happy. The more gold they had the slaves collect, the less happy they were," said Coyote.

"They had feelings of scarcity when they had so much. Sad, just sad," said Coyote, as he shook his head.

"They were trying to appease Ferdinand and Isabella, the rulers of Spain. They are the ones who wanted Columbus to seek riches. That was part of the agreement when they funded the expedition. He was following orders," stated Eagle.

"They were doing just that, following orders."

"When we visited the French settlement, those settlers seemed to be more content than Columbus and his people," stated Coyote.

"Yes. They did seem to be more content. The villagers didn't practice the form of leadership that the Ojibwe did, but they seemed to be more civilized. They appeared to have fun dancing and playing music. Everybody helped one another and each did their part for the community. The children attended learning institutions called schools and helped out by doing whatever they could."

"Why were they happier than Columbus and the men under his command? Let's examine that," said Eagle thoughtfully.

After a pause, Eagle went on to recall, "First of all, there wasn't this gold seeking. Together they built homes, the town hall, and a fortress surrounding the village. Things were in order and a few people weren't trying to obtain all the wealth. There was none of this slave business, and the villagers gladly helped their neighbors. They lived in a community and everyone had the community's best interest in mind. They even planted community gardens."

"It appears that greed had something to do with the unhappiness that Columbus and his people were experiencing?" asked Coyote.

"I think it has a lot to do with it," replied Eagle.

"Why do you think they were so cruel to the native people?" asked Coyote.

"I think it was because they thought the native people were less than human and undeserving of the same rights as humans," replied Eagle.

"That still doesn't make sense. Anyone could tell they were human. They had legs, arms and walked upright. Why would anyone think they were anything but human?" said Coyote as he pawed the ground trying desperately to come up with an answer.

"Well, it's like this: if they believed the native people weren't human, it would excuse them of any wrongdoing. Weak, self-serving people usually find it easier to blame others for their own mistakes than to take responsibility for their own actions, no matter how severe," replied Eagle as a stern look crossed her face.

"I don't have a lot of patience with such people. There is no excuse for treating anyone with cruelty, and no excuse for Columbus's bad behavior. Columbus worked for what appeared to be very heartless people. They owned him," stated Coyote.

"I would not sell my soul to anyone," said Eagle.

"Me either."

"The native people jumped to the aid of anyone they thought could use their help. As a rule, they were usually so generous, willing to do what it took. They even served in the war with the union troops to free the slaves. The Indian people often turned the other cheek," said Coyote.

"Remember that terrible story we were told by the Creator about that man named Willem Kieft? If I remember right, he was the second governor of New Netherlands around the year 1641. He promised some men an opportunity to earn a reward for the collection of scalps of Indian people who resided on Staten Island. Men were hired to collect scalps from the native people and were given money for each "hostile" Indian scalp that was turned in by the bounty hunters. It didn't take these hunters long to figure out that the government agents could not tell the difference between a scalp from a hostile Indian to one who was on friendly terms. Many innocent tribal people from peaceful villages were killed for the sake of collecting a bounty. The French hired Indians to collect the scalps of their enemies, and the

English did the same against the French. I am bringing up the taking of scalps because Indian people were blamed for the starting of this practice. Indian people did scalp their foes, but only to prove that vengeance took place against those who have committed wrongdoings towards someone in the tribe. The practice of collecting scalps and turning them in for money continued until the late 1800s," Coyote looked at Eagle to see what her reaction was to what he told her.

She appeared to be deep in thought, and then a grimace crossed her face as she looked down.

Eagle and Coyote moved from the edge of the cliff, then settled down near a small tree to rest and continue contemplating their past experiences. The sun was cresting over the horizon. Custodians were sweeping the cement and spraying the surfaces of the Mt. Rushmore walkway. The marble tops of the displays situated below a large marble wall were being cleaned and polished. They sparkled brightly as the sun peaked to greet the day. The men's shadows stretched across the pavement of the walkway. The front gate was not open for business yet. It was early April. The famous tourist site was only open for a few hours a day. Business hours would increase Memorial Day Weekend. Mountain goats grazed on the side of the cliff and on both sides of the drive to the main gate. Eagle and Coyote were gazing at a mountain goat, wondering how this animal would taste and how difficult it would it be to catch this beast. It had been two days since they satisfied their pallets. They were long overdue.

"We can proceed with this discussion after we take care of a physical need. My stomach is speaking to me loud and clear, and it's all I can think about," said Coyote.

"I'm feeling the same way," replied Eagle.

After they satisfied their appetites, they sat down near the base of a large tree to commence their discussion about their past travels.

"I am thinking about the vast differences that have occurred between the various types of people we have observed. We need to continue analyzing various situations to discover what has worked and what hasn't. Let's move onto the time when we infiltrated that boarding school. That was an experience and a half."

"Where do we begin?" inquired Coyote.

Eagle stared blankly ahead while she tapped her talon on a stone surface, and Coyote sat and tapped his paw on the ground. Both were deep in thought while they reminisced about their boarding school experience.

"You know what comes to mind when I think about the time we spent at the boarding school? I wonder how the students got through some of the awful experiences. Most of the children built such strong alliances with other children. It must have given them strength, supporting one another. They were so creative about it. Sometimes it was just through the light tapping of a pencil eraser on a desk, when one of their peers was being verbally and physically abused in front of the classroom by a cruel teacher. Other times, it was by sending messages through eye contact or making sure someone had food to eat when they were sent to bed without supper. The children stuck together through thick and thin," said Eagle.

"They only had each other. It didn't appear they got to see their parents or any other family members very much. They must have been very lonely,"

"Yes. However, some of the children were farmed out to their grandparents and other caregivers during the summer months," replied Coyote.

"I remember that. What was that all about?" asked Eagle.

"I don't know," replied Coyote.

"It wasn't bad enough they were abused in every way by many of the nuns and priests who worked there. Some of the children had to live without their parents during the summer months too. I felt so bad for the children who had to go to a boarding or residential school. I learned from others whom the Creator sent on similar missions that the same horrible things were happening at other schools, including those in Canada. Remember the meeting with Creator when we had to report our experiences and what the others were saying?"

"Yes. I remember. Where did they find the people who worked at those places? Did the job description include provisions such as must have a terrible disposition and be capable of performing atrocities against children?" said Coyote as he shook his head at his own morbid sense of humor.

"Must have. Some of those people were down right mean. It's as if cruelty was their art; however, at the risk of minimizing the terrible acts that some of those school employees did, there were some employees, although only a few, who were nice to the children. However; their kind behaviors were overshadowed by the heinous acts of the other employees."

"Well, let's get on with this discussion. What worked for the children who were sent to these institutions was their support for one another and their resiliency," said Coyote.

"Yes, they did appear to be tougher than the average child. Still, what we are seeing today is a high rate of child abuse and neglect amongst the tribal population as well as for other races," stated Eagle.

"There is also a high rate of alcoholism and drug abuse, which usually appears to go hand in hand with domestic violence," retorted Coyote.

"Remember that young man who broke into our home when we were living on the reservation? He was looking for our prescription drugs. I don't know what he was going to do with the drugs if he would have gotten them, but it couldn't have been good," said Eagle.

"He seemed desperate. It appeared that he was going to be a hurting soul if he didn't get his hands on those drugs."

"How sad to have to rely on such things to get though life," said Eagle.

"I like how that situation turned out with the family we helped. They really got their life together and we ended up supporting each other. I think we are on to something when we mentioned how important the support was for the children at the boarding schools" said Coyote.

"We had a lot of fun with that family once they decided to stop abusing one another and start getting the help they needed. It's like they had forgotten how to have fun," said Eagle.

"Having fun with your family is so important. We loved learning how to play those board games with them, and how much fun it was to go for walks or play in the park."

"It is important to find fun activities the whole family can enjoy like the horseshoe game we introduced to them," said Eagle.

"The Creator told me how he liked my sense of humor. He told me humor is a good way to deal with things life can throw at you," said Coyote.

Eagle was smiling at Coyote as she remarked, "Yes. Life is good at throwing you curve balls when you least expect it."

"A little baseball humor Eagle. If you keep it up, you just may end up with a sense of humor, too."

"I've got to lighten up some. I get so worried when things aren't going well. I forget when we are in our human forms that it's okay to make mistakes, as long as we admit and take ownership for our mistakes and learn from them. When I'm in my Eagle form, I do what comes naturally, and it seems like I am not as susceptible to making mistakes."

"I think you are wound a little tight when you're in your Eagle form, too."

"I know I could be a little more fun. I don't have to be so serious all the time," said Eagle.

"To your credit, I realize you have a lot on your shoulders, being responsible for passing on wisdom and all. Just don't forget to look at the lighter side of things now and again. It would make life more pleasant for you and those around you."

"Point taken," said Eagle as she looked thoughtfully towards the horizon.

"I can't believe I am saying this, but let's continue reminiscing. I want to discuss our time in tribal court," said Coyote.

"I learned a lot from that experience, too. Alcoholism was one of the topics we discussed earlier. The White family had a lot of issues, and alcoholism was just one of them. A common factor was the boarding school experience of the children's grandparents."

"Do you think that's when the problems began?" asked Coyote.

"I don't know. My gut feeling tells me that was when Frank was introduced to sexual abuse and after that things began to really go downhill. Remember when Frank said he tried to tell his mother that he was sexually abused at the boarding school, but Alice wouldn't believe him. Now Alice is feeling some regret," stated Eagle.

"The grandfather was abused by his stepfather, and then the grandfather abused the father of the White children. The abuse can go on and on if the root cause of the problems is not resolved."

"What happened to the grandfather of the White children was terrible. Then he had no one to talk to and no one to validate his feelings about the sexual abuse he endured while he was at that awful institution. He didn't get any help regarding what he went through. On top of things, he masked whatever pain he was feeling by using alcohol," said Eagle as she fought back her feelings of frustration.

"To the point he killed himself by drinking himself to death."

"The emotional trauma inflicted at the boarding and residential schools has caused so much destruction. It destroyed the foundation of many families," Eagle said as she looked at Coyote in a way to prompt him to add more to the conversation.

He took the bait. "You are so right. Who can measure the amount of damage that was done? The children who attended these schools were told they were worthless, and the way of life of their families was wrong. Every day they were told they were bad because of whom they were. What did that do to their self image?" asked Coyote.

"Not to mention they were shown how to be a parent by people who were abusers."

"Why were the white people so abusive to the children in those institutions?" asked Coyote.

"I think it is because they felt they were following the word of God. They thought they were better than the children they were placed in charge of. And they thought they were doing right to make the children carbon copies of themselves," said Eagle.

"I want to add more to this picture we are trying to paint. The Europeans meaning the English, the Pilgrims, Dutch, French, and people from other countries ran from wherever they were from to escape the horrible conditions that existed there. But what did they do instead of learning from these experiences? They brought sicknesses with them to the Americas," said Eagle.

"What sicknesses are you talking about, Eagle?"

"I mean the pestilence, the greed, the pettiness, and the self centeredness. You know an all for one instead of one for all mentality, and the need to control everything in sight."

"What do you mean by pestilence?"

"That is referring to the epidemics of disease that spread through the Indian people like wild fire. Entire civilizations were wiped out," replied Eagle.

"Now that you mention it, I recall what one of our peers reported about what Cortez did to the Aztec empire. If I remember right, he gave the Aztecs blankets with the small pox disease on them. It wiped out thousands, said Coyote."

"The Europeans did the same to many Indian people in the Americas. The Odawa Indians near the Petoskey in Michigan were given little metal boxes by the British and told not to open the boxes until they returned to their home community. These boxes contained small pox spores and as a result, thousands of Odawa people died," retorted Eagle.

"So let me get this right. The Europeans killed the tribal people in the Americas through blankets infested with sickness, other fake gifts; by placing them on useless plots of land, killing most of the buffalo, thus starving them; by using land near reservations as dumping grounds for toxic chemical waste; using the children in Alaska as lab rats to test medications that may have been laced with the HIV virus, and if that wasn't enough, they inflicted the boarding and residential schools on these people as well."

Eagle went on to say "Yes, and it all started because they misinterpreted the Bible to suit their own selfish desires. They believed they were the superior race. Most of the atrocities were committed in the name of God. Even the Pope at one time gave his blessing to use whatever means possible to ensure the native people followed the rulings of the European governments. Greed and control was part of that faulty belief system also. We can't forget that."

"Okay, I want to end this discussion, so let's surmise what we have learned from our experiences. First of all, the Indian people had a system of leadership that worked. They were respectful to one another. There were battles, but these were between the various tribes and not within the tribes themselves. They worked together as a community by supporting one another through good and bad times. That support was essential for their survival and appears to be lacking today. Humor is also essential. That's from my private experience, but I do think it needs to be noted."

"Duly noted," said Eagle as she prompted Coyote to continue with a nod of her head. When it came to her peers, Eagle was so quick to step in and add things. She was turning over a new leaf and wanted to hear more about what others had to say.

Impressed by Eagle carrying out what she promised she would do, Coyote added, "The community effort definitely needs to be a prominent suggestion when we meet with Creator to give him our report. We need to stress the importance of everyone needing to be there to help their neighbors, family members and anyone else who needs a hand. It worked well when we helped our neighbors on the reservation, and we did it without passing judgment."

"May I add something?" asked Eagle politely.

"Sure. I would love to hear what you have to say."

"We can't forget to mention that the elders need to be called upon more often. They have such a wealth of information because of their many life experiences."

"Good point. I will make sure that is noted."

"We've talked about support, community effort, humor and elders. Is there anything else we are forgetting?" asked Eagle.

"We do need to mention the unresolved emotional trauma that has permeated throughout the generations and that needs to be addressed. Also, there is the need for a lot of people in North America to adopt better parenting practices."

"Another good point," stated Eagle.

"I think we need to emphasize that practices of genocide, assimilation, and discrimination have caused harm to all. Plus, we need to point out that there needs to be a shift in values from being greed based to people based. How we can benefit others is another way of looking at things, and not how can I get more control and resources so that I can acquire more and more. It is so important to examine your life to learn what has worked and what hasn't worked. And then to come up with new ways of doing things, if necessary."

"You are so right."

"People need to be kinder to one another," said Coyote.

"Another good point, Coyote. I think we are armed and ready to submit our final report to the Creator," said Eagle.

Chapter XII
One Step at a Time

The Rebirth of Communities
Eyes and hearts wide open,
past trauma in the forefront,
not clouded by denial.
Hurt souls seek healing

Communication is being restored,
between all races and genders.
Taking care of our four selves.
No more discrimination.

Families reconnecting,
hope replaces violence,
not only surviving, thriving,
the rebirth of communities.

      The Native American population is considered the most neglected minority in the United States. Unemployment, substance abuse, and school dropout rates are among the highest in the nation. Indian people struggle with epidemic levels of diabetes, cancer, and heart disease. Another tragic circumstance is the high amount of parental rights being terminated, predominantly the result of substance abuse issues faced by many Native American parents. The Indian Child Welfare Act was enacted in 1978 to reunify Indian families. The act has resulted in little to no success with reducing the high rates of child abuse and neglect concerning the Native American population. Other problems faced by Indian people are high levels of mental health issues and domestic violence. In spite of everything they have been subjected to, the Native American people and remnants of their culture still exist.

It has been said that Indian people do not process alcohol as well as white people, and they are more apt to become dependent on alcohol. Harold reported that his parents filled the void with alcohol when Indian spiritual practices were outlawed in Canada and the United States. Since many Indian people are dealing with anxiety based issues, alcohol and drugs are often used to self-medicate. The problems leading to substance abuse go even deeper than that. Post Traumatic Stress Disorder (PTSD) and other anxiety based symptoms such as shame are often coupled with substance abuse. These problems will not be resolved until everything is put on the table and understood. Denial of the harmful effects of past actions serves as a barrier to recovery. Denial usually does not work in any circumstance for anyone. Problems that are not dealt with only get worse.

Victor Frankl, neurologist and psychiatrist, developed logotherapy. The premise of this therapy is based on admission of specific fears. Most individuals will tell themselves not to be afraid before standing in front of an audience or group, which ends up applying more pressure on the speaker. With Frankl's logotherapy, if stage fright is the individual's fear, the individual acknowledges it and gives the fear attention. Telling themselves they are going to be nervous has proven to provide relief for stage fright. Also, informing the audience about the speaker's nervousness provides relief for some of the tension the presenter may be feeling. The point is the admission of shortcomings does relieve stress and provides a way for enlisting support.

    Carl Hammerschalg makes the statement that it is not enough to acclaim one's monsters in private or in the confines of a therapist's office. An individual needs to openly admit to others about the issues they have been dealing with, even challenges such as sexual abuse needs to come to be brought out in the open. Remember Oprah Winfrey's testimonial in public about the sexual abuse she was subjected to as a child. Public statements can make people more accountable for their own recovery, as well as clicit support. The first order of business is to acknowledge current feelings or conditions. In the case of Indian people acknowledging the grim effects of historical trauma is the sad reality, based on an inability of a downtrodden people to overcome a vast amount of despair. Other lost skills involve the ability to be solution focused and the knowledge of how to apply the use of proactive attempts at handling any problem. The move from survival mode to thriving can be a long, arduous journey. It is, however, a journey that can be undertaken if people receive the support needed to achieve their goal to thrive. Three steps are recommended to begin the process of recovery and maintain an overall sense of well-being.

Step One: Identifying the Sources of Chronic Emotional Pain

Social service programs and other service providers have not been able to reduce the high rates of domestic violence, suicide, child abuse and neglect for Native Americans because they have been applying a band aid to symptoms and not addressing the problems lending to these hardships. For example, tribes have implemented drug elimination programs to offer alternative behaviors to replace or deter adolescents from turning their lives over to addictions, primarily substance abuse. Substance abuse is only a symptom of much deeper problems. Exploring the past of families and individuals with a fine tooth comb is a good start. Bring attention to all factors associated with any negative effects at any point in time, past or present.

The types of trauma the individual, parents, grandparents and other family members experienced throughout their lifetime needs to be understood. Were the grandparents or parents forced to attend a boarding or residential school? Did the fathers and grandfathers serve in any wars? Did the individual suffer abuse, including sexual abuse, and neglect? Have they witnessed or have been the target of domestic violence? Does the individual have a problem with anger or uncontrolled rage? Did they lose any family member or friend to substance abuse? Did the individual lose anyone to suicide? Individuals need to examine their lives closely to see if these circumstances have occurred in their life and the lives of family members or others of significance. How have these experiences affected them personally?

Some PSTD and shame inducing encounters and occurrences are unique to Native Americans, such as Indian boarding and residential schools and reservation experiences. There was also the enforced restrictions on family contact, the speaking of family languages, and the practice of spiritual beliefs. These cumulative traumas from a loss of their identity and culture to a lack of family cohesiveness concerning Indian families have had a long-lasting and devastating effect on Indian people. A higher percentage of Indian men have served in the armed forces, leading to PTSD, which plagues a great number of veterans. Layers upon layers of trauma have been inflicted on Native Americans, from historical trauma to the distress they face today. Tribal reservations are heavily populated by individuals who have a personal history of attending boarding and residential schools or they have suffered at the hands of parents and grandparents who were forced to attend.

Before the years of technological advancements, formal education, and the preoccupation with material wealth, people knew what was of real significance in their lives. Living in communities interconnected with the people who resided in these locales. Stories were told and the storyteller's spirit was intertwined within the mystery of the story being told. Now with the era of instant communication, it's difficult to make that connection. Communication problems also developed as a result of children not being permitted to talk at the boarding and residential schools. How could they learn to communicate? Communication deficiencies are endemic throughout all Indian communities, and appear to be a problem across most cultures. Young people of all ages are addicted to technological devices, such as cell phones, computers, and Xboxes. Many people would rather text or read an email than pick up a phone or speak in person.

Another example of why anxiety based issues exist is shame based, the result of when one of their parents or themselves were called a "dirty savage," "drunken Indians" or other disparaging remarks. The effects of their parents' shame were passed down from generation to generation. These disapproving attacks also happened through their own self-hatred and the hatred of other Indian people, bred throughout history by the various forms of discrimination, genocide, and assimilation. Where did the parent who attended these boarding and residential schools learn his or her parenting skills? What if that parent raged unexpectedly or was withdrawn because of PTSD issues because of this parent's childhood history of abuse and neglect? What would a child learn from that kind of treatment? Would a child be able to form healthy, trusting relationships with others? In the *Remnants of a Shattered Past* chapter, the following effects of the acts of discrimination, genocide and assimilation were covered. These included:

- Pedagogy of the Oppressors
- The Impact of Shame and Post Traumatic Stress Disorder
- The Long-lasting Effects of Sexual Abuse

- Residential School and Boarding School Syndromes
- Malignant Trauma
- Ethnostress
- Historic Traumatic Transmission/Intergenerational Stress
- Loss of Culture
- Loss of Communication Skills

Many Indian people suffered at the hands of self-serving individuals. Some of the people in authority may have had well-meaning intent for what they did in the past. Whatever the reason for any destructive acts, the results of such acts have had long- lasting negative effects. The basic needs of the oppressed, such as love and nurturance were often not met when they were children. Also, other basic needs were neglected or pushed aside, and the end product is ethnostress. These unmet needs include:

- Being seen.
- Being heard in communication.
- Knowing their communication is accepted and believed.
- Knowing that others have faith and trust in them.
- Being allowed to take a place in the world.
- Feeling secure about, and at peace with one's self.

- Feeling that one's existence is not detrimental, but beneficial to the important people in one's life.[140]

It is very important to take note of the above losses and negative effects and give careful consideration to each and every one of them. All of the aftereffects of the various acts of abuse and discrimination need to be considered a part of the root cause behind today's high rates of alcoholism, suicide, poverty, domestic violence, child abuse and neglect.

The end results of anxiety based problems faced by the oppressed and the oppressors involve some or all of these personality traits:

- High Level of Creativity/Imagination
- Rigid Thinking
- Excessive Need for Approval
- Extremely High Expectations of Self
- Perfectionism
- Competent, Dependable "Doer"
- Excessive Need to Be in Control
- Suppression of Some or All Negative Feelings
- Tendency to Ignore the Body's Physical Needs[141]

To serve as a disclaimer to the above information, it needs to be noted that if anyone possesses any of these traits, it does not mean the individual suffers from anxiety based disorders and phobias. Some of the above results may not be considered negative side effects in and of themselves. However, if any of the results mentioned above are not harnessed and utilized properly, each of these results can be detrimental to the individual who possesses it. Take, for example, the shame issue as it relates to development of one's self-concept by how much they do for others. That person will end up ignoring their body's physical needs because the needs and wants of others have become paramount. A person may have undiagnosed PTSD as a result of chronic abuse and is suffering from hypertension, and high blood sugar that could lead towards the development of diabetes. However, this individual is suffering from his adrenals being stuck in the fight or flight mode and may need to address adrenal and cortisol issues instead. The real problem was not being taken care of and the person is suffering from insomnia, and other difficulties due to the excessive adrenal output and adrenal fatigue and is still feeling terrible because only the symptoms were being treated, not the main problem.

  As mentioned earlier, an Indian person may have been raised by a parent who was suffering from PTSD and as a result that parent was emotionally absent. His or her emotional needs as a child were not met. The history of each individual must be examined thoroughly. What trauma did this individual and others such as his or her grandparents and parents suffer that may have caused personal problems to surface? Healing and recovery can occur more efficiently once the individual gets to the bottom of things and develops the courage to heal.

Step Two: Healing, Recovery and Growth

In order to adhere to a healing process, it is vital to make <u>a decision to heal</u>, make the determination that <u>everyone deserves to heal</u>, decide it is <u>never too late to heal</u>, and understand that <u>it's not going to be easy</u> walking on the road to healing. Getting ready and motivated to begin the healing process needs to start with a plan of action. Set easy, short-term goals and list the steps it will take to achieve these goals. Find a person or group that can support one's efforts. Experiment for a month or two to determine if a program fits the needs and goals that have been set. Be sure to allow time to adjust to all healing efforts. It is important to be flexible and leave room for error. Visualize success.

Healing Rituals:

The individual needs to set up a ritual involving healing and place personal care in the forefront. Healing rituals may contain, but are not limited to, specific locations, props, personal support, healing words, and farewells to past traumatic events. Specific locations refer to a place where someone may have experienced trauma, serve as a way of coming to terms with the traumatic event, or alternately represent a place in which an individual feels safe. Flowers, candles, photographs and written speeches or sayings may serve as props. Personal support comes from people who demonstrate love and support. Photographs of caring individuals or remembrances of lost loved ones may provide comfort. These are some of the many ways to say farewell to past trauma. A suggestion could be to draw pictures of the feelings associated with traumatic events and either burying, burning or tearing and disposing of these memories as a way of providing solace. These rituals move healing forward when they are used on a regular basis.[142]

Meditation:
Another way to seek a more peaceful state is through meditation. It can be done in different ways, and it is more important to practice meditation than to primarily focus on technique. One can meditate while walking, sitting still, lying down or any other way in which the individual feels comfortable. Find a peaceful location and meditate and clear the mind of all intrusive thoughts. A good idea is to set up a specific time to meditate, such as right after waking up in the morning or before going to sleep. At the risk of sounding like a commercial, just do it.

Alternative Treatments:
For many people who are suffering from mental health issues, medicines used in the healing process can have serious side effects. Alternative forms of treatment, such as energy balancing exist that do not have these side effects. One form of energy balancing is Reiki massage, which is becoming more and more well known. It is a non-invasive form of treatment involving Therapeutic Touch techniques, coupled with the redirection of energy, positive intention, and other ancient techniques. Another alternative to modern allopathic medicine is the use of traditional healing services.

Medicine men and women still provide healing assistance, and many tribes provide these services for tribal members. These providers meet with individuals or groups of people to explore the problems someone may be facing. As far as groups are concerned, talking circles are often held to gain support and guidance. A feather or another object is passed around, and everyone gets a chance to speak when they are holding the feather. An Indian person may bring a question about a health problem they are facing or difficulties with a specific relationship. The medicine man or group will ponder the question and possibly beat a drum and smoke a pipe to seek guidance from the Great Mystery on how to help that person. A person may request a healing sweat lodge ceremony be held to assist with their healing. Herbal medicines may be provided to address ailments. An Indian person may be given instruction on what herbs and plants to seek to provide healing.

The Importance of Maintaining Cultural Identities:
Sometimes people can be their own worst enemy and do the opposite of what is needed. For example, many European Americans have lost touch with their cultural origins. A person of European descent once said "What about the white people? We left our families of origin to move to this country and forego our cultural ties to those communities we left behind. We have suffered also." Yes, many Euro-Americans did suffer. All of the people in the world resided in some form of tribal community during the distant past. For the sake of becoming mobile societies, people have lost valuable connections to their cultural roots.

To address spiritual deficiencies, individuals can explore their cultural roots. According to tribal ancestors, spirituality was of the utmost importance and needed to be developed fully starting at a young age for children. Children were encouraged to become aware of their dreams and learn how to examine the latent and manifest messages relayed by their dreams. Vision quests, fasting and other forms of communicating with one's higher power were strongly encouraged. All inanimate objects and animate beings possessed spirits requiring mutual respect and honor. Much of this close connection to the spiritual realm was lost through the legislation that banned traditional spiritual practices for Native Americans.

 Building a strong spiritual connection can provide strength and hope during difficult times. It can serve as a reminder that good and beautiful things co-exist in a world with violence and suffering. Spirituality is unique and personal and can be achieved in many ways, from a walk in the woods or belonging to a church, to participating in a 12 Step program. Prayer and meditation are other ways to seek spiritual solace. A life force does exist that makes things grow, makes rain, rivers, mountain ranges, and the perfect banana. Childbirth is another representation of the miracle and mystery of life. Spirituality is the maintaining of a connection to a part of each individual who wants to seek a healthy, integrated, fully alive life.

 The results of the Aboriginal Healing Project in Canada demonstrated the importance of returning to one's cultural heritage. As part of this healing project, cultural interventions were applied along with modern day, traditional, and/or alternative therapies. Cultural identities were reaffirmed through activities such as pow wows, feasts, immersion in traditional art, language, dancing, storytelling, music, and drumming. These activities provided a source for empowerment and were considered an essential component to holistic healing.[143]

Personal Empowerment:
    Instilling empowerment is a vital step for anyone who has faced the effects of any form of trauma. Empowerment is usually best served on a platter of useful educational tools that have the potential for meeting a specific individual's needs. Libraries, book stores, the offices of healers and mental health counselors, tribal social service departments, and Internet sources can serve as locations for securing the necessary educational tools to assist one with the healing process. This involves taking care of one's four selves: physical, emotional, spiritual and intellectual. Others like to refer to having three selves: mind, body and spirit. The emotional and spiritual sides can be lumped together because each one feeds the other. If one's emotional well-being has been negatively impacted, the rest of the individual is off balance physically, spiritually and intellectually.

    Chronic stress damages the body, mind, spirit and emotional state. Historical trauma has led individuals to feel that they are in constant danger and/or distress. As a result of this stress it has been demonstrated that the following symptoms may occur, but not limited to: gastrointestinal distress; high blood cholesterol; insomnia; low back pain; decreased immune system; and high blood pressure. Some of the ways to counteract these harmful effects are: making a commitment to self, work, family, and other important aspects of one's life; maintaining a sense of personal control over one's life; and achieving the ability to see change as a challenge to overcome the barriers to achieving balance and contentment.

Emotional Intelligence:

Emotional intelligence is considered one of the most important qualities to possess when it comes to surviving in all social relationships. It is associated with the ability to perceive, access, and manage one's personal emotions. Emotional intelligence also includes possessing an understanding of the emotions experienced by others and by groups of individuals. Fortune 500 groups include questions on interview forms to evaluate the most viable applicants to fill their employment positions by assessing their level of emotional intelligence. People do not need to be experts in the area of emotional intelligence. However, at the very least, one needs to have an understanding of personal emotions and why these emotions are occurring. For example, what is behind one's anger, sadness or feelings of depression? It is also vital to take steps to protect an individual's emotional well-being, even if it means leaving a situation that may be causing harm to a person's psyche.

It is imperative to learn to recognize and name feelings. Naming emotions leads to a sense of control over them. When noticing feelings it is important to observe the process without passing judgment. It is okay to feel a certain way without feeling guilty. An individual's feelings are not right or wrong, they just exist as a result of one's perception of a circumstance.

Feelings normally make sense once examined. Something happens, the situation is thought about, and feelings occur. Try to identify the thoughts associated with the feelings or the trigger that may be related to past trauma. Reminding oneself that these feelings and thoughts are safe now is very important. Writing out troublesome thoughts in a journal is a great releasing activity. It is important to develop skills that assist with managing symptoms associated with a variety of stress related mental health issues, such as PTSD.

Survival Skills for the Healing Process:
Undergoing the healing process can be a daunting task. The task involves the understanding and treatment of the harmful effects relating to years of trauma or current harmful situations. Rehashing hurtful memories can lead to the resurfacing of the feelings relating to past traumatic events.

Survival skills for healing can be established, and these may include:
- Overcoming isolation by developing a support system, learning how to ask for help, and assessing current relationships.
- Getting enough sleep and proper nutrition are imperative to the achievement of a healthy and satisfying lifestyle.
- Exercising to alleviate stress. (Make sure to consult a physician before undergoing an exercise regime.)
- Letting go of resentments.

- Living the examined life, looking at what works and doesn't work concerning the living of a healthy lifestyle, and making adjustments.
- Setting healthy boundaries.
- Improving communication skills.
- Exploring activities that are not destructive, such as playing games, being creative, listening to or playing music, and other forms of enjoyable activities.
- Practicing gratitude and applying humor as much as possible.
- Becoming involved in community activities to instill and participate in acts of giving.

Therapeutic Interventions:

Do not under estimate the value of counseling. Recently, it has been discovered that PTSD can be caused by chronic abuse. Therapeutic treatment of PTSD and other mental health issues can be enhanced when the therapist applies sound treatment practices. Best practice is when the therapist shares control with the client possessing primary control. Also in best practice, the therapist explores any fears associated with treatment and is skilled in forging a strong therapeutic partnership. Mutual respect is vital for sustaining and maintaining all relationships at a healthy level.

The Importance of Proper Nutrition and Exercise:
    Many tribes provide nutritional services and exercise facilities for their tribal members. Other ways exist for people to obtain nutritional information, such as the Internet and health departments. Health departments are prevalent all over the country. Walking can be a great way to deal with stress and work on one's spirituality at the same time. Being one with nature can promote a sense of well-being and also provide the privacy necessary to commune with an individual's higher power.

    Everyone who has engaged in regular types of exercise, either moderate or more strenuous, knows how effective it is in reducing stress. Exercise has been known to reduce muscle tension and other symptoms associated with stress without the side effects of medication. It can improve self-esteem and overall general mental health, reduce blood pressure, increase energy levels, improve immunity, strengthen the heart, improve the quality of sleep, and encourage weight loss. Exercise can expend and dissipate the energy of a stress reaction, assist with returning the body to a more restful state, and also serves as a distraction from everyday problems. Exercise can assist with the achievement of a better frame of mind when problems occur. People who participate in exercise activities on a regular basis are more productive by accomplishing more in less time. Start an exercise program by determining a specific comfort level, and build up gradually to more strenuous activity over time.

    Please consult with a health care provider prior to beginning an exercise program.

The Benefits of Forgiveness:
Forgiveness of those who have personally caused harm to an individual, the individual's family or significant others can serve as a release. In the *Course of Miracles* "all dis-ease comes from a state of unforgiveness," and it is further explained that "whenever we are ill, we need to look around to see who it is that we need to forgive." Louise L. Hay also adds that the very person an individual finds hardest to forgive is the one needed to be let go of the most. Forgiveness has nothing to do with condoning unjust and unkind behaviors, it means letting things go. [144]

True forgiveness of self and others involves confronting the truth about the harmful situation and then feeling the emotions associated with the situation head on, not holding back at all. By experiencing feelings as deeply as possible, even feelings of anger towards the individual who may have caused harm can be released. Remember, everyone makes mistakes. Generally, it is more harmful for the person who is holding onto the resentments than the person who appears to have caused the resentment. Everyone has been hurt at one point or another. Life is unfair. People will hurt others and there will not always be an understanding as to why. Release those hurt feelings. Holding onto resentments is linked to several physical problems consisting of, but not limited to, increased blood pressure, weakened immune system, depression and impaired memory. "Bitterness is like

drinking poison and waiting for the other person to die."
145

Examination of feelings concerning forgiveness towards one's parents is a necessary component to the healing process. Everyone who wants to be mentally healthy need to come to terms with their parents whether they consider them to have been either good or bad parents. Children do not possess the intellectual and emotional tools to admit their parents' harmful behaviors are not the result of something the child has done. When parents are at war with each other, a child's loyalties are strained. This is most likely the case in a majority of households because of the high divorce rate. Many Native American households are plagued with poverty, domestic violence, substance abuse, child abuse and neglect and can oftentimes feel like a war zone.

The boarding and residential schools encouraged children to feel contempt and hatred for their parents, and self-hatred was promoted. As a result of these negative thoughts and feelings, added to the experiences of multiple forms of abuse, self-damaging behaviors occur, especially substance abuse to self-medicate, numbing the pain. It is important to accept what has occurred during one's childhood. With a caring support system, one can experience all the feelings head on from joy to sorrow. Mourning a lost childhood is vital to overcome childhood trauma. Most people have set beliefs of how parents should treat their children. When parents fall short of these beliefs, the adult child often feels cheated.

Hay is experienced in providing services to those who are suffering from poor health, lack of money, unsatisfactory relationships, or even repressed creativity and ties these problems with not loving the self. Holding oneself hostage to resentments is associated with not loving the self. Hay suggests that individuals need to love, accept, and approve themselves just as they are and individuals need to consider that no matter where they are in their growth, that they are a work in progress. Self-approval and self-acceptance are a couple of the main ingredients that can lead to positive changes in every area of one's life. That process can begin with never criticizing oneself. Self criticism can lock individuals into the pattern they are trying to change, which is oftentimes referred to as a self-fulfilling prophecy. If a person tells him or herself that they possess these negative characteristics, they become the very things they are trying to avoid or disapprove. [146]

Overcoming Sexual Abuse:

History is repeating itself in many of the homes of Indian people, as well as people of all races. Sexual abuse raised its ugly head too frequently for children who resided at the boarding and residential schools. Every child was sexually abused and/or witnessed children being taken away at night. It is recommended that anyone who has been exposed to or suffered from sexual abuse should seek mental health counseling and follow all the recommendations portrayed in this chapter as well as in other valuable sources. One recommended source is *The Courage to Heal: A Guide for Women Survivors of Child Sexual Abuse.* This book would also benefit the male segment of the population. First and foremost, individuals who have experienced this kind of abuse must not blame themselves and must not feel they are crazy. Sexual abuse can cause a whole host of problems within one's psyche. In the *Remnants of Shattered Past* chapter a long list of possible effects was included involving sexual abuse.

When individuals are in the survival mode, their systems are in a state of chaos, and they usually are experiencing deep pain, emotionally and often physically. If one could visualize their mental, emotional, spiritual and physical state, especially if they have suffered from chronic trauma, it would appear as a disorganized mess. A good example of this state might be the condition of a teenager's room after a long period of time of not picking up after themselves. Just like the teenager's messy room, nothing is accounted for or where it should be. Try to find the lost white sock in that mess. It's next to impossible. With PTSD and shame issues, for example, one's coping skills have been overwhelmed. When a trigger is encountered, it is next to impossible to pull out of someone's skills the necessary tool to handle that specific trigger. The tools may be disorganized and have been worn to the point of being non-usable after years of over use. It is important to develop new coping skills to prevent any future damage as the result of further attacks on one's psyche.

Step Three: Prevention

Healing can be enhanced with the aid of appropriate coping skills. These skills can serve to prevent further harm to one's emotional being. Developing a sound coping plan is essential for maintaining the balance attained after dealing with or resolving mental health issues. Part of the plan may include set, self-instructional statements, which can provide assistance with navigating through future difficult experiences. Imagine stressful situations and apply the process of eliminating fruitless thoughts and actions. A common feature of trauma victims is their inability to look at the future with positive anticipation. They approach the future with a gloom and doom attitude such as "I'll never be all right," which is a fruitless thought. The preplanned thought process will include what to do with stress provoking situations that may occur in the future. What the stress level was before, during and after the feared circumstance needs to be carefully examined.

The feared situation can be broken down into manageable parts. Picture a positive event before and after the feared situation, an experience that was less stress provoking. Place more importance on the positive events and less on what is fearful. Break the feared situation into incremental portions and think about what is needed for each section. Most difficult feelings such as fear, frustration, anxiety, worry, anger, jealousy, loneliness and envy can be addressed by taking the following steps:

- Take care of one's physical self through nutrition, exercise, and getting enough sleep.
- Avoid toxic and harmful situations.
- See difficult situations as possible blessings in disguise.
- Make a plan for recovery and set up a support system. Part of the support system needs to include alternative activities to replace the destructive ones such as the use of alcohol.
- Isolate the feeling that one wants to be free from; identify triggers for the feeling; frame the feeling from a spiritual perspective.
- Make a spiritual connection to center oneself by meditating, listen to one's intuition, practice gratitude, and help others (redirects thoughts).

Alcohol use can be replaced with a whole host of activities. What one enjoys doing can be explored. For many Indian people, alcohol took the place of spiritual practices when they were outlawed. Removal from their cultural heritage along with the consequences of chronic trauma has led Indian people to use alcohol as a method of self-medicating to deaden the pain. However, once people are undergoing the healing process, they can take part in other activities that are less damaging. If money is an issue, go for a walk instead of being immobilized on the sofa.

Other options for entertainment might be board games or sports. Reconnecting with the outside world is very important. Volunteering in programs that provide service to others, such as community activities is excellent for building one's self-esteem. People need people. All people are meant to be social beings. Seek peers who will provide support, encouragement, and aid in the building of self-esteem.

  Explore a variety of ways to be creative, then create. It will improve the health of relationships and provide something interesting to share with others. When discussing creativity with an elder, the elder relayed, "The Creator wants us to be creative, hence the name Creator." One can find a vast amount of satisfaction in exploring various kinds of creativity. It can serve as a release for pent up feelings by expressing oneself with different forms of art, such as painting, sculpting, drawing and writing. Navajo people are renowned for the weaving of rugs, and making silver jewelry and pottery to provide for their families, serve as a source of income, and to serve as an alternative to other damaging activities. Indian people from other tribes have done similar creative work. One Navajo man said he replaced his alcohol problem with artwork. What a beautiful way to seek healing and remain healthy.

  Another vital point that needs to be presented is to not take oneself too seriously. It is all right to make mistakes, and seeing life through the lens of humor provides an escape valve from life's pressures. By being able to laugh at oneself, an individual can become more candid and self-accepting. A link exists between humor, truth and self-esteem, and when one is in control of life, she or he can laugh at themselves more. The more serious the subject, the more potential it has to be humorous. Problems need to exist in order for there to be humor. Store humorous memories and pull them out when life throws curve balls.

    Financial problems have been identified as the reason why most divorces occur and why there is disharmony in a home. Money problems can be the source of anxiety, insomnia and depression, because money represents security, control and power. Many people let income serve as a form of identification of who has succeeded and who has not. Realize that no amount of income will ever be large enough. People with large incomes also suffer from various mental health issues. Overspending can result in loss of self esteem and self value.

    Ways of overcoming budgeting problems are to seek assistance from community resources that provide budgeting education, set up a budgeting plan, and find ways to enjoy life without spending a lot of money. The best things in life are not things. Ways of getting the most for your money include visiting thrift shops to supply the family's needs. Purchasing generic brands is another way to save money. Priorities should be set concerning wants versus needs. Wants need to be considered of lesser importance than needs. With the push for immediate gratification in this country, this is easier said than done. More importance has been placed on junk food, television viewing and video game playing than on the significance of adequate nutrition and exercise.

Setting boundaries may be difficult for people who have been sexually abused or have suffered other forms of mental distress. However, clear emotional boundaries enable individuals to experience themselves as separate from others. Others do not think or feel as they do, interests and needs are different, and do not necessarily reflect on the person of interest. It may be helpful to think of one's self as a beautiful home, lovely inside and out. This home is a place of joy and comfort, a safe place with strong doors and windows from which to explore the world. Around the home is a sturdy fence. Each individual has the authority to decide who may enter their home including a guest, neighbor, friend, or family member. Past trauma blew open the doors, and a feeling of powerlessness overcame the security of his/her home. However, now this individual is in control. Setting strong boundaries enables one to assume responsibility for his or her actions and attitudes. Realize one does not have to assume responsibility for the action of others. [148]

Depression can be completely destructive to anyone who is plagued with its effects resulting from physical and psychological causes. Ways to become less vulnerable to depression are: Attend to the basics of sleep, diet and exercise; and clarify values and goals. Do things that are pleasurable such as dancing, listening to music or whatever is enjoyable and not harmful to one's well-being. When an individual is off balance, it is often due to what is valued being in contradiction with what one is actually doing.

If an individual is suffering from deep depression it is also important to: Seek professional help, create rewards for small achievements, reduce tasks to manageable amounts, and do not try to do too much. Build supportive relationships. When making the attempt to dig out of depression, use a diary to log how time is spent, rate the activities to determine skill level and enjoyment, troubleshoot if mastery and enjoyment are an issue, and develop plans on how to spend the day. Naming or labeling one's depression also gives the individual more control of their life. Accept the fact that everyone's life comes with bumps and hardships.

Learning how to "fight" may prevent more harm to an individual's psyche. Naming of one's feelings and using "I" messages during heated exchanges are good forms of self defense. Saying things like "you make me…" or "you are…" may put someone on the defensive. When people are defensive, they feel as if they have been backed into a corner and have to come out swinging to protect themselves. People often say things they regret before they have had a chance to calm down. A good rule of thumb is to take an intermission for a short period of time, an hour or so, or perhaps even a day, and then regroup when tempers have subsided. Then discuss the problem in a calmer fashion. Enhanced people skills will create a more meaningful connection with others.

Listening is the essential skill when it comes to building strong, healthy relationships. However, researchers have documented that approximately 75% of what is spoken is ignored, misunderstood, or forgotten. In carrying dialogue, while one person is expressing what is on his or her mind, the other should be carefully examining what is being said. Imagine being present during an important conversation about a problematic situation. If a stressful feeling has been shared by the speaker, it would be disheartening and difficult to believe anything has been heard if the listener's reaction is automatic or unconscious. The most skilled listener is one who can focus intently on the speaker's words as well as the deeper meaning behind them, and then express an understanding of the meaning and words. In most conversations there must be a grain of truth to find, decipher, and then reflect back. If the verbal exchange is volatile, disarm the outraged person by responding in a calm, respectful manner. For conversations to be mutually effective there must be give and take, not one in which only one opinion matters. When these listening skills are used, communication can sound like a well-orchestrated symphony.

  Gratitude is essential and a great way to diffuse any uncomfortable feelings one is experiencing. It is impossible to be grateful and angry at the same time. Gratitude is a positive way to counteract the anger an individual may be feeling towards the people who have inflicted harm on them. Individuals need to count their blessings. An individual can start with feeling blessed for even the small things, such as having a roof over one's head and thinking about how difficult it is for the homeless people in the world. It has been noted that people who tend to be more optimistic have fewer health problems and live longer.

Associated with gratitude to a large degree is the changing of life stories. Life stories are usually based on fiction that is developed from personal perceptions. That is why a brother may see the experiences of his childhood completely different from what his sister may seem them as. Try changing these stories to having a positive ending or teaching a valuable lesson and see what happens. Earlier there was information regarding experiencing feelings towards traumatic events fully. That needs to be done first and then change personal views of life stories. Turn the stories into humorous anecdotes on how to address problems life may throw your way. Also, look at life as one's own creation.

Try to turn the problems that have surfaced from past experiences into lessons. "Mistakes are only mistakes if you don't learn from them." These lessons can be learned by leading the examined life. That means involving the examination of all things an individual has experienced, good and bad. Deb Ford wrote a book entitled *Spiritual Divorce,* and this book could be used in numerous stress causing situations, not only divorce. According to Ford, there are no accidents. If someone was married to a batterer, for example, why did this occur? What needed to be learned from that situation? This question can be applied to the batterer as well as the battered. A person's world is filled with a wealth of experiences to be examined. A multitude of opportunities exist to counteract the harmful effects caused by chronic and acute episodes of trauma.

Step Four: Rebuilding Communities

     The Anishanaabeg existed in a life that was peaceful and harmonious within their village with a feeling of connectedness and congeniality before the onset of the European invasion. Everyone worked together to supply the needs of the whole village. Sometimes there were battles between opposing tribes over resources; however, amongst the tribal villages there was a cohesive balance and respect for all of the village dwellers. Leaders were chosen due to their wisdom and care for the well-being of all of the tribal members. Each tribal member had a specific role within the tribe and that role was honored and respected by the other villagers. Everyone listened to others' opinions and thoughts and these ideas were formulated into possible solutions to various problems or possibilities for the future.

     Today, many people of all races need to replace isolation and self involvement with caring and connectedness. Technology has run rampant and instead of globalization making people feel more connected, its driving people further and further apart. A multitude of people are sitting in front of computers, holding cell phones while texting and monitoring email accounts. So many people are mesmerized by these technological advances and have lost touch with meaningful relationships with others, a relationship that involves a complete psychological, spiritual, and emotional commitment.

Social service agencies, hospitals, neighborhoods, businesses, corporations, and governments operate in their own worlds, and are primarily concerned with their own purpose. A high importance is placed on efficiency in regards to providing services, working near one another without overlapping. It's an assembly line approach, fix the problem move onto the next problem, and so on. The term possibility hasn't even entered most of the minds of these service providers. Everyone is problem focused.

Peter Block made mention in his book *Community: The Structure of Belonging* about the aspect of fragmentation relating to the gaps between various sectors in the United States, sectors being defined as neighborhoods, businesses, governments, and social welfare agencies. A definite separation is occurring between all these entities, and they are operating independently of each another. The people of this country are fragmented into pieces. This dilemma is occurring as a result of the individualistic mindset influenced by the media and the isolation experienced by many in this country due to a lack of connectedness.[149]

The power of language is something that requires attention. Dialogue and communication are important tools for improvement. A shift in speaking and listening is essential for any meaningful transformation to happen. There can be a change in conversation to evolve from conversations that are held on a regular basis to those in which something new can be created in the world. This new type of conversation can bring into question how much value is placed on personal stories, the positions taken, concern about the past, and a way of being in the world. Personal worldviews are strongly associated with reflections of the past, and these thoughts and ideas can be brought into the future context. That is when problems can be transformed into possibilities.

People from different ethnic groups, especially Indian people, are still living on the fringe of society, being marginalized and treated as if they have nothing worthy to offer. Rules, mandates, legislation and other forms of control have rendered the provision of social welfare systems useless. These services are not addressing the needs of the people. The needs involve care, generosity, and a feeling of connectedness, the care and generosity of people who altruistically provide for others without concern of receiving payment of any sort, only for its own sake.

Block states that individuals need to decide to be accountable to one's commitments to others and the community and country as a whole. President John F. Kennedy said, "Ask not what your country can do for you, ask what you can do for your country." Too much responsibility is placed on the leaders in this country. If things do not improve or go wrong, people are quick to blame one man for the mistakes of many. The definition of a citizen is one who is willing to be accountable for and makes a commitment to the well-being of the whole. An atmosphere of generosity towards others, and a collective mindset of possibility are some of the ingredients for a well-balanced community. The persons residing on the margins need to be brought to the center to be enlisted in this campaign. They are citizens with valuable insight to share. "When we are open to thinking along the line that citizens create leaders, that children create parents, and that the audience creates the performance, we create the conditions for the widespread accountability and the commitment that emerges from it."

There needs to be a transformation from independence to interdependence. People need people. When Block referred to systems, he listed them as an organized group of well-funded professionals who provide services to a caseload of clients. Systems can provide services, but not care. He mentioned that these clients received services; however, their lives primarily remained the same. Block suggested that what was missing was the associational life, one in which a group of individuals come together as volunteers to do public good. Another missing element is that communities can come together and solve problems for themselves. Ownership in any project leads to one desiring that the project is successful. [150]

Realistically, there is a need for the entire population to earn an income to pay for taxes, utilities, and other necessities. These needs are not going to disappear. Many small groups of individuals donating their time after hours spent earning an income is feasible. A neighbor stopping by to see if he or she could use help with anything from house repair to assisting with the care of children. Count the hours spent watching one meaningless show after another on television. Communities are built by focusing on people's gifts rather than on their deficiencies. "In the community and volunteerism, deficiencies have no market value; gifts are the point. Citizens in community want to know what you can do, not what you can't do."[151] Volunteering to help others is very rewarding and there are so many ways to do so. If everyone in the community volunteered to help others, including those in need, think about how wonderful things could be.

Syracuse Cultural Workers suggested ways in which to build a community:

"Turn off you TV*Leave your house*Know your neighbors

Look up when you are walking*Greet people

Sit on your stoop*Plant flowers*Use your library

Play together*Buy from local merchants*Share what you have

Help a lost dog*Take children to the park*Garden together

Support neighborhood schools*Fix it even if you didn't break it

Have potlucks*Honor elders*Pick up litter*Read stories aloud

Dance in the street*Talk to the mail carrier*Listen to the birds

Barter for your goods*Start a tradition*Ask a question

Hire young people for odd jobs*Organize the block party

Bake extra and share*Ask for help when you need it

Open your shades*Sing together*Share your skills...
Listen before you react to anger*Mediate a conflict
Seek to understand*Learn from new and uncomfortable angles
Know that no one is silent though many are not heard*
Work to change this."

In conclusion, this chapter was not meant to solve all problems existing today, but to make the point that there is a need to find out why problems such as the high rates of child abuse, neglect and alcoholism still exist for so many Indian people. The problem goes much deeper than depression, substance abuse, or learned behaviors. A multitude of people may be suffering from the ills of PTSD, shame and/or malignant trauma, and these mental health problems are not being addressed. The residential and boarding school syndrome involves a host of mental health issues that permeate today's society. Lack of communication skills has also caused much angst along with the loss of culture. Problems can only be addressed when they are acknowledged correctly. A transformation from seeing these issues as problems to viewing them as possibilities to enhance positive growth can occur. It is reassuring to know that the future for many is within the scope of hope.

Notes

Introduction

[1] American Psychological Association. (Volume 35, No.9, October 2004). *Statistics show mental health services still needed for native populations.* Retrieved November 4, 2009, from http://www.apa.org/monitor/oct04/servicew.html.

[2] J. Dale-Burton, (November 5, 2010). *Suicide prevention program waging its war.* Win Awenen Nisitotun.

[3] M. Berry & C. Reynoso (Chairperson and Vice Chairperson), et. al., (September 2004). *Broken Promises: Evaluating the Native American Health Care System.* Washington, DC: U.S. Commission on Civil Rights.

[4] J. Redfied, (1997). *The Celestine Vision: Living the New Spiritual Awareness.* New York: Warner Book, Inc.

[5] D. Sharpes, (Vol. 19, No. 1, October 1979). Journal of American Indian Education. *Federal Education for the American Indian.* Retrieved on 8/25/2009 from http://jaieasu.edu/v19/V19S1fed.html.

[6] D. Kipper & S. Whitney, (2010). *The Addiction Solution.* New York: Rodale, Inc., 197-202.

[7] Ibid, 200.

Chapter I: Beginnings

[8] Andrews,T. (2006). *Animal Speak: The Spiritual and Magical Powers of Creatures Great and Small.* Minnesota: Llewellyn Publications, 262-264.

[9] Ibid, 303-304.

[10] The bags were referred to as Mide bags. Everyone with the exception of childen in the village carried a medicine bag. These bags were connected to the legend tied with the four Mide manido with the colors of the dawn painted on their foreheads carrying the live otters. The bags have been made of weasel skin, bear skin, wildcat skin, mink skin and the skin of a rattlesnake. Densmore, F. (1979). *Chippewa Customs.* Minnesota: Minnesota Historical Society Press, 93.

[11] Ibid, 70–71.

[12] Densmore explained how the young girls were watched closely by the parents. He also described the issue of jealousy between the young girls and how this led to spirited fighting. Densmore, F.

(1979). *Chippewa Customs*. Minnesota: Minnesota Historical Society Press, 1979, 72-73.

[13] Hilger included information different types of ceremonies such as neighbors, both men and women, as soon as they heard the sound of a gun would go to the home of the newborn baby. They would gather outside of the wigwam near the place in which the baby was lying on the inside and would shoot their guns and would pretend they were going to snatch the child. The other villagers would tap the baby and tell it to be strong. Water was thrown on the intruders by the mother and her relatives. The father or any of his relatives would not partake in this ceremony. They were running around the baby to protect the baby. Even though this ceremony was not carried out often, when it was the child would do well and become a warrior or some other important person such as a leader of the village. Hilger,M. (1992). *Chippewa Child Life and Its Cultural Background*. Minnestota: Minnesota Historical Society Press, 19.

Chapter II: Traditional Period

[14] Benton-Banai,E. (1981). *The Mishomis Book: The Voice of the Ojibway*. Minnesota: Indian Country Press, Inc., 89-93.

[15] Peacock, T. and Wisuri, M. (2002). *Ojibwe Waasa Inaabidaa: We Look In All Directions*. Minnesota: Afton Historical Society Press, 23.

[16] Benton-Banai, E. (1981). *The Mishomis Book: The Voice of the Ojibway* (Minnesota: Indian Country Press, Inc., 1981), 75-79.

[17] Peacock, T., and Wisuri, M. (2002). *Ojibwe Waasa Inaabidaa: We Look In All Directions*. Minnesota: Afton Historical Society Press, 28.

[18] Ibid, 64-89.

[19] Peacock, T.and Wisuri, M. (2002). *Ojibwe Waasa Inaabidaa: We Look In All Directions*. Minnesota: Afton Historical Society Press, 64-77.

[20] Hilger,I. *Chippewa Child Life and Its Cultural Background*. Minnesota: Minnesota Historical Society Press,58.

[21] Benton-Banai, E. (1981). *The Mishomis Book: The Voice of he Ojibway*. Minnesota: Indian Country Press, Inc., 30-35.

[22] Densmore, F. (1979). *Chippewa Customs* .Minnesota: Minnesota Historical Society Press, 52.

Chapter III: Eagle and Coyote Travel with Columbus
[23] D'Souza, D. (1995). *The End of Racism.* New York: Simon and Schuster, 35.
[24] Columbus was very aware of Ferdinand's and Isabella's commercial desires, so he had to get to work and capture the trusting Indians. It was estimated there were two to four million inhabitants on what is known today as Haiti. Recent estimate brings the number of inhabitants to eight million. By 1520, the population was reduced to 20,000 inhabitants. Wilson, J. (1998) *The Earth Shall Weep: A History of Native America..* New York: Grove Press, 34.
[25] Bigelow, B., and Peterson, B. (Eds.). (1998). *Rethinking Columbus: The Next 500 Years.* Wisconsin: Rethinking Schools, 19.
[26] Fernandez-Armesto, F. (1991). *Columbus.* Oxford: Oxford University Press, 67-69.
[27] "The idea of reading this document could genuinely absolve the Spanish from all responsibility for their action now seems completely mad – and, indeed, it had its critics at the time, notably the great humanitarian churchman Bartolome' de las Casas, who said it make him wonder whether to 'laugh or cry.' But at some level, if only the level of wishful thinking, it clearly satisfied some urgent need for the Conquistadores: in a world of manic legalism, where only adherence to the outward forms of the true faith was ultimately important and where everything could be forgiven by following a church-sanctioned mechanism, it was able to assure them of the justice of their cause and the salvation of their souls." Wilson, J. (1998) *The Earth Shall Weep: A History of Native America.* New York: Grove Press, 36.
[28] Ibid.
[29] Columbus used the Chip log and Reel to measure the speed of the ships he sailed. The speed was based on the knots of the rope that was released from a large reel. *Chip Log.* Retrieved on June 18, 2009 from http://en.wikipedia.org/wiki/Chip_log.
[30] Tirado, T. (2000). *Christopher Columbus.* Retrieved on June 6, 2008 from http://www.millersville.edu/~columbus/columbus.html.
[31] Ibid.

Chapter IV: Eagle and Coyote's Adventures with French Settlers
[32] Conlan,R. (1994). *People of the Lakes: The Native Americans.* Virginia: Time-Life Education, 141.

[33] Nies, J. (1996). *A Chronology of a Culture's Vast Achievements and Their Links to World Events.* New York: Ballentine Books, 75-98.
[34] Conlan, R. (1994). *People of the Lakes: The Native Americans.* Virginia: Time-Life Education, 133.
[35] The Jesuits learned the Indian languages and it was suggested that the Indian people kept their cultures in tact while they converted to Christianity. O'Brien, G. (2008). *World History Timeline, The Timeline of Native Americans: The Ultimate Guide to North America's Indigenous Peoples.* San Diego: Thunder Bay Press, 81.
[36] The purpose and reasoning behind the Jesuit order in the chapter entitled *The Company of Ignatius* was delineated as all on earth was considered subordinate and those who were divined to spread the word of the Gospel were chosen to do so. There was an election for General of the Jesuits orders and these were elected positions. Martin, M. (1987). *The Jesuits: The Society of Jesus and the Betrayal of the Roman Catholic Church.* New York: Simon and Schuster,188-199.
[37] Nies, J. (1996). *A Chronology of a Culture's Vast Achievements and Their Links to World Events.* New York: Ballentine Books, 132.
[38] Wikipedia. Retrieved on May 7, 2010 from http://en.wikipedia.org/wiki/newfrance.org.
[39] Conlan, R. (1994). *People of the Lakes: The Native Americans.* Virginia: Time-Life Education, 142.

Chapter V: Power and Control Through Patriarchal Domination and the Church
[40] Howard-Brook, W. (2001). *The Church Before Christianity.* New York: Orbis Books, 2.
[41] Corey, G., Corey, M., and Callanan, P. (1998). *Issues and Ethics: In the Helping Professions.* California: Brooks/Cole Publishing Company, 82-83.
[42] Williston, R., (2003). *Native American Spirituality:A Walk in the Woods.* Ohio: Rainbow Light and Company.
[43] Fox, M. (1988). *The Coming of the Cosmic Christ.* San Francisco: Harper Collins, 11-34.
[44] Blond, A. (1994). *The Private Live of the Roman Emperors.* London: Constable and Robinson Ltd., 178 – 185.
[45] Marshall, D. (2007). *The Truth About Jesus and the Lost Gospels.* Oregon: Harvest House Publishers, 6.
[46] Ibid, 23.

[47] Ibid, 71.
[48] Freke, T., and Gandy,P. (1999). *The Jesus Mysteries: Was the "Original Jesus" a Pagan God?* New York: Three Rivers Press, 6-8.
[49] Prophet, M., and Prophet, E. (1988). *The Lost Teachings of Jesus: Missing Texts, Karma, and Reincarnation.* New York: Summit University Press, 173-179.
[50] Thorn, J. *Early Quaker History.* Retrieved on August 9, 2010 from http://thorn.pair.com/earlyq.htm.
[51] Podles, L. (2008). *Sacrilege: Sexual Abuse in the Catholic Church.* Maryland: Crossland Press.
[52] Buechner, F. (1993). *Wishful Thinking: A Seeker's ABC.* San Francisco: Harper Collins Publishers, 27-28.
[53] Greeley,A. (2007). *Jesus: A Meditation of His Stories and His Relationship with Women.* New York: Tom Doherty Associates, LLC, 58-106.
[54] Marshall, D. (2007). *The Truth About Jesus and the Lost Gospels.* Oregon: Harvest House Publishers, 49.
[55] Pavlac, B. *Timeline for the Witchhunts.* Retrieved on November 23, 2010 from http://departments.kings.edu/womens_history/witch/worigin.html
[56] Bonfanti,L. (1992). *The Witchcraft Hysteria of 1692: Volume 2.* Massachusetts: Old Saltbox Publishing.
[57] Spong,J. (2005). *The Sins of the Scriptures: Exposing the Bible's Text of Hate to Reveal the God of Love.* New York: Harper One, 68-100.
[58] Marshall, D. (2007). *The Truth About Jesus and the Lost Gospels.* Oregon: Harvest House Publishers, 124.
[59] Williston, R., and Williston,M. (2009). *The Ancient Roots of Christianity: A Native American's Look Through Christianity.* Ohio: Rainbow Light and Co.,178.
[60] Buechner, F. (1993). *Wishful Thinkig: A Seeker's ABC.* San Francisco: Harper Collins Publishers, 96.
[61] Marshall,M. (2007). *The Truth About Jesus and the Lost Gospels.* Oregon: Harvest House Publishers, 44-45.
[62] Ibid, 33.
[63] Ehrman, B. (2009). *Jesus, Interrupted: Revealing the Hidden Contradictions in the Bible.* New York: Harper Collins Publishers, 19-20.
[64] Ehrman, B., (2009). *Jesus Interrupted: Revealing the Hidden Contraditions in the Bible.* New York: Harper Collins Publishers, 6-7.

[65] Keller,T. (2008). *The Reason for God: Belief in an Age of Skepticism.* New York: Riverhead Books, 103.
[66] James, R., and Williston, M. (2009). *The Ancient Roots of Christianity: A Native American's Look Through Christianity.* Ohio: Rainbow Light and Co., 30-32.
[67] Fox, M. (1988). *The Coming of the Cosmic Christ.* San Francisco: Harper Collins, 11-34.

Chapter VI: The Realization of Manifest Destiny
[68] Diamond, J. (1999). *Guns, Germs, and Steel: The Fates of Human Societies.* New York: Simon and Schuster, 197.
[69] Holms, T. (1996). *Strong Hearts Wounded Souls: Native American Veterans of the Vietnam War.* Texas: University of Texas Press, 83-89.
[70] Hall, M., Schaessens, C., Connelly, K., & Connelly, R.(Eds.). (2007). *Great American Documents: The Landmark Documents in Our History.* London: Quercus Publishing, 29.
[71] Ellis,J. (2007). *American Creation.* New York: Vintage Books, 131 – 132.
[72] Utter,J. (1993). *American Indians: Answers to Today's Questions.* Nebraska: University of Oklahoma,86.
[73] Ellis,J. (2007). *American Creation.* New York: Vintage Books, 135.
[74] Ambrose, S. (1996). *Undaunted Courage: Meriwther Lewis, Thosmas Jefferson, and the Opening of the American West.* New York: Simon and Schuster Paperbacks, 154.
[75] Merk,F. (1963). *Manifest Destiny and Mission in American History.* Toronto: Random House of Canada Limited, 24-60.
[76] Ambrose, S. (1996). *Undaunted Courage: Meriwther Lewis, Thomas Jefferson, and the Opening of the American West.* New York: Simon and Schuster Paperbacks, 13-14.
[77] Sugden,J. (1997). *Tecumseh: A Life.* New York: Henry Holt and Company, 215.
[78] Henry Schoolcraft accomplished many things from exploration and geologic survey to many published works. He served at Fort Brady in Sault Ste. Marie, Michigan. Fort Brady was established to preclude British peril against the Ojibwe following the war of 1812. Schoolcraft was married to Jane Johnston. She was the daughter of John Johnston, a successful Scots-Irish fur trader. Her mother was Susan Johnston, daughter of an Ojibwe chief. Schoolcraft served as

an Indian agent. He published Journal of a Tour into the Interior of Missouri and Arkansaw in 1821. Parker, R. (2007). *The Sound the Stars Make Rushing Through the Sky: The Writings of Jane Johnston Schoolcraft.* Pennsylvania: University of Pennsylvania Press, 1-44. Wikipeia. *Henry Schoolcraft.* Retrieved May 7, 2010 from http://en.wikipedia.org/wiki/HenrySchoolcraft.

[79] Nies,J. (1996). *Native American History: A Chronology of a Culture's Vast Acheivements and Their Links to World Events.* New York: Ballantine Books, 242 – 243.

[80] Nabokov, P. (1992). *Native American Testimony: A Chronicle of Indian-White Relations from Prophecy to the Present, 1492*-2000. New York: Penguin Books, 145- 151.

[81] Ibid.

[82] Dewing,R. (2000). Wounded Knee II. South Dakota: Pine Hill Press Inc., 3-4.

[83] Ambrose,S. (2000). *Nothing Like It in the World: The Men Who Built the Transcontinental Railroad 1863-1869.* New York: Simon and Schuster Paperbacks, 17-22.

[84] Prucha,F. (2000). *Documents of United States Indian Policy.* Nebraska: University of Nebraska, 166.

[85] Ibid, 170-173.

[86] Nies, J. (1996). *Native American History: A Chronology of a details about more than sex to permanently change the color of forCulture's Vast Acheivements and Their Links to World Events.* New York: Ballantine Books, 17-22.

[87] Holms,T. (1996). *Strong Hearts Wounded Souls: Ntive American Veterans of the Vietnam War.* Texas: University of Texas Press, 179.

[88] Churchill, W. (1997). A Little Matter *American History: A Chronology of a Culture's Vast Acheivements and Their Links to World Events.* New York: Ballantine Books, 328.

[89] Holms, T. (1996). *Strong Hearts Wounded Souls: Native American Veterans of the Vietnam War.* Texas: University of Texas Press,104.

[90] Churchill, W. (1997). A Little Matter *American History: A Chronology of a Culture's Vast Acheivements and Their Links to World Events.* New York: Ballantine Books, 328.

[91] Holms, T. (1996). *Strong Hearts Wounded Souls: Native American Veterans of the Vietnam War.* Texas: University of Texas Press, 175.

[92] Ibid, 173.

[93] Dewing, R. (2000). Wounded Knee II. South Dakota: Pine Hill Press Inc., 21 – 28.

[94] Holms, T.(1996). *Strong Hearts Wounded Souls: Native American Veterans of the Vietnam War.* Texas: University of Texas Press, 173-174.
[95] Churchill, W. (1997). *A Little Matter of Genocide: Holocaust and Denial in the Americas 1492 to the Present.* San Francisco: City Lights Books, 249.
[96] Ibid, 249.

Chapter VII: Eagle and Coyote Infiltrate the Holy Childhood Boarding School
[97] Child, B. (2000). *Boarding School Seasons: American Indian Families, 1900-1940.* Nebraska: University of Nebraska Press, 43. .
[98] Reyhner, J. and Eder, J. (2004). *American Indian Education: A History.* Oklahoma: University of Oklahoma Press, 134 – 140.
[99] Archuleta,M., Child, B., and Lomawaima, T. (2000). *Away from Home: American Boarding School Experiences 1879-2000.* Arizona: Heard Museum.
[100] An interview was conducted in 2009. Harold is a member of the First Nations Tribe in Sault Ste. Marie, Ontario, Canada who attended the Shenwauk Residential School in the 1950's. He was given a number which was 59 for most of the time he attended. The importance of being given a number and importance not placed on one's name is paramount. The name was the only thing an Indian person owned and special ceremonies were attached to receiving one's given name.
[101] Stanton, A. (July 7, 2008). Northern Express. *Wounded Souls. By Anne Stanton.* Retrieved on September 9, 2008 from http://www.northernexprss.com/editorial/features.asp?id=3241.
[102] Stanton, A. (June 30, 2008). Northern Express. *Unholy Childhood.* Retrieved on September 9, 2008 from http://www.northernexprss.com/editorial/features.asp?id=3240.
[103] Churchill, W. (2004). *Kill the Indian, Save the Man.* San Francisco: City Lights Books, 62.
[104] An interview was conducted with Jennifer in 2001. She is a member of the Sault Ste. Marie Tribe of Chippewa Indians and attended the Holy Childhood boarding school located in Harbor Springs, Michigan in the 1940's.
[105] An interview with Tim was conducted in 2001. He is a member of the Sault Ste. Marie Tribe of Chippewa Indians and attended the Holy Childhood Boarding School in Harbor Springs, Michigan during the

1960s. Tim claimed that being at the boarding school made him very ill for a long time.

[106] An interview was conducted with Kent in 2001. He is a member of the Sault Ste. Marie Tribe of Chippewa Indians and attended the Holy Childhood boarding school in the late 1940's and early 1950's. During an interview, he claimed that he suffers from fear of the dark as the result an incident in which he was locked in the dark basement.

[107] An interview with Sheila was conducted in 2009. Sheila attended the Shenwauk Residential School in Canada during the 1960s.

[108] Child, B. (2000). *Boarding School Seasons: American Indian Families, 1900-1940.* Nebraska: University of Nebraska Press, 45.

[109] Ibid, 32.

[110] An interview was conducted with Jeff in 2001. He had a lot to say about his experience at the federal boarding school in Mt. Pleasant Michigan. Jeff relayed that he does not regret having been sent to that school. The school, according to Jeff, afforded him with financial opportunities and got him away from his father who appeared to have had problems with alcohol.

[111] Kipper, D. and Whitney, S. (2010). *The Addiction Solution.* New York: Rodale, Inc., 239.

Chapter VIII: Life on the Rez

[112] Holms,T. (1996). *Strong Hearts/Wounded Souls: Native American Veterans of the Vietnam War.* Texas: University of Texas Press, 22.

[113] Sandefur, G. *American Indian Reservations: The first underclass areas?* Retrieved on May 14, 2010 from http://www.irp.wisc. Edu/publications/focus/dfs/foc121f.pdf.

[114] Wikipedia. *What was the first Indian reservation?* Retrieved on May 14, 2010 from http://wiki.answers.com/Q/What_was_the_first_Indian_reservation.

[115] Mukhopadhyay,S. (July 31, 2007). *Native American Women, Domestic Violence and Congress.* http://www.racewire.org/archives/2007/07/native_american_women_domestic.html.

Chapter IX: Eagle and Coyote's Day in Tribal Court

[116] Indian Country Today. *Exploring the Prevalence of Domestic Violence Against Native Americans.* Retrieved on March 7, 2010 from

http://www.indiancountrytoday.com/internal?st=print&id=79410797
&path=/archive.
[117] Child Maltreatment2007. *Race and Ethnicity of Victims.*
Retrieved on March 3, 2010 from
https//mail.google.com/mail/?ui=2&ik=6ebf51b2d4&view=att&th=1
272ae9909c632b&att...

Chapter X: Remnants of a Shattered Past
[118] Kersting, K. (September, 2005). *Suicide Prevention Efforts Needed, American Indian Psychologist Tells Policy-Makers.* Retrieved on June 19, 2007 from http://www.apa.org/monitor/sep05/suicide.html.
[119] Churchill, W. (2004). *Kill the Indian: Save the Man.* San Francisco: City Lights Books, 6-7.
[120] Holm, T.(1996). *Strong Hearts Wounded Souls: Native American Veterans of the Vietnam War.* Texas: University of Texas,116.
[121] Eyaa-keen Centre Inc. *Historic Traumatic Transmission (HTT): What is It?* Manitou, Canada: Eyaa-keen Centre Inc.
[122] O'Brien,G. (2008). *World History Timeline: The Timeline of Native Americans – The Ultimate Guide to North America's Indigenous People.* San Diego: Thunder Bay Press, 184.
[123] Freire,P. (1993). *Pedagogy of the Oppressed.* New York: Continuum International Publishing Group, Inc., 30
[124] Ibid,58
[125] Ibid, 59.
[126] Moore, M. (2003). *Genocide of the Mind.* New York: Thunder's Mouth Press, 307-308.
[127] Steffen described seven sources of shame. These included faulty learning, excessive negative feedback, poor decision-making, being a victim of circumstance, false identity, inaccurate perceptions, and loss of social status or recognition. In regards to faulty learning, sometimes the wrong information was received or untrue information was believed to be true. Excessive negative feedback referred to being told on several occasions that they, as children and adults, were unworthy or incompetent. An inability to believe in one's capabilities may lead to difficulty of making sound decisions. Being the victim of circumstance referred to someone whom expected bad circumstances to continue because they have occurred in the past. This state of affairs has been tied with the feelings of constant gloom and doom about the future and is closely tied with shame. Steffen, C. (1999).

Dancing Through the Darkness: The Cognitive Treatment of Shame. Illinois: Reaching Potentials Press.
[128] Holm, T. (1996). *Strong Hearts Wounded Souls: Native American Veterans of the Vietnam War.* Texas: University of Texas, 8-11.
[129] Ibid, 8-11.
[130] Ibid, 139.
[131] Bass, E., and Davis,L.(2008). *The Courage to Heal: A Guide for Women Survivors of Child Sexual Abuse.* New York: Harper Collins Publishers, 6.
[132] Ibid, 6-8.
[133] Ibid, 4.
[134] Churchill, W. (2004). *Kill the Indian: Save the Man.* San Francisco: City Lights Books, 68.
[135] Petoskey, W. (2009). *Dancing My Dream.* Michigan: Read the Spirit Books, 13.
[136] LaMothe, R. (1999). The Absence of Cure: The Core of Malignant Trauma and Symbolization. *Journal of Interpersonal Violence,* 11.
[137] Ibid,6.
[138] Antone, R., Miller, D., and Myers, B. (1986). *The Power Within People.* Ontario: Peace Tree Technologies, Inc., 8.

Chapter XI: A Journey's End
[139] Kersting, K. (September 2005). *Suicide Prevention Efforts Needed, American Indian Psychologist Tells Policy-Makers.* Retrieved on June 19, 2007 from http://www.apa.org/monitor/sep05/suicide.html.

Chapter XII: One Step at a Time
[140] Antone,T., Miller,L., and Myers,B. (1986). *The Power Within People: A Community Organizing Perspective.* Ontario: Peace Tree Technologies, Inc.R.
[141] Peuifoy, R. (1995). *Anxiety, Phobias and Panic: A Step-by-Step Program for Regaining Control of Your Life.* New York: Warner Books, 8-10.
[142] Schiraldi, G. (2000). *The Post Traumatic Stress Disorder Sourcebook: A Guide to Healing, Recovery, and Growth.* New York: McGraw/Hill, 231 – 235.
[143] Archibald,L. (2006) *Final Report of the Aboriginal Healing Foundation, Volume III : Promising Healing Practices in Aboriginal Communities.* Ontario: Aboriginal Healing Foundation.

[144] Hay,L. (1999). *You Can Heal Your Life.* California: Hay House, Inc., 22.
[145] Weaver, J. (2006). *Having a Mary Spirit: Allowing God to Change Us from the Inside Out.* Colorado: Waterbrook Press, 152-157.
[146] Hay,L. (1999). *You Can Heal Your Life.* California: Hay House, Inc.,23.
[147] Schiraldi,G. (2000). *The Post Traumatic Stress Disorder Sourcebook: A Guide to Healing, Recovery, and Growth.* New York: McGraw/Hill, 355.
[148] Ibid, 53.
[149] Block, P. (2009). *Community: The Structure of Belonging.* San Francisco: Berett-Loehler Publishers, Inc., 1-7.
[150] Ibid, 13.
[151] Ibid, 12.

Appendix A

History of Federal Indian Education Policy
Historical Events in Indian Education

"The Following is a chronological view of the development of Indian Education during the past 200 years. Since at least 1775 American Indian have had an ongoing, albeit tenuous relationship, with the United States Government. While a concerted federal effort at educating the Indian has occurred only within the last fifty years, it has originated from the following historical events." (National Advisory Council on Indian Education, 1993).

1775 Continental Congress approves $500 to educate Indians at Dartmouth College
1778 September 17, 1778, the first treaty between the United States and an Indian Nation.
1802 Congress approves appropriations for Indian education not to exceed $15,000 annually "to provide civilization among the aborigines."

1818 Congress authorizes a civilization fund in the amount of $10,000 to convert Indians from
Hunters to agriculturalists.
1819 Congress passes a law on March 3, 1819 which states that the act was "designed to Provide against the further decline and final extinction of the Indian tribes adjoining

The frontier settlements of the United States, and for introducing among them the habits And arts of civilization."

1870 Congress authorizes appropriations of $100,000 to operate federal industrial schools for Indians.

1871 Congress ends authority to make treaties with Indian tribes and nations.

1890 Federal tuition offered to public schools to educate Indian children.

1892 Congress authorizes the Commissioner of Indian Affairs to make and enforce regulations on Indian student attendance including the authority to withhold food and services from families that resist the "educational program" by refusing to send their children to school.

1906 Congress abolishes Oklahoma Cherokee school system.

1921 Congress passes the Snyder Act of 1921 which instructed the Secretary of Interior "to Direct, supervise, and expend such moneys as Congress may from time to time appropriate, for the benefit, care and assistance of Indians through the United States." The monies could be used for "general support and civilization, including education."

1928 Meriam Report to Congress, which influenced a change in Indian education policies.

1934 Congress passes the Johnson O'Malley (JOM) Act which authorizes contracts for welfare
and educational services, and which was used to entice public school districts to assume more responsibility for providing an elementary and secondary education for Indian children who reside on Indian reservation lands.

1950 Congress amends Public Law 874 otherwise known as Impact Aid which provides federal subsidizes to public school districts to educate children residing on federal lands including Indian reservations.

1951 Congress passes a program to relocate Indians away from reservations.

1964 Congress passes Economic Opportunity Act which provides for Indian children and Adults to participate in Head Start, Upward Bound, Job Corps, Vista, and the Indian Community Action Program.

1965 Congress passes the Elementary and Secondary Education Act which is intended to benefit socially and economically disadvantaged youth. Titles I and III of the act was
Amended to include Bureau of Indian Affairs (BIA) schools.

1966 Rough Rock Demonstration School which is the first modern day Indian controlled
School funded by the federal government opens within the Navajo Nation.

1967 Special Senate Subcommittee on Indian Education is established by Senate Resolution 165.
1968 Navajo Community College as the first tribally controlled Indian community college is Established in the Navajo Nation.
1969 Indian Education: A National Tragedy – A National Challenge, the Special Senate Subcommittee Report on Indian Education is released.
1970 Rama Navajo High School which is the first Indian controlled contract high school opens.
1971 Navajo Nation establishes the first comprehensive tribal education department which Contracts to administer the Bureau of Indian Affairs Office Title I Program and Higher Education Grants Program.
1972 Congress passes the Indian Education Act which creates an Office of Indian Education Within the U.S. Office of Education, defines Indian to include members of state recognized Indian tribes and descendents of Indians, establishes a quasi-entitlement program for Indians attending public schools, and establishes a National Advisory Council on Indian Education.
1975 Congress passes the Indian Self-Determination and Education Assistance Act which opens up contacting.
1978 Congress passes the Indian Education Amendments which establishes standards

for BIA schools, institutionalizes BIA school boards, requires formula funding in BIA schools, and provides for increased Indian involvement in the use of Impact Aid funds.

1988 Congress passes Public Law 100-297 which reauthorize the Indian Education Act and calls for a White House Conference on Indian Education.

1989 Salt River Pima Maricopa Indian Community, through agreement with Mesa Public Schools (Arizona), gains control over Impact Aid.

1991 Indian Nations at Risk Task Force created by Secretary of Education issues report.

1991 White House Conference on Indian Education held resulting in 114 recommendations.

1990 The National Advisory Council on Indian Education recommends to the Congress that Indian education be a federal entitlement program
(National Advisory Council on Indian Education, 1993).

Glossary

Acculturation - The exchange of cultural features that results when groups of individuals having different cultures come into continuous first hand contact; the original cultural patterns of either or both groups may be altered, but the groups remain distinct.

Anishanaabe(g) – An Ojibwe word meaning the original people.

Anxiety Disorder - A mental illness characterized by persistent and/or excessive anxiety. In addition to PTSD, anxiety disorders included generalized anxiety disorder, obsessive-compulsive disorder, panic disorder, and phobias. PTSD is the only anxiety disorder which includes a stressful event(s) as one of its diagnostic criteria.

Assimilation - The process whereby a minority group gradually adopts the customs and attitudes of another culture.

Boundary – An abstract delineation between parts of a system or between systems, typically defined by implicit or explicit rules regarding who may participate and in what manner.

Culture - The customary beliefs, social forms, and material traits of a racial, religious, or social group. The characteristic features of everyday existence shared by people in a place or time.

Discrimination - The unjust or prejudicial treatment of different categories of people or things, esp. on the grounds of race, age, or sex.

Dissociation – A mental process whereby one attempts to escape distressing memories or situations. One's mind might appear to separate from distressing bodily experience. Or the mind might separate traumatic memories from the main body of consciousness. These "dissociated memories" are stored in a fragmented way and often intrude into awareness in distressing ways.

Emotional Intelligence - An ability to identify, assess, and control the emotions of oneself, of others, and of groups.

Foreshortened Future – The sense that a normal or pleasant future will not exist as the survivor seems to focus on the injury caused by the traumatic event and the likelihood that unpleasant outcomes will occur.

Genocide - The deliberate and systematic extermination of a national, racial, political, or cultural group.

Gitchi Manito – An Ojibwe word meaning the Creator or the "Great Mystery."

Healing – The process of becoming whole again; uniting pieces of self that have been shattered by trauma.

Historical Trauma – Collective and cumulative emotional wounding across generations that results from massive cataclysmic events. The trauma is held personally and transmitted over generations. Thus, even family members who have not directly experienced the trauma can feel the effects of the event generations later. The multi-generational aspects of trauma continue to be treated as secondary, and, consequently the behavior of many children of survivors of massive trauma is misunderstood and not treated appropriately. (Maria Yellow Horse Brave Heart, PhD.)

Hypervigilance – The extreme caution survivors take to protect against further harm, or the fearful anticipation of real or recalled threats.

Manifest Destiny - The belief or doctrine, held chiefly in the middle and latter part of the 19th century, that it was the destiny of the U.S. to expand its territory over the whole of North America and to extend and enhance its political, social, and economic influences.

Numbing – A shutdown of emotions or memory in order to protect survivors from distressing feelings.

Patriarchal Domination – Represents all the social mechanisms that produce or reproduce and exert male dominance over women.

Post Traumatic Stress Disorder – The understandable response to an overwhelmingly stressful event(s). The symptoms of the resulting emotional wounding include re-experiencing the event(s) in distressing ways, emotional and physical arousal, and attempts to distance oneself from reminders of the event(s).

Recovery – A return to a former state or healthy state of functioning.

Shame - A painful emotion caused by a strong sense of guilt, embarrassment, unworthiness, or disgrace.

Stress – The response of the body to a threat. Concerning anxiety disorders, the stress response becomes exaggerated, too easily triggered, and/or chronic. Because the mind and body are connected,

physical arousal is accompanied by emotional arousal and sometimes behavioral changes.
Systematic Relaxation – Forms of relaxation that are structured and practiced regularly, such as meditation, and progressive muscle relaxation. These practices tend to reduce physical and emotional arousal, and can be an important part of a survivor's coping and recovery.
Trigger – A cue that reminds one of a traumatic event and elicits distressing intrusions.

Bibliography

Adams, D. (1995). *Education for Extinction: American Indians and the Boarding School Experience 1875-1928.* Kansas: University of Kansas Press.

Allen, P. (1992). *The Sacred Hoop: Recovering the Feminine in American Indian Traditions.* Boston: Beacon Press.

Ambrose, S. (2000). *Nothing Like It in the World: The Men Who Built the Transcontinental Railroad 1863-1869.* New York: Simon and Schuster Paperbacks.

Ambrose, S. (1996). *Undaunted Courage: Meriwether Lewis, Thomas Jefferson, and the Opening of the American West.* New York: Simon and Schuster Paperbacks.

Amnesty Magazine. *Soul Wound: The Legacy of Native American Schools.* Retrieved on February 20, 2010 from http://www.amnestyusa.org/amnestynow/soulwound.html.

Andrews, T. (1993). *Animals Speak: The Spiritual and Magical Powers of Creatures Great and Small.* Minnesota: Llewellyn Publications.

Antone, R., Miller, L. and Myers, B. (1986). *The Power Within People: A Community Organizing Perspective.* Ontario: Peace Tree Technologies, Inc.

Archibald, L. (2006). *Final Report of the Aboriginal Healing Foundation (Volume III):Promising Healing Practices in*

Aboriginal Communities. Ontario: Aboriginal Healing Foundation.

Archuleta, M., Child, B. and Lomawaima, T. (Eds.) (2000). *Away from Home: American Boarding School Experiences (1879-2000).* Arizona: Heard Museum.

Bigelow, B. and Peterson, B. (Editors). (1998). *Rethinking Columbus: The Next 500 Years.* Wisconsin: Rethinking Schools.

Blond, A. (1994). *The Private Lives of the Roman Emperors.* London: Constable and Robinson Ltd.

Bonfanti, L. (1992). *The Witchcraft Hysteria of 1692: Volume 2.* Massachusetts: Old Saltbox Publishing.

Bordewich, F. (1996). *Killing the White Man's Indian: Reinventing Native Americans at the End of the Twentieth Century.* New York: Anchor Books.

Bower, J. (2007). *Beliefs that Changed the World.* London: Quercus Publishing.

Bradshaw, J. (2005). *Healing the Shame That Binds You.* Florida: Health Communications, Inc.

Brown, D. (1970). *Bury my Heart at Wounded Knee: An Indian History of the AmericanWest.* New York: Henry Holt and Company.

Buchanan, P. (2007). *The Day of Reckoning: How Hubris, Ideology, and Greed Are Tearing America Apart.* New York: Thomas Dunne Books.

Buechner, F. (1993). *Wishful Thinking: a*

Seeker's ABC. San Francisco: Harper Collins Publishers.

Butler, G. and Hope, T. (2007). *Managing Your Mind: The Mental Fitness Guide.* New York: Oxford University Press, Inc.

Campbell, J. and Moyers, B. (1988). *The Power of Myth.* New York: Anchor Books/A Division of Random House, Inc.

Chadwick, O. (1995). *A History of Christianity.* New York: St. Martin's Press.

Chansonneuve, D. (2005). *Reclaiming Connections: Understanding Residential School Trauma Among Aboriginal People.* Ontario: Aboriginal Healing Foundation.

Child, B., (2000). *Boarding SchoolSeasons: American Indian Families, 1900-1940.* Nebraska: University of Nebraska Press.

Child Maltreatment 2007. *Race and Ethnicity of Victims.* Retrieved on March 3, 2010 from https//mail.google.com/mail/?ui=2&ik=6ebf 51b2d&view=att&th=1272ae9909 c632b&att...

Chinmoy, S., (1974). *Yoga and the Spiritual Life.* New York: AUM Publications.

Chopra, D. (2009). *The Ultimate Happiness Prescription.* New York: Harmony Books.

Churchill, W. (1997). *A Little Matter of Genocide: Holocaust and Denial in theAmericas 1492 to the Present.* San Francisco: City Lights Books.

Churchill, W. (2004). *Kill the Indian, Save the Man.* San Francisco: City Lights Books.

Clifton, J., Cornell, G. and McClurken, J.

(1986). *The People of the Three Fires: The Ottawa, Potawatomi and Ojibway of Michigan.* Michigan: The Michigan Indian Press Grand Rapids Inter-Tribal Council.

Copeland, M. and Harris, M. (2000). *Healing the Trauma of Abuse: a women's workbook.* California: New Harbinger Publications, Inc.

Cousins, N. (1988). *The Biology of Hope and the Healing Power of the Human Spirit.* New York: Penguin Books.

Crosby Jr., A. (2003). *The Columbian Exchange: Biological and Cultural Consequences of 1492.* Westport: Praeger.

Deloria, V. (2003). *God is Red: A Native View of Religion.* Colorado: Fulcrum Publishing.

Deloria, V. (1997). *Red Earth/White Lies: Native Americans and the Myth of Scientific Fact.* Colorado: Fulcrum Publishing.

Deloria, V. (2006). *The World We Used to Live In.* Colorado: Fulcrum Publishing.

Densmore, F. (1979). *Chippewa Customs.* Minnesota: Minnesota Historical Society Press.

Dewing, R. (2000). *Wounded Knee II.* South Dakota: Pine Hill Press Inc.

Diamond, J. (1999). *Guns, Germs, and Steel: The Fates of Human Societies.* NewYork: W.W. Norton and Company.

Dove, P. (2010). *Laughter, Tears, Silence: Expressive Meditations to Calm Your Mind and Open Your Heart.* California: New World Library.

D'Souza, D. (1995). *The End of Racism*. New York: Simon and Schuster.

Dowd, G. (1992). *A Spirited Resistance: The North American Indian Struggle for Unity, 1745-1815*. Baltimore: The John Hopkins University Press.

Eastman, C. (2010). *Living in Two Worlds: The American Indian Experience*. Indiana: World Wisdom, Inc.

Ehle, J. (1988). *Trail of Tears: The Rise and Fall of the Cherokee Nation*. New York: Anchor Books/Doubleday.

Ehrman, B. (2009). *Jesus, Interrupted: Revealing the Hidden Contradictions in the Bible*. New York: Harper Collins Publishers.

Ehrman, B. (2005). *Misquoting Jesus: The Story Behind Who Changed the Bible and Why*. New York: Harper Collins Publishers.

Ellis, J. (2007). *American Creation*. New York: Vintage Books.

Emmons, H. (2010). *The Chemistry of Calm*. New York: Simon and Schuster, Inc.

Engel, B. (2006). *Healing Your Emotional Self: A Powerful Program to Help You Raise Your Self-Esteem, Quiet Your Inner Critic, and Overcome Your Shame*. New Jersey: John Wiley and Sons, Inc.

Evans, P. (1996). *The Verbally Abusive Relationship: How to recognize it and how to respond*. Massachusetts: Adams Media Corporation.

Eyaa-keen Centre Inc. (2003). *Historic*

Traumatic Transmission (HTT): What is It? Manitou, Canada: Eyaa-keen Centre, Inc.

Farmer, S. (2006). *Animal Spirit Guides.* California: Hay House, Inc.

Fernandez-Armesto, F. (1991). *Columbus.* Oxford: Oxford University Press.

Fixico, D. (2000). *The Urban Indian Experience in America.* New Mexico: University of New Mexico Press.

Fletcher, J. (2006). *Reclaiming Our History.* Ontario: Otisiabi Matriarchal Society and Ojibway and Cree Cultural Centre.

Fox, M. (1988). *The Coming of the Cosmic Christ.* San Francisco: Harper Collins Publishers.

Freke, T. and Gandy, P. (1999). *The Jesus Mysteries: Was the "Original Jesus" A Pagan God?* New York: Three Rivers Press.

Gardner, D. (2008). *The Science of Fear.* New York: Penguin Group, Inc.

Garst, S. (1965). *Red Cloud.* Chicago: Follett Publishing Company.

Giago, T. (2006). *Children Left Behind: The Dark Legacy of Indian Mission Boarding Schools.* New Mexico: Clear Light Publishing.

Godin, S. (2008). *Tribes: We Need You to Lead Us.* London: Penguin Books.

Gombrich, E. (1985). *A Little History of the World.* New Haven: Yale University Press.

Greeley, A. (2007). *Jesus: A Meditation on*

His Stories and His Relationships with Women. New York: Tom Doherty Associaties, LLC.

Hall, M., Schaessens, C., Connelly, K., and Connelly, R. (Cambridge Editorial Partnership)(2007). *Great American Documents: The Landmark Documents in Our History.* London: Quercus Publishing.

Hammerschlag, C. (1992). *The Theft of the Spirit: A Journey to Spiritual Healing.* New York: Simon and Schuster Inc.

Hay, L., (1999). *You Can Heal Your Life.* California: Hay House, Inc.

Hanh, T. (2007). *The Art of Power.* New York: Harper Collins Publishers.

Hilger, I. (1992). *Chippewa Child Life and Its Cultural Background.* St. Paul: Minnesota Historical Society Press.

Hitchens, C. (2007). *God is Not Great: How Religion Poisons Everything.* New York: Hachette Book Group.

Holms, T. (1996). *Strong Hearts/Wounded Souls: Native American Veterans of the Vietnam War.* Texas: University of Texas Press.

Howard, H. (1971). Sacajawea. New York: MJF Books – Fine Communications.

Howard-Brook, W. (2001). *The Church Before Christianity.* New York: Orbis Books.

Indian Country Today. *Exploring the Prevalence of*

Domestic Violence Against Native Americans. Retrieved on March 7, 2010 from http://www.indiancountrytoday.com./internal?st=print&id=79410797&path=/archive.
Jacobs, A. (2009). *The Essential Gnostic Gospels.* London: Watkins Publishing.
Jacobsen, W. and Coleman, D. (2006). *So You Don't Want to Go to Church Anymore.* California: Windblown Media.
Johnson, T. (1997). *We Hold the Rock: This is the Beginning of Our Fight for Justice And Self-Determination (The Indian Occupation of Alcatraz, 1969 to 1971).* San Francisco: Golden Gate National Parks Association.
Johnston, B. (1988). *Indian School Days.* Norman: University of Oklahoma Press.
Johnston, B. (1982). *Ojibway Ceremonies.* Nebraska: University of Nebraska Press.
Johnston, B. (1976). *Ojibway Heritage.* Nebraska: University of Nebraska Press.
Jones, D. (1977). *Arrest Sitting Bull.* New York: Charles Scribner's Sons.
Karen, R. (2001). *The Forgiving Self: The Road from Resentment to Connection.* New York: Doubleday.
Keller, T. (2008). *The Reason for God: Belief in an Age of Skepticism.* New York: Riverhead Books.
Kenney, S. and Kinsella, H. (Editors)

(1997). *Politics and Feminist Standpoint Theories.* New York: The Haworth Press, Inc.

Kingma, D. (2010). *The Ten Things to Do When Your Life Falls Apart.* California: New World Library.

Kipper, D. and Whitney, S., (2010). *The Addiction Solution.* New York: Rodale, Inc.

Kluger, R. (2007). *Seizing Destiny: The Relentless Expansion of American Territory.* New York: Vintage Books.

Levine, M. (2006). *The Price of Privilege: How Parental Pressure and Material Advantage Are Creating a Generation of Disconnected and Unhappy Kids.* New York: Harper Collins Publishers.

Lieberman, D. (2002). *Make Peace with Anyone: Breakthrough Strategies to Quickly End Any Conflict, Feud, or Estrangement.* New York: St. Martin's Press.

Littlefield, H. (2001). *Children of the Indian Boarding Schools: 1879 to present.* Minneapolis: Carolrhoda Books, Inc.

MacArthur, J. (2002). *Twelve Ordinary Men: How the Master Shaped His Disciples for Greatness, and What He Wants to Do with You.* Tennessee: Thomas Nelson.

Mann, C. (2005). *1491: New Revelations of the Americas Before Columbus.* New York: Alfred A. Knopf.

Marshall, D. (2007). *The Truth About Jesus*

and the Lost Gospels: A Reasoned look at Thomas, Judas, and the Gnostic Gospels. Oregon: Harvest House Publishers.

Martin, M. (1987). *The Jesuits: The Society of Jesus and the Betrayal of the Roman Catholic Church.* New York: Simon and Schuster Paperbacks.

Matthiessen, P. (1991). *In the Spirit of Crazy Horse.* New York: Viking Penguin.

McNally, D. (1990). *Even Eagles Need a Push: Learning to Soar in a Changing World.* New York: Bantam Doubleday Dell Publishing Group, Inc.

Merk, F. (1963). *Manifest Destiny and Mission in American History.* Toronto: Random House of Canada Limited.

Miller, J. (1996). *Shingwauk's Vision: A History of Native Residential Schools.* Toronto: University of Toronto Press.

Moore, M. (Editor). (2003). *Genocide of the Mind.* New York: Thunder's Mouth Press.

Mukhopadhyay, S. *Native American Women, Domestic Violence and Congress.* Retrieved on March 7, 2010 from http://www.racewire.org/archives/2007/07/native_american_women_domesic.html.

Nabokov, P. (1992). *Native American Testimony: A Chronicle of Indian-White Relations from Prophecy to the Present, 1492-2000.* New York: Penguin Books.

Nies, J. (1996). *Native American History:*

A Chronology of a Culture's Vast Acheivementes and Their Links to World Events. New York: Ballantine Books.

O' Brien, G. (2008). *World History Timeline: The Timeline of Native Americans (The Ultimate Guide to North America's Indigenous Peoples.* San Diego: Thunder Bay Press.

Orloff, J. (2009). *Emotional Freedom: Liberate Yourself from Negative Emotions and Transform Your Life.* New York: Harmony Books.

Overy, R. (2010). *The Times Complete History of the World.* London: Times Books.

Padus, E. (1986). *The Complete Guide to Your Emotions and Your Health: New Dimensions in Mind/Body Healing.* Pennsylvania: Rodale Press.

Page, J. (2003). *In the Hands of the Great Spirit: The 20,000 Year History of American Indians.* New York: Free Press.

Pagels, E. (1995). *The Origin of Satan.* New York: Vintage Books.

Paquin, R. and Doherty, R. (1992). *Not First in Nobody's Heart: The Life Story of a Contemporary Chippewa.* Iowa: Iowa State University Press.

Parker, D. (2007). *The Sound the Stars Make Rushing Through the Sky: The Writings of Jane Johnston Schoolcraft.* Pennsylvania: University of Pennsylvania Press.

Peacock, T. and Wisuri, M. (2002). *Ojibwe*

Waasa Inaabidaa: We Look In All Directions. Minnesota: Afton Historical Society Press.

Petoskey, W. (2009). *Dancing My Dream.* Michigan: Read the Spirit Books.

Peurifoy, R. (1995). *Anxiety, Phobias, and Panic: A Step-by-Step Program for Regaining Control of Your Life.* New York: Warner Books.

Picknett, L. (2003). *Mary Magdalene.* New York: Carroll and Graf Publishers.

Picknett, L. and Prince, C. (2008). *The Masks of Christ: Behind the Lies and Cover-ups About the Life of Jesus.* New York: Simon and Schuster.

Podles, L. (2008). *Sacrilege: Sexual Abuse in the Catholic Church.* Maryland: Crossland Press.

Poland, S. and McCormick, J. (1999). *Coping with Crisis: Lessons Learned.* Colorado: Sopris West.

Prophet, M. and Prophet, E. (1988). *The Lost Teaching of Jesus: Missing Texts – Karma and Reincarnation.* New York: Summit University Press.

Prucha, F., (2000). *Documents of United States Indian Policy.* Nebraska: University of Nebraska Press.

Rakove, J. (2009). *The Annotated U.S. Constitution and Declaration of Independence.* Massachusets: The Belknap Press of Harvard University Press.

Reyhner, J. and Eder, J. (2004). *American*

Indian History: A History. Oklahoma: University of Oklahoma Press.

Rinaldi, A. (1999). *My Heart Is on the Ground: The Diary of Nannie Little Rose, a Sioux Girl.* New York: Scholastic, Inc.

Schiraldi, G. (2000). *The Post Traumatic Stress Disorder Sourcebook: A Guide to Healing, Recovery, and Growth.* New York: McGraw/Hill.

Sharpes, D. *Federal Education for the American Indian.* Journal of American Indian Education/Arizona State University. Retrieved on 8/25/09 from http://jaie.asu.edu/v19/v19S1fed.htm

Silko, L. (2006). *Ceremony.* New York: Penguin Books.

Spong, J. (2005). *The Sins of the Scripture: Exposing the Bible's Texts of Hate to Reveal the God of Love.* New York: Harper One.

Steffen, C. (1999). *Dancing through the Darkness: The Cognitive Treatment of Shame.* Illinois: Reaching Potentials Press.

St. Pierre, M. and Long Soldier, T. (1995). *Walking in the Sacred Manner.* New York: Simon & Schuster.

Stanton, A. (August 4, 2008). *The Legacy of Holy Childhood.* Retrieved on September 9, 2009 from http://www.northernexpress.com/editiorial/features.asp?id=3302.

Stanton, A. (July 7, 2008). *Wounded Souls.* Retrieved on September 9, 2009 from http://www.northernexpress.com/edit

iorial/features.asp?id=3241.
Stanton, A. (June 30, 2008). *Unholy Childhood.* Retrieved on September 9, 2009 from http://www.northernexpress.com/editorial/features.asp?id=3240.
Steffen, C. (1999). *Dancing through the Darkness: The Cognitive Treatment of Shame.* New Lenox, Illinois: Realizing Potential Press.
Stout, M. (2005). *The Sociopath Next Door.* New York: Broadway Books.
Stout, M. and Kipling, G. (2003). *Aboriginal People, Resilience and the Residential SchoolLegacy.* Ontario: Aboriginal Healing Foundation.
Sturtevant, W. (Ed.) (1988). *Handbook of North American Indians: History of Indian-White Relations (Volume 4).* Washington, D.C.: Smithsonian Institute.
Sugden, J. (1997). *Tecumseh: A Life.* New York: Henry Holt and Company.
Thorton, R. (1987). *American Indian Holocaust and Survival: A Population History Since 1492.* Norman: University of Oklahoma Press.
Tirado, T. (2000). *Christopher Columbus.* Retrieved on June 6, 2008 from http://www.millersville.edu/~columbus/columbus.html.
Tolle, E. (2008). *Oneness with All Life.* New York: Penguin Group, Inc.
Tomkins, S. (2005). *A Short History of*

Christianity. Michigan: William B. Eerdmans Publishing Company.

Trafzer, C., Keller, J., and Sisquoc, L. (2006). *Boarding School Blues: Revisiting American Indian Educational Experiences.* Lincoln: University of Nebraska Press.

Twenge, J. and Campbell, W. (2009). *Living in the Age of Entitlement: The Narcissism Epidemic.* New York: Free Press.

Utter, J. (1993). *American Indians: Answers to Today's Questions (Second Edition).* Nebraska: University of Oklahoma Press.

Waldman, C. (2006). *Encyclopedia of Native American Tribes (Third Edition).* New York: Checkmark Books.

Warren, W. (1984). *History of the Ojibway People.* St. Paul: Minnesota Historical Society Press.

Weaver, J. (2006). *Having a Mary Spirit:Allowing God to Change You From the Inside Out.* Colorado: Waterbrook Press.

Whitfield, C. (1987). *Healing the Child Within: Discovery and Recovery for Adult Children of Dysfunctional Families.* Florida: Health Communications, Inc.

Wikpedia. *Chip Log.* Retrieved on June 18, 2009 from http://en.wikipedia. org/wiki/Chip_log.

Williston, R. (2003). *Native American Spirituality: A Walk in the Woods.* Ohio: Rainbow Light & Company.

Williston, R. and Williston, M. (2009). *The*

Ancient Roots of Christianity: A Native American's Look Through Christianity. Ohio: Rainbow Light & Company.

Wilson, J. (1998). *The Earth Shall Weep: A History of Native America.* New York: Grove Press.

Wright, J. (1996). *The Crooked Tree: Indian Legends of Northern Michigan.* Michigan: Thunder Bay Press.

Wright, R. (2009). *The Evolution of God.* New York: Little Brown and Company.

Zander, R. and Zander, B. (2000). *The Art of Possibility: Transforming Professional and Personal Life.* Boston: Harvard Business School Press.